Reshaping Education in the 1990s

Reshaping Education in the 1990s

Perspectives on Secondary Education

Edited by

Christopher Pole
and
Rita Chawla-Duggan

 Falmer Press

(A member of the Taylor & Francis Group)
London • Washington, D.C.

UK	Falmer Press, 1 Gunpowder Square, London
USA	Falmer Press, Taylor & Francis Inc., 1900 Frost Road, Suite 101, Bristol, PA 19007

First published in 1996

A catalogue record for this book is available from the British Library

Library of Congress Cataloging-in-Publication Data are available on request

ISBN 0 7507 0 528 0 cased
ISBN 0 7507 0 529 9 paper

Jacket design by Caroline Archer

Typeset in 10/12 pt Garamond by
Graphicraft Typesetters Ltd., Hong Kong.

Printed in Great Britain by Biddles Ltd., Guildford and King's Lynn on paper which has a specified pH value on final paper manufacture of not less than 7.5 and is therefore 'acid free'.

Contents

Contents

Acknowledgment

The papers in this volume derive from the CEDAR 1994 Conference at the University of Warwick.

We would like to thank the authors who have contributed to the volume, CEDAR staff for their help and advice in the planning and delivery of the conference and Falmer Press for their patience.

We are especially indebted to Janet Flynn and Sylvia Moore for their secretarial and administrative expertise in relation to the conference and this volume.

Christopher Pole
Rita Chawla-Duggan

List of Abbreviations

BEMAS	British Educational Management and Administration Society
CBI	Confederation of British Industry
CCMS	Council for Catholic Maintained Schools
CEDAR	Centre for Educational Development Appraisal and Research
CTC	city technology colleges
DENI	Department of Education for Northern Ireland
DFE	Department for Education
DMR	devolved management of resources
DSM	devolved school management
EBD	educational and behavioural difficulties
EIS	Educational Institute of Scotland
EIU	economic and industrial understanding
ELB	education and library board
ERA	Education Reform Act
ERO	Education Reform Order
ESRC	Economic and Social Research Council
EWO	Education Welfare Officer
FE	further education
FRS	Fellow of the Royal Society
FTE	full time equivalents
GM	grant maintained
GMI	grant maintained independent
GMS	grant maintained status
GNVQ	General National Vocational Qualification
HE	higher education
HMI	Her Majesty's Inspectorate
IIEP	International Institute for Educational Planning
IT	information technology
LEA	local education authority
LMS	local management of schools
MSC	Manpower Services Commission
MVA	Multi Variate Analysis
NAHT	National Association of Head Teachers
NC	national curriculum
NCPE	national curriculum for physical education

NICER	Northern Ireland Council for Educational Research
NIESR	National Institute of Economic and Social Research
NUT	National Union of Teachers
OECD	Organization for Economic Cooperation and Development
OFSTED	Office for Standards in Education
PASCI	Parent and School Choice Interaction (study)
PE	physical education
PGCE	Postgraduate Certificate in Education
PIC	Private Industry Council
PTA	parent-teacher association
SAT	standard assessment testing
SCOTVEC	Scottish Vocational Education Council
SEB	Scottish Examination Boards
SEN	special educational needs
SHA	Secondary Heads Association
SOEID	Scottish Office Education and Industry Department
TEC	Training and Enterprise Council
TVEI	Technical and Vocational Education Initiative

List of Figures and Tables

Introduction

Christopher Pole and Rita Chawla-Duggan

Introduction

In common with many other countries, education in the United Kingdom has undergone major change in recent years. Although the 1988 Education Reform Act is now some eight years old the effects of the wide ranging changes which it introduced are still being worked through in many areas of educational provision. The changes have had implications across all phases of education and have impacted upon its provision, content and management. The Act was designed to bring about major structural change (Simon, 1988) to a system which was seen as poorly managed by LEA administrators at some distance from schools and colleges, as failing to ensure all pupils received a curriculum which would equip them adequately for life after school and denied parents both a choice in the education of their children and a voice in its management (Knight, 1990). Any piece of legislation which set out to tackle these major issues collectively would necessarily be of substantial scale and scope.

In the spring of 1994 the Centre for Educational Development Appraisal and Research (CEDAR) held its fifth conference which took as its theme changing educational structures: policy and practice. Many of the papers presented at the conference dealt with issues arising from the changes brought about by the 1988 Act. The papers in many cases; reported on research which had been carried out in schools and colleges after the passing of the 1988 Act and as such they represent some of the first research based commentaries on the impact of the Act. Approximately 80 papers were presented in parallel streams at the conference and this collection is one of two which brings together debate, key questions and knowledge about issues which are central to the provision and experience of education in the United Kingdom.

In this volume the focus is upon changes which have occurred and are occurring in the secondary sector whereas issues relating to primary education are addressed in the companion volume (Chawla-Duggan and Pole, 1996). While papers at the conference covered a wide range of issues, those selected for inclusion in this volume relate to three key areas of post-ERA education provision and management. The book is, therefore, divided into three sections which address these three areas. In Part I three chapters address issues relating to schooling and the creation of an education market. In Part II four chapters examine different aspects of changes which have occurred in the governance of schools and in Part III the focus is upon experience of local school management.

Although there are three separate parts to the volume the themes with which they deal are interrelated. While on the one hand they could be seen to engage with notions of democratizing schooling by placing more control in the hands of parents, headteachers and the forces of the market, on the other they could equally be seen to relate to notions of competition, a reduced responsibility for the state in education and an increase in bureaucracy at the level of school management. Their integration (Simon, 1988) is a clear reflection of the ways in which the different aspects of the 1988 Reform Act work together to achieve fundamental change in the provision, management and experience of education.

Schooling and the Market

In Part I the chapter by Woods, Bagley and Glatter reports on a longitudinal study of parents and school choice. The focus is upon the ways in which secondary schools have responded to greater competition for pupils. The authors put forward the hypothesis, which they test by means of several school case studies, that where there is a quasi-market for pupils then changes which schools make in order to attract them tend to be concerned with traditional academic issues, practices and values. For example exam performance, homework and ability setting are cited as instances of such changes. One of the conclusions to be drawn from the chapter is that competition leads to an homogenization of provision around fairly narrow definitions of what is good educational practice and what are acceptable educational values for schools to hold. The implications to be drawn from this research are that competition for pupils has the potential to stifle innovation, leaving schools no option but to play safe in their approaches to teaching and learning, school organization and management if they wish to succeed in attracting large numbers of pupils and the per capita funding which accompanies them. The chapter links to important questions, therefore, about competition, markets and a quest for conservatism in education, fostered by the need for secondary schools to attract and keep pupils.

In the second chapter Jamieson examines examples of convergence between the economic and education systems. He contends that as the economy becomes more complex then the relationship between the two systems also becomes more complex. He develops the argument that the marketization of education may mean that schools now have more in common with private enterprise. Jamieson argues that marketization can enable schools to realize their power in their relationship with the economy. He says, for example, that many schools are larger than most local businesses with more staff and a higher turnover. His argument is that marketization of education has produced a shift from the curriculum as the focus of education–business links to a greater emphasis on the school in local social and economic restructuring.

Jamieson also spends some time questioning whether marketization of education has actually happened. This is an issue that is paralleled in the last of the chapters in this first part by Blyth and Milner. They examine the extent to which the education market includes the often diverse needs of different kinds of pupils. Their concern is with pupils as commodities as they examine issues of school efficiency, school exclusion and per capita funding.

Collectively, the three chapters are important in examining questions of choice, access to schooling and notions of consumerism. They suggest a form of commodification (Chitty, 1989; Jones, 1989; Hatcher, 1994) of education as schools package a homogenized form of schooling in their bid to attract clients.

Changing School Governance

The 1988 Education Reform Act also brought significant changes to the role of school governors (Deem, 1990). The Act increased their powers and responsibilities in such a way as to make them legally responsible for the activities of their schools and for the management of their finances. On the one hand such changes could be seen as examples of increased local democracy, with those directly involved in the school being responsible for the decisions and management by which it operates, particularly as parents were to constitute a greater part of governing bodies. Alternatively, the new arrangements could be seen as a measure to further remove local education authorities from the decision-making processes *vis à vis* schools and to reduce the responsibilities of the state. Moreover, while parents were ensured representation on governing bodies, there have been divisions of opinion as to whether this requirement would prove to be more inclusive or exclusive with regard to the social class, ethnic and gender composition of governing bodies. While optimists, e.g. Eggleston (1988), have drawn attention to the possibility for greater diversity which the Act brought, pessimists or realists, e.g. MacNeil (1988), have reminded us of key sociological factors which would ensure that such diversity would indeed be unlikely in most schools.

In addition the issues of democracy, decision-making and state responsibility, which have been raised in relation to changes in school governance, have been played out in a more concentrated fashion in relation to the emergence of grant maintained schools (Fitz *et al.* 1993; Angus, 1994). The possibility of shedding virtually all local education authority involvement in schooling has been presented to headteachers and governors as a central plank of the 1988 legislation. While take-up of grant maintained status was slow at first, the years since 1988 have seen further inducements (Power *et al.* 1994) and changes to procedures both to encourage schools to opt out and to make the process involved more straightforward. The creation of this new kind of state independent school gives rise to a range of questions (Rogers, 1992) central to the administration, management and composition of state education.

Many of the central issues which underpin the introduction of grant maintained schools and changes to school governance are addressed by the four chapters in the second part of the volume. Part II also includes a view of school governance from Northern Ireland and an analysis of devolved management in Scotland.

In her chapter on the involvement of lay people in site based management of schools Rosemary Deem draws parallels between England and Australia and the United States of America. She compares power structures and discusses the ways in which they have changed. Her central concern is with the democratization of school management as she poses questions about the ways in which governors are appointed rather than elected. Her research leads to the conclusion that those who become school governors are from a fairly narrow stratum of society and are comprised principally by those who have the time and the material resources to allow them to take on what can be a demanding and time consuming role. While the role for governors now embraces finance, school organization and delivery of the national curriculum, Deem believes that a degree of confusion exists amongst many governors who find their task somewhat daunting. Moreover, her research has shown that most governors do not involve themselves with matters relating to teaching and learning and are unsure of their relationship with teachers and pupils. Her conclusion is that despite the rhetoric of involvement and democracy, lay governors have little effect in shaping education.

Several of the themes addressed by Deem are also present in the chapter by McKeown, Donnelly and Osborne. However, their specific concern is with school governing bodies in Northern Ireland and the changes which were brought about by the 1989 Education Reform Order (ERO). The chapter is a welcome contribution to the literature on school governance in Northern Ireland about which there has been little research to date. The authors develop their work to suggest that the increased responsibility for governors has, under some circumstances, led to a tension between governing bodies and headteachers. Where this occurs, the school may become a site of conflict as the forces of the new democracy are tested out.

A Scottish perspective on changes in school governance is provided in the chapter by Arnott, Rabb and Munn. Their examination of devolved school management (DSM) *vis à vis* Scottish school boards reveals many similar issues to those arising from the introduction of local management of schools (LMS) in England and Wales. Their chapter draws on research conducted in three geographical areas of Scotland and discusses the new roles for parents, headteachers and local authorities under DMS. In addition to issues related to the location of power and the capacity for decision-making under the new arrangements, the authors also point to evidence that DMS with its link to formula funding (Levacic, 1993) has brought about particular image-management strategies as schools seek to attract and hold onto funds. The chapter also casts some doubt over the extent to which school governors have real power in schools. Their research shows that governors tend to defer to headteacher judgment on key issues.

Issues of devolved school management are taken further in the next chapter by Power, Halpin and Fitz as they consider the English experience of grant maintained schools policy. The chapter picks up on many of the themes already raised in the volume and which encapsulate the intentions, focus and implications of the 1988 Education Reform Act. For example, their concern is with parental empowerment and choice, the role of the head, curriculum and pedagogy. The authors deploy their research evidence to suggest a considerable difference between the rhetoric of grant maintained status and the experience of it. They conclude that in relation to parental involvement, curriculum and pedagogy, little change can be discerned in grant maintained schools. Their conclusion is that grant maintained schools policy has resulted in a consolidation of hierarchies within schools with headteachers continuing in much the same way as ever when it comes to decision-making and parents tending to defer to the authority of the teacher.

The chapters in this second part of the volume pose some serious questions about the extent to which new arrangements for school governance in England, Scotland and Northern Ireland are achieving any real change in the distribution of power in education. The evidence presented tends to suggest a rhetorical rather than a real shift of power to parents and governing bodies, with, moreover; a fairly narrow representation of parents in terms of key social characteristics. Given the chapters concentrate upon actual experiences of new arrangements for governance, they demonstrate little real change despite the elaborate structures put into place by the various Education Reform Acts in England, Scotland and Northern Ireland.

The theme of experience and rhetoric rather than reality also provides the foundation for the final section of the volume which is concerned with local management of schools.

Experiencing Local Management

While education management may be seen as a key aspect of the first two parts of the volume the final part addresses the changes brought about by the introduction of LMS head-on, by examining the experiences of those directly involved in this aspect of devolved management. The integrated nature of the 1988 Education Reform Act means that many of the themes already addressed in the volume are revisited in the context of LMS. For example questions of autonomy and the capacity of heads and governors to make real decisions are posed alongside questions of per capita funding and the implications for budget management. Again, the chapters in this section highlight the difference between the rhetoric and the reality of changes which have occurred post-1988.

Part III begins with Julia Evetts's chapter on the role of the headteacher under LMS. Evetts argues that in respect of the day to day work activities the occupational culture of headship has changed fundamentally. Using detailed interviews and follow-up postal questionnaires with 20 headteachers, Evetts argues that LMS has necessitated a new kind of headteacher: one whose time is taken more by aspects of budgetary and corporate managerialism and less by traditional aspects of the role such as leadership. Her research signals a significant change for headteachers to a role which those with traditional expectations may find difficult. An emphasis on bureaucracy, finance and administration may be far removed from experience as a classroom teacher to the extent that questions need to be posed about the career paths for headteachers and whether the traditional route of working up through the ranks provides appropriate experience and training for the position of headteacher. Furthermore, an emphasis on budgetary and corporate managerialism may mean the position is less attractive to those whose interests lie with teaching. The title Head*teacher* may have become a misnomer.

The theme of budgetary and corporate managerialism is pursued in the second of the chapters in this part. Huckman and Fletcher are concerned with the school as a unit of production and their chapter, which is based on a two year study of LMS in two schools, focuses upon internal decision-making processes in the context of cost effectiveness and cost efficiency for schools. The language used in the chapter may seem to have more in common with accountancy than with processes of schooling, but it is nevertheless consistent with the rational planning strategies in which their schools engaged and with the structures now put into place by financial devolution. In this context of efficiency and financial effectiveness, the chapter raises some serious questions about school effectiveness and the ways in which the quality of education in secondary schools is demonstrated via balance sheets and league tables. The chapter introduces the notion of product assessment and again, while the language may seem somewhat clinical for what is a social process, it would seem to be quite appropriate for the ethos of the education market and the homogenization of provision discussed in earlier chapters of the volume.

In the penultimate chapter Sally Brown provides a view of recent changes in school management in Scotland. While many of the themes are familiar, for example, consumerism, competition, efficiency and enterprise, there are also some important differences from the situation in England and Wales. For example Brown informs us that technology academies (CTCs) failed to take off in Scotland due to a lack of private finance and were therefore, abandoned. The Scottish national curriculum is less prescriptive than the English, being based on guidelines rather than orders and there are no published league tables. Brown believes a period of policy hysteria has underpinned developments in Scotland as schools have endured multiple innovations, frequent policy switches and a lack of educational coherence. With regard to self-government, Brown reports that this has barely taken off in Scotland as schools have been reluctant to break links with local authorities.

The final chapter is provided by Dawn Penney and John Evans. Their concern is with the internal markets which, under LMS, have developed within individual schools. Using examples from physical education, their chapter shows how competition for resources within schools has intensified. Rather than removing constraints which were previously imposed by local authorities, LMS has simply substituted a set of internal constraints for teaching staff as they vie for resources with each other based on various funding formulas devised and applied internally by schools. The chapter raises important questions about provision of the curriculum (Fowler, 1990), particularly in relation to less favoured or what might be perceived as less important components of it. Where resources are scarce, perhaps due to a failure by unpopular schools to attract large numbers of pupils (Levacic, 1993), it may be that schools are only able to adequately resource those areas of the curriculum which are mandatory. Consequently it is the national curriculum subjects which have the greatest influence on internal school markets. As a result, this may mean that some schools are only able to offer a relatively narrow curriculum.

In total, this volume provides a critical view of the new shape of education in the United Kingdom. It poses important questions about the experience of education from the perspective of teachers, heads, governors and parents. As the chapters draw on empirical research, the book provides an opportunity to gauge the actual outcomes of 1980s education legislation against the aspirations which underpinned it.

So far, the 1990s has been an important decade for secondary education – one where expectations have been high, where established structures have been challenged and where the responsibilities of the state have been modified. The decade has brought widescale change and a degree of uncertainty, which for some of those involved, has been difficult to accept. The chapters in this volume provide an opportunity, therefore, for reflection, and taking stock of how far education has changed since the watershed year of 1988 and on this basis, looking towards the implications of the changes for the further development of secondary education into the twenty-first century.

References

Angus, L. (1994) 'Sociological analysis and education management: The social context of the self-managing school', *British Journal of Sociology of Education*, **15**, 1, pp. 79–92.

Chawla-Duggan, R. and Pole, C. (eds) (1996) *Reshaping Education in the 1990s: Perspectives on Primary Education*, London, Falmer Press.

Chitty, C. (1989) *Towards a New Education System: The Victory of the New Right?* London, Falmer Press.

Deem, R. (1990) 'The reform of school governing bodies: The power of the consumer over the producer', in Flude, M. and Hammer, M. (eds) *The Education Reform Act 1988, Its Opinions and Implications*, London, Falmer Press.

Eggleston, J. (1988) 'The new education bill and assessment – Some implications for black children', *Multicultural Teaching*, **6**, 2, pp. 24–6.

Fitz, J., Halpin, D. and Power, S. (1993) *Grant Maintained Schools: Education in the Market Place*, London, Kogan Page.

Fowler, W. (1990) *Implementing the National Curriculum*, London, Kogan Page.

Hatcher, R. (1994) 'Market relationships and the management of teachers', *British Journal of Sociology of Education*, **15**, 1, pp. 41–62.

Jones, K. (1989) *Right Turn*, London, Hutchinson.

Knight, C. (1990) *The Making of Tory Education Policy in Post-War Britain*, London, Falmer Press.

Levacic, R. (1993) 'Assessing the impact of formula funding on schools', *Oxford Review of Education*, **19**, 4, pp. 435–58.

MacNeil, C. (1988) 'The national curriculum: A black perspective', *Multicultural Teaching*, **6**, 2, pp. 14–17.

Power, S., Fitz, J. and Halpin, D. (1994) 'Parents, pupils and grant-maintained schools', *British Educational Research Journal*, **20**, 2, pp. 209–26.

Rogers, M. (1992) *Opting Out: Choice and the Future of Schools*, London, Lawrence and Wishart.

Simon, B. (1988) *Bending the Rules: The Baker 'Reform' of Education*, London, Lawrence and Wishart.

Part I

Schooling and the Market

Chapter 1

Dynamics of Competition – The Effects of Local Competitive Arenas on Schools

Philip A. Woods, Carl Bagley and Ron Glatter

Introduction

A major thrust of government reforms in education since 1988 has been to introduce a more competitive, market-like environment for schools. Key elements in this process include: open enrolment, by which schools and LEAs (local education authorities) are prevented from limiting admissions below their full capacity; local management of schools, through which responsibility for budgets and management more generally is devolved to schools; moves to diversify school provision, through, for example, grant maintained status and the creation of technology schools; and the publication of more information for parents, such as league tables of examination results and other data about schools.

To assess whether these reforms are achieving the intended aim of creating a vibrant market in schooling and, thereby, making schools more consumer-responsive and raising educational standards requires monitoring and investigation over a period of time. The PASCI (Parental and School Choice Interaction) study is seeking to meet, in part, this requirement. It is a major longitudinal investigation of the interaction between parental choice of school and school decision-making.[1] It is focusing on how secondary schools respond to competition (including how they obtain, interpret and act upon clues regarding parental preferences, and what factors constrain them in reacting to such information) and how parents react to these responses (including their perception of choice and constraints upon it).

The exploratory phase (which undertook methodological groundwork and pilot fieldwork in preparation for the study's main phase) ran from 1990 to 1992. The three-year main phase began in 1993. As choice and competition in schooling is characteristically local in nature, we have sought in the study to focus on what we have termed *local competitive arenas* (Glatter and Woods, 1994). Such arenas are areas of varying sizes and natures within which schools draw from a largely common population of parents and children. Research

Figure 1.1 Local Competitive Arenas – Processes of Interaction and Influence

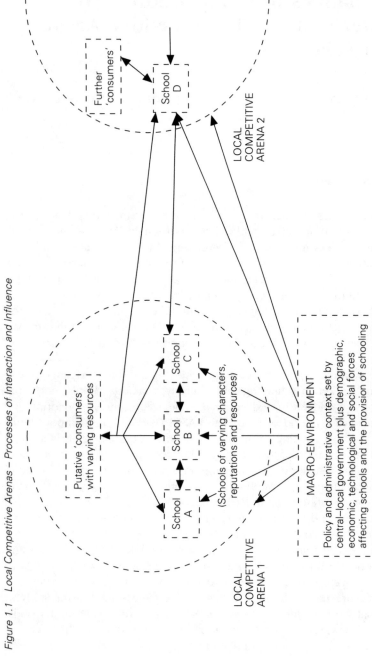

Key INTERACTION PROCESSES
     INFLUENCE PROCESSES

Source: Glatter and Woods 1994

activity (using multiple methods of investigation) is being undertaken in three contrasting case study areas concurrently over the three years 1993 to 1995. Each area:

- resembles as closely as possible a competitive arena in which secondary schools draw from a largely common population of parents;
- contains three to six secondary state schools (plus feeder schools) at which a series of interviews with school personnel are being undertaken and competitive responses by the secondary schools monitored;
- is the focus for three annual surveys of parents choosing a secondary school, using both self-completion questionnaires and personal interviews.

Local competitive arenas are not in practice discrete entities. Their boundaries will tend to overlap and individual family perceptions of the area in which they may choose schools will vary according to such factors as access to transport. Nevertheless, the notion of local competitive arenas is, we believe, a useful means of conceptualizing competition in schooling and of organizing empirical work investigating the impact of policies aimed at enhancing competition.

Local competitive arenas are subject to both distinctive (and interacting) internal influences and to external influences from wider political, administrative and other factors. These wider factors emanate from what has been termed the macro-environment. Figure 1.1 seeks in a preliminary way, and through an element of simplification, to help organize our thinking about the forces and influences affecting choice and competition in schooling.

There is a huge variety of such arenas around the country, varying, for example, in socioeconomic character and population density. In extreme cases, where the population is very thinly spread, there may be no competitive arena at all, but this is unusual. We feel the figure is useful in delineating a number of the interactive relationships on which our study focuses. The model, as represented in the figure, is not intended to be comprehensive and is at an early stage of development. We will return to the model below.

The introduction of market forces into schooling does not produce approximately private markets, but instead heavily conditioned *quasi-markets*. In this chapter we will provide impressions of the effects of quasi-market pressures on schools, drawing on our 1993 fieldwork data (and, where relevant, pilot fieldwork undertaken in 1991). These impressions will be set in the context of the schools' local competitive arenas.

Impressions from 1993 Fieldwork with Schools

In 1993 a total of 76 interviews were carried out with staff (mainly senior management) in the 11 secondary schools participating in the study. Using this

Figure 1.2   Typology of School Responses

Response	Purpose and scope
Competitive within these three main types of activity can be distinguished	To increase or maintain the number of pupils at the school
• substantive change	• includes changes in the school's central educational activities (such as curriculum and teaching methods) and the way it organizes itself; also includes changes in intake selection and character of school
• environmental 'scanning and interpretation' (environmental scanning)	• concerned with how a school perceives its 'market', finding out what influences parents' school preferences
• promotional activity	• action intended to raise the school's profile, improve its image
Income-enhancing	To secure income over and above the school budget based on formula-funding, through fund-raising, sponsorship deals, and so on
Efficiency-increasing	To get the most out of the school budget and concentrate resources on the school's central educational activities
Political	To influence politicians and/or officials and encourage them to make changes (such as in the funding formula) which will benefit the school
Collaborative	To obtain benefits from working in cooperation with other schools: cooperation can be concerned with achieving any of the above aims; includes cooperative action aimed at eliminating or reducing competition

Source: Woods 1994a

data we have sought to identify how these schools are responding to government attempts to create a more competitive environment. All names below are fictitious. A typology of school responses developed as part of the PASCI study is being used as an analytic framework (Woods 1994a; Glatter and Woods 1995). The typology is set out in Figure 1.2.

Marshampton

Marshampton is a town of approximately 100,000 people. A high proportion of its employment emanates from national government agencies and engineering firms, with an above-average representation of professional and middle-class households.

It has a long history of competition between schools (both state and private – the latter nevertheless educating less than 10 per cent of pupils in Marshampton). One of the secondary schools is an academically-selective grammar school (Salix Grammar) taking pupils from age 11 to 18. This school is not currently involved in the study. The remaining five are comprehensive (all-ability) schools. In 1991, pilot fieldwork was undertaken in Marshampton at three of these schools (Thurcleigh Hill, Daythorpe and Endswich). At that time, Marshampton secondary schools were widely seen as being in a 'pecking order' headed by Salix Grammar, followed (in descending order) by Bridgerton (11–18), Thurcleigh Hill (11–16), Daythorpe (11–16) and Endswich (11–16). These last four are all involved in the study's main phase. The fifth school in the study is a church school, St Asters Catholic School (11–16), which gives priority to Catholic pupils in its admission policy, though its intake is by no means exclusively Catholic. St Asters has similar reputational problems to Daythorpe and Endswich.

By 1991, Salix Grammar was the only school in Marshampton that had opted for grant maintained (GM) status. Since then, all the remaining secondary schools have opted for GM status. The predominant incentive for going GM appears to be financial, ahead of other reasons such as the feeling that the county is being 'dismembered' and the belief that GM status will allow the school to appoint administrative/financial staff to whom responsibilities can be delegated. However, there are perceived competitive advantages: it is believed to improve the school image ('grant maintained' sounds good to parents – or so it is thought); extra money allows improvements, e.g. in school reception areas; and it allows the possibility of introducing a sixth form (more on this below).

The schools we visited in 1991 had undertaken a range of promotional initiatives, including improved school brochures, more active links with feeder schools and advertising in the local press (Woods, 1993a). Attention to the importance of school-promotion is evident in the current phase of our study too. Emphasis on active contacts with primary schools is prominent amongst this promotional activity. Although it is stressed by some interviewees that promotion is not the prime reason for these links, they are clearly of great significance to those schools under greatest pressure – St Asters, Daythorpe and Endswich – in seeking to attract parents and children.

It is noteworthy that Bridgerton, which is consistently oversubscribed and has been the most popular of the town's comprehensive schools, has become more conscious of the need to promote itself. One initiative it has taken is, in September 1993, to hold its first open evening for parents (other schools already held such evenings as a matter of course). The headteacher believes that attitudes in the school are changing:

> I think probably there has been a shift in the attitudes of staff over a period of time . . . I think the teaching staff . . . found it difficult to come to terms with the notion that we had to sell ourselves and that we had to compete. And there was no easy relationship between that and jobs and finance and all the rest of it. Now I think people do realize that. (headteacher, Bridgerton, 1993)

This change at Bridgerton is related to greater competition from other Marshampton comprehensives. Thurcleigh Hill has increased its attractiveness and there are signs of its becoming closer to Bridgerton in image and factors such as GCSE pass rate. Thurcleigh Hill's intake has risen since 1985 so that it is now admitting pupils up to its standard number. Bridgerton and Thurcleigh Hill are the more academically-orientated of the town's comprehensives.

There are indications of substantive changes which are related to some degree to the more market-like environment intended for schools. We highlight here certain changes which have a bearing on the schools' academic policies and practices. Results from the 1991 pilot fieldwork indicated that at Thurcleigh Hill changes in examination and homework policy had taken place as a result of parental pressure. In consequence, the school's own examinations were made more formal (so as to prepare pupils for public examinations) and a more organized system of homework was introduced. Our 1993 fieldwork suggests that other schools, as a result of Marshampton's heightened competitive environment, may be focusing to a greater extent than previously on matters to do with examinations and homework policy, and that this also may be giving encouragement to banding or setting of pupils according to ability: Bridgerton has introduced homework diaries and is planning to review its policy on setting (with a view, possibly, to extending it); St Asters is engaged in a campaign to improve examination results and a review of homework policy is being considered; Endswich believes that banding of pupils, introduced in 1991, has helped to improve its examination results.

It is important not to overstate changes such as these. They appear to be in part a result of a belief amongst school decision-makers that their school must be attractive to parents. But, it is difficult to distinguish the effect of the local quasi-market from other influences acting upon schools and to gauge the full impact of such changes on the conduct and ethos of the schools concerned. Research activity is continuing in the schools to explore these matters further and to follow up policy changes planned by schools. This activity is also following up other apparent substantive changes relating, for example, to curricular provision and class sizes.

A significant change is being considered by Daythorpe and Endswich. It has long been felt at these schools that the absence of a sixth form markedly reduces their attractiveness to parents (only Salix Grammar and Bridgerton have sixth forms currently). Each of the headteachers says that they plan to introduce a sixth form which would concentrate on GNVQs. This is based on a belief that rising demand for vocational qualifications cannot be fully met by Marshampton's further education college. These plans, while tentative at present, symbolize what may be a widening division between the academically-orientated, high-in-the-pecking-order schools on the one hand, and the more vocationally-orientated, less popular schools on the other.

Initiatives in environmental scanning are much more patchy than in school promotion. Most effort has been put in by St Asters where one of the deputy headteachers had undertaken a research study of perceptions of the school and where she also monitors the numbers of children in primary schools and baptismal records. Plans at Endswich (mooted in 1991) to send questionnaires to parents were not acted upon. Elsewhere, there appears little to report (though Daythorpe did introduce an interesting programme of 'listening to pupils' which involved senior staff asking pupils in their final year for their views of the school). School decision-makers characteristically rely on ad hoc and informal feedback concerning how parents perceive the school and prospects for future demand on places.

Endswich has the most formidable task in responding to the impact of quasi-market forces. It has the worst reputation in the town, which is compounded by location and transport problems: it is on the edge of town, lacks good bus routes and is reached via a poor, run-down estate. The headteacher also sees it as suffering from the difficulties of perceiving and conveying indicators of 'quality education': crude exam results favour Salix Grammar and Bridgerton, but Endswich has (and according to the head the LEA has produced evidence of this) superior 'value-added' performance. In addition to all this, the school has financial problems (£100,000 overdraft) and its intake has fallen substantially from 151 in 1991 to 112 and 116 in 1992 and 1993 respectively. Its plans involve obtaining GM status and changing its name in order to distance itself from its poor reputation (both of these things were done in 1994), and adding sixth form provision as noted above. Apart from these planned changes, the impression gained at Endswich is of a school that (at least till now) has tended to deal less positively and systematically with its difficulties than many other schools. This is in part due to the consequences of financial constraints which have included staff redundancies.

At St Asters, for example, the approach appears more positive. Its intake is consistently below its standard number and there is a perception that the school is not ensuring that a sufficient proportion of its Catholic community is sending its children to the school. But, as indicated above, a 'market research' exercise has been undertaken to which the headteacher responds in this way:

> I think it's led to a higher profile being given to disciplinary matters and uniforms since these are the most obvious visual ways in which a school's reputation is judged. It certainly focused minds on the importance of academic attainment as well and a great deal is currently going into analysing the examination results each year, discussing them with departmental heads, looking at ways in which these can be sustained and improved, and also in increasing an awareness on the part of all the staff that it's very important to hold up high expectations for children. (headteacher, St. Asters, 1993)

The extent to which this articulation of change represents a real change in the school and is successful in achieving the school's marketing goals will be monitored during the remaining period of the study (as will indications of substantive change in other schools). In particular, we will be investigating whether there is a general trend in Marshampton schools towards emphasizing what might be termed traditional academic issues – examination success, homework, banding/setting of pupils and strong discipline. In the 1991 pilot fieldwork, the caring and pastoral aspect of schools was emphasized by many senior staff interviewed and one school (Daythorpe) saw this as part of its competitive strategy (Woods 1992, 1993a). This aspect has been more muted during the most recent fieldwork. While it would be wrong to conclude that schools are in any way less caring, it raises the question of whether there has been a significant shift in emphasis as a result of Marshampton's quasi-market.

East Greenvale

East Greenvale is an administrative district of Greenvale LEA. It is a semi-rural area consisting of three small towns and a large number of villages. The education system in the area is organized as a 'pyramid' with an upper school (13–18 years) at the pyramid head, taking pupils at age 13 (Year 8) from its feeder middle schools and the latter receiving pupils at age 9 from their feeder first schools. This organization does not affect parents' rights to school choice, although the vast majority of pupils transfer from their feeder middle to their pyramid upper school.

There are three LEA-controlled upper schools in East Greenvale: Dellway, Molehill and Elderfield, one in each of the small towns. All three schools are broadly similar in character, offering a comprehensive education for a wide ability range of pupils, and placed in the lower-middle of the academic league table (for Greenvale LEA).

The schools' similarity and location, and the LEA system of school place allocation, means that the schools tend to serve their own communities, and while they do not achieve their admission limits they are assured of a constant and sufficiently high intake of pupils to feel financially secure. There is very little evidence of competition between the three schools. A cordial and to a limited extent collaborative relationship has evolved, based on a mutual understanding that the present system brings shared benefits. School collaboration is not seen as a response to competition. Nevertheless, its existence enables the headteachers to share their concerns about an increasingly competitive environment. For example, the headteachers who meet regularly on an informal basis share confidential information on such issues as the use of exam boards and exam performance. They have a 'gentleman's agreement' not to use these figures either for or against one another, and to keep each other informed of any moves within their governing bodies towards grant maintained status. Sixth form students have the opportunity to take A-level courses at each others' schools, although none is currently doing so.

At present there is no immediate pressure or perceived need by any of the schools to make substantive changes. The primary response is a promotional one geared towards maintaining a strong relationship with their pyramid feeder middle schools and ensuring that parents choose to remain within the existing LEA system of school allocation.

As a consequence, and in keeping with the collaborative relationship between the schools, there is an informal agreement that any promotional activity is confined to their own feeder middle schools. Promotional activities include production of school brochures and promotional videos, open evenings, increased links with feeder middle schools, open forums for middle school parents, regular features in the local press and improvements to school appearance (repainting, displays).

While activities such as open evenings and links with primary schools were happening before attempts to introduce competition, senior staff acknowledge an increased recognition of their promotional value in addition to their always-acknowledged educational value. Consequently, greater attention and planning is given to the promotional side of any linkage than had previously been the case.

The headteacher at Molehill reported that he had 'been picking up vibes' from middle school parents that the school was not doing enough to promote itself. He responded by introducing an open forum for parents from the feeder middle schools – an opportunity to visit Molehill, to listen to him and his deputy and to ask any questions and raise any issues about the school. This exercise is not only promotional but also provides feedback on parental perspectives. Molehill has also introduced a series of promotional 'roadshows' which visit Year 7 pupils and their parents in the feeder middle schools. Ad hoc feedback from parents at the open forum and discussion with staff at the feeder middle schools prior to a visit, mean that the format and issues discussed at each roadshow vary depending on the school being visited. For example, if parents are concerned about transport to Molehill then that is the main issue discussed. The roadshows show a school using promotional activities and scanning and interpretation exercises to complement one another. The decision by Molehill to visit Year 7 pupils (rather than Year 8) was something new, the headteacher believing it was now important to provide parents with information about the school as soon as possible. This new strategy was treated with some suspicion by staff at Dellway, who required reassurance that such action was confined to Molehill's feeder schools.

All three headteachers recognize that if one of their schools were to go grant maintained or the LEA admission system were to change, then the present cooperative relationship between them could easily dissolve. The potential fragility of this situation has led to an increased sensitivity by senior staff to any actions which might be construed as competitive. For example, at present Elderfield gains approximately 30 pupils who transfer at age 9 from one of Dellway's lower pyramid schools to one of their pyramid feeder middle schools. This is creating a tension area between the schools as Dellway now visits Elderfield's middle school to encourage pupils to transfer back into their pyramid. In effect Dellway is having to fight a rearguard action against increased competition between middle schools for lower school pupils.

Similarly, the accepted protocol amongst upper schools in Greenvale LEA is for school brochures to be only given to middle school pupils who, because of where they live, are likely to attend their upper. A neighbouring upper school (on the boundary of Molehill's catchment area) recently broke with this tradition and decided to give its brochure to all the pupils in a middle school. This action resulted in a meeting between the schools at which it was agreed that in future all pupils, regardless of where they lived in Greenvale would receive a brochure. The response to this incident reveals once again the sensitivity of schools to any action which might be construed as competitive. This sensitivity is even more acute when it involves middle schools on the periphery of their pyramid catchment areas, as it is in these areas that parents have the greatest opportunity to choose between different schools.

Northern Heights

Northern Heights is a local competitive arena within Northborough LEA. It is an area which displays many of the forms of social deprivation and disadvantage characteristic of parts of urban Britain, with above-average proportions of working-class households, poor quality housing, high rates of unemployment, and so on. There is an identifiable ethnic minority community in Northern Heights (approximately 5 per cent of the population), which is predominantly of Bangladeshi origin.

Northborough LEA has operated a system of open enrolment since 1977 whereby parents can choose any four schools in the LEA which they then rank in order of preference. This well-established practice means that schools in Northern Heights are used to operating in a competitive environment. However, the introduction of LMS, and in particular the linking of school funding to pupil intake, has undoubtedly heightened the competition between schools, especially as some are now fighting for their economic survival. Senior staff believe they are now working in what a headteacher and a deputy from one school described as a 'dog eat dog' situation.

Northern Heights has three LEA-controlled secondary schools: Braelands, Newcrest Technology School and Leaside. Braelands is in a semi-rural location on the boundary of Northern Heights and of Northborough LEA. It is at the top of the academic league table and is oversubscribed, attracting pupils from throughout Northern Heights, other parts of Northborough and increasingly from an adjoining LEA.

Senior staff are committed to maintaining, and if possible enhancing the academic reputation of the school. This they seek to achieve largely through promotional activities (school brochures, primary school visits, open evenings) which stress the academic nature of the school. Promotional links with primary schools are targeted at those which the school sees as providing 'the sort of pupils' (academic achievers) and type of parents (middle-class) the school wishes to attract. This promotional work is coordinated by a teacher with a marketing brief.

As an oversubscribed institution with a strong academic record, no substantive change to its curriculum or organization is seen as necessary. The school is perceived as already providing what parents want. Parents who have selected the school are asked to fill in a form to indicate the reasons for their choice. This monitoring (scanning) seeks to ensure that the school is maintaining its existing standards and is continuing to attract the 'right sort' of pupils and parents.

Due to its strong market position as an academic school, Braelands does not view itself to be in competition with either Newcrest Technology School or Leaside, both of which it sees as catering for the needs of different pupils (less academic) and parents (more working-class). The major competition for Braelands is identified as three grant maintained schools outside Northern Heights in Northborough LEA who similarly promote themselves as academic, schools.

Newcrest Technology School is located in the central urban area and is the main school serving the ethnic minority community with around 20 per cent of its intake being pupils of Bangladeshi origin. It is in the lower half of the league table and struggles to maintain its admission level at the standard number of 180.

The school, while placing an emphasis on the caring and pastoral aspect of schooling, is keen to attract more academically able pupils in order to improve its league table position which it sees as important in influencing parental choice. For this reason Braelands rather than Leaside is seen as its major competitor in Northern Heights.

Receipt of money under the Technology School Initiative led to the school's adopting its present name. This was complemented by the introduction of a new school uniform and the development of substantive changes involving a greater focus on technology across the school curriculum. The school believes that this strategy coupled with the delivery of more vocational courses will not only solidify its traditional parental support from the surrounding urban area, but also encourage parents to choose the school whose children might otherwise have attended Braelands. The promotional activities undertaken by Newcrest Technology School (similar in form to those of Braelands) stress the message and image of a 'technology award winning school'.

As a school in financial difficulty, the sale of the new school uniform and the hiring-out of the school's sports facilities helps to pay for these promotional activities, particularly school brochures. The lack of additional sources of income means that Leaside cannot afford to produce and distribute brochures so widely.

Scanning and interpretation of parental perspectives is less formal and more ad hoc in the case of Newcrest (and Leaside) than in that of Braelands. Senior staff stress the schools' strong and close association with their parents. Both schools have an open door policy towards parents and staff make frequent visits to parents' homes. The close proximity of the schools to pupils' homes (not the case at Braelands) add to this sense of familiarity; as the deputy at Newcrest remarked 'We know our area'.

In the context of this relationship senior staff at Newcrest were confident that the school's increased emphasis on technology would succeed. As the deputy observed, 'We talk to our parents and we convince them that that's what they want . . . If you've got a product to sell you can mould people into receiving that product'.

The vigorous promotional and substantive activity at Newcrest Technology School contrasts sharply with the response of Leaside. This school is situated in the middle of a large run-down 1960s housing estate (also called Leaside) set apart from the main urban area and is largely reliant for its admissions upon the support of parents from its immediate feeder primaries. It is at the bottom of the academic league table and is undersubscribed by 50 per cent.

Senior staff are resigned to the fact that in its present predicament the school is unable to attract parents who do not live on the Leaside estate. The reasons given for this are the school's relatively isolated location, the estate's bad reputation, the school's lack of funds, and its inadequate staffing levels, all of which combine to make it difficult to promote the school and undertake any substantive changes to the school's curriculum and organization.

Newcrest Technology School and Braelands do not seek to attract pupils from the Leaside estate. The major reason for this is that Leaside's intake of pupils, many from socially disadvantaged backgrounds and requiring strong pastoral and remedial support, are not the sort either Braelands or Newcrest Technology School want to attract. For the same reason they share a common interest with Leaside in ensuring that despite its low pupil intake and large number of surplus places it nonetheless remains open. Senior staff at Newcrest Technology School are particularly supportive of Leaside and offer facilities and equipment to the school. At a macro level there is no political desire on behalf of the Labour controlled council to close the school which is in a strong Labour area. Moreover, school rolls in Leaside estate primary schools are now rising.

Discussion

In all of the case study areas, it is evident that schools generally are actively promoting themselves and utilizing a range of means to this end. Prominent amongst these is the use and development of links with feeder schools. Such links – involving staff visiting feeder schools and in some cases pupils from the latter visiting the secondary or upper schools – are not new. But where they have existed there is greater awareness of their potential for promoting the image of the school and encouraging a favourable attitude towards it. In some cases steps have been taken to initiate links, or to formalize ties, with particular feeder schools.

This emphasis on promotion, and the importance attached specifically to nurturing contacts with feeder schools, contrasts with the relative paucity of attention given to environmental scanning. Schools are keen to promote themselves, but much less likely to initiate ways of finding out how parents view the school and how it might accommodate their expressed wishes and concerns. Part of the explanation for this is likely to be an inherent professional reluctance to be led by 'consumers' rather than driven by the profession's own expertise (a reluctance not confined to the teaching profession). But there may be an additional factor shaping the way schools respond to the quasi-market: a tendency to interact more readily with and take notice of other institutions, in preference to amorphous and more difficult-to-reach individuals (parents).

This line of thought prompts us to suggest that school personnel are more likely (for practical purposes) to see the school as inhabiting an environment of institutions and that in consequence there may be a tendency in some schools to be 'institution-responsive' rather than 'consumer-responsive'. Thus schools pay particular attention to their feeders and to other secondary schools. School managers have a view of where they fit into the pecking order of schools in their area. They tend to be aware of what other schools are doing, particularly new departures in promotional activity, and sometimes will respond – by following suit or, possibly, contacting the school if they believe the action oversteps the mark in some way. There are instances where commonly-held views amongst schools affect decision-making. In Marshampton, for example, all schools attach great importance to having a school uniform and none alone would depart from this – indeed, the tendency is to upgrade or renew emphasis on the uniform and there is almost a ratchet effect (as one does it, others follow). Whether this is what parents and pupils want is another matter.

Seeing themselves as part of a group of existing institutions, and as occupying a particular place within this, has implications for perceptions of what competitive responsiveness can achieve. Schools do not compete as equals. Some schools suffer from poor reputation, difficult location, financial limitations and other negative factors, while others are more positively endowed. It is enormously difficult for the schools with many or all of the most negative characteristics to compete with schools enjoying the most positive advantages. It may be possible for a school, however, to move up the pecking order one or two places – to overcome a short gap between it and another school. This appears to be the case with Thurcleigh Hill in Marshampton, for example, which has moved closer to Bridgerton (the town's most popular comprehensive). The context formed by other schools interacts with a school's own characteristics and resources to define the scope for competition, responsiveness and achievable change.

There is no clear-cut trend amongst schools with regard to substantive changes. There is less evidence of mutual (interschool) influence with regard to substantive change, as compared with the mutual monitoring of promotional activities (noted above). In East Greenvale, there is very little market-driven substantive change at all. This is as one would expect, since there is considerably less scope for parental choice and for competition in this area because of its semi-rural nature. Elsewhere there are signs of substantive change which we are investigating further through continuing research activity.

It is possible to suggest a hypothesis at this stage. This is that, where there is an active quasi-market, substantive change tends to be concerned with traditional academic issues (such as examination performance, homework, setting according to ability, etc.) and/or with 'hard' curriculum areas such as technology (support for aspects of this hypothesis is evident from other work – Gewirtz *et al.* 1994, for example). This suggests, as a corollary, that concern with the caring aspect of a school (what elsewhere has been characterized as the 'human warmth' aspect of schooling – Woods, 1993b; Woods and Woods, 1994) is given less prominence. These tendencies – if confirmed – are not necessarily the result of responsiveness to parental preferences. As we have noted, environmental scanning is limited. Moreover, influences emanating from the macro-environment have important consequences. For example, central government has decreed that league tables of school examination performance should be published. These may not be the most influential sources of information for parents (Woods, 1994b) but there are indications that they are significant for senior management in schools. A further example is the emphasis placed by central government on technology initiatives. Such developments may have the effects of making the school system more sharply tiered and reducing the practical possibilities for schools to appeal to a broad market in academic and social terms (Glatter, 1993). We shall be interested to see whether such trends are visible in our case study areas in the remaining period of the PASCI study.

The continuing work of the study's main phase will also allow us to refine the diagrammatic representation of local competitive arenas and the macro-environment (Figure 1.1). For example, it is clear from the results to date that the relationship with feeder schools is a significant one. This mediates or replaces the interactive relationship with putative 'consumers' in the figure – or it might co-exist with direct contacts with parents and families. Its importance suggests that it should be incorporated in the figure. Our fieldwork experience to date also reinforces the point that local competitive arenas have overlapping boundaries. They are intersecting circles rather than discrete entities. Boundaries are fluid and strong influences can move across them. Thus Daythorpe School in Marshampton sees itself as benefiting from the declining reputation of a secondary school outside the town. Similarly, Braelands School in Northern Heights looks to three grant maintained schools outside the area as its most potent sources of competition, rather than the two schools within it which it sees as catering for a different type of pupil. Generally, the interaction *between* secondary schools in relation to competition appears highly significant, and this may need to be reflected more clearly in the figure.

Finally, and perhaps of greatest importance, the specific historical, political and cultural context of particular local arenas is not shown explicitly. In a sense, this inhabits the space outside the boxes but within the circles, framing and influencing (along with the macro-environment) the processes of family choice and school response which are the focus of the PASCI study. The contexts of the three case study areas within the study contrast starkly with one another, shaping the nature of the quasi-market and the character of the choice offered to families in each area. Whether this indicates desirable diversity between different areas, or unacceptable variation based on the chance factor of where one happens to live, is a central issue for debate arising from the operation of the new market model of schooling.

Note

1   The PASCI study is funded by the UK Economic and Social Research Council (ESRC) (ref. R000234079). A briefing paper about the project and a publications list can be obtained free of charge from: Caroline Dickens, CEPAM, School of Education, The Open University, Milton Keynes, MK7 6AA, United Kingdom.

References

GEWIRTZ, S., BOWE, R. and BALL, S. (1994) 'Choice, competition and equity: Lessons from research in the UK', paper presented at American Educational Research Association Conference, New Orleans, LA, April.

GLATTER, R. (1993), 'Choice of What?', *Education*, p. 331, 29 October.

GLATTER, R. (1995) 'Partnership in the market model: Is it dying?' in MACBETH, A., McCREATH, D. and AITCHISON, J. (eds) *Collaborate or Compete? Educational Partnerships in a Market Economy*, London, Falmer Press.

GLATTER, R. and WOODS, P.A. (1994) 'The impact of competition and choice on parents and schools', in BARTLETT, W., LEGRAND, J., PROPPER C. and WILSON, D. (eds) *Quasi-Markets in the Welfare State*, Bristol, SAUS Publications.

WOODS, P.A. (1992) 'Empowerment through choice? Towards an understanding of parental choice and school responsiveness', *Educational Management and Administration*, **20**, 4, pp. 204–11.

WOODS, P.A. (1993a) 'Responding to the consumer: Parental choice and school effectiveness', *School Effectiveness and School Improvement*, **4**, 3, pp. 205–29.

WOODS, P.A. (1993b) 'Parental Perspectives on Choice in the UK: Preliminary Thoughts on Meanings and Realities of Choice in Education', paper presented at American Educational Research Association Conference, Atlanta, GA, April.

WOODS, P.A. (1994a) 'School responses to the quasi-market' in Halstead, J.M. (ed) *Parental Choice and Education*, London, Kogan Page.

WOODS, P.A. (1994b) 'Parents and Choice in Local Competitive Arenas: First Findings from the Main Phase of the PASCI Study', Paper presented at American Educational Research Association Conference, New Orleans, LA, April.

WOODS, P.A. and WOODS, G. (1994) 'The challenge of the spiritual: Spirituality in UK schools', *Holistic Education Review*, **7**, 3, pp. 17–24.

Chapter 2

Education and Business: Converging Models

Ian Jamieson

Introduction

The relationship between the economic system and the education system has long been the object of intense study because of its inherent complexity. As countries industrialized the function of education became gradually differentiated from other subsystems, that is it took on a semi-autonomous form, differentiated from the family on the one hand and the economy on the other. Such an evolution will always involve tensions between the different subsystems, between say home and school, and, the subject of this particular chapter, between the economic system and the education system.

Education has always contributed, either consciously or unconsciously, to the working of the economy. This is inevitably the case given that the outputs of one system – 'educated people' – became the inputs to the economic system. As the economy itself becomes more complex, creating an increasingly complicated and differentiated range of jobs, then it is likely that the articulation between the two systems will become more difficult. These difficulties will grow if certain other conditions are also thought to hold. First, if the contribution of human capital to the productivity of the economy is thought to grow in importance compared to other functions. As 'knowledge' is hypothesized to be a vital factor in an advanced economy, then this condition is thought to hold for most of the OECD economies. Second, if the economy of a particular country is thought not to be performing comparatively well, then the educational input (both 'flow' factors and 'quality' factors) is likely to be closely scrutinized. The final condition potentially exacerbating the relationship is if those working in the educational system, that is the teachers and administrators, are thought to be either out of touch with the needs of the economy, or out of sympathy with those needs. For example, teachers might place the personal or cultural development needs of their students over any more utilitarian economy related needs.

The argument is simply that the relationship between the education system and the economy is inherently problematic in an advanced industrial society. In any particular country there is usually debate about the 'goodness of fit', that is the articulation between the two systems. It is possible to see countries at various points along a 'goodness of fit' continuum. At one end there are countries like Japan or Germany, which are thought to have educational and economic systems which fit tolerably well together; in the middle we perhaps have the Scandinavian countries like Denmark and Sweden, and at the other end of the continuum we have countries like the US and the UK, or perhaps more precisely, England and Wales (Skilbeck *et al.,* 1994).

Of course concepts like 'fit' make certain interesting assumptions about the mode(s) of articulation between the two systems. They assume, for example, that we know what good or bad fits look like, that is, that we have some generally acceptable models of this process. Until recently the debate has not been conducted around models of education–economy articulation. In practical terms 'goodness of fit' has been deduced from the messages sent by employers and other end-users to schools and colleges, or to their trade and professional associations. In these terms, a system which has a good fit turns out to be little more than that employers and other end-users of the immediate products of the system are satisfied, or have no immediate complaints. In the UK and US, where system articulation is thought to be poor, much of this view derives from employer complaints about the quality and volume of new entrants to employment (see summaries of these concerns in two seminal documents: MSC, 1981; National Commission on Excellence in Education, 1983).

Arguments about system articulation which revolve around employer judgments are not necessarily unsound. Indeed it is generally recognized that if the system of employer signalling and education receptivity was improved then the system as a whole would benefit. In practice the system is unsatisfactory on a number of counts. First, there are sampling problems. The view of system operation is not often based on systematic samples of employer opinion, rather it is based on a few well publicized examples of employer dissatisfaction. In order for employer data to be sound from a sampling point of view we would require systematic data collection across different industries, and firms within those industries, suitably differentiated by generic job type.

Even if the macro sampling problem could be overcome there would still be a micro sampling problem. We might summarize the problem by asking, who exactly is the employer in the phrase 'employer opinion'? In other words, who inside a company would have reliable and valid knowledge about the congruence of an entrant's competencies and the demands of the job? Whatever our answer is to that question, and that may not be straightforward, and may vary by position from company to company, are we happy that those who answer recruitment satisfaction questions on behalf of their companies have such knowledge?

There are some studies which are thought to produce reliable and valid knowledge about education–economic congruence, for example, the studies of Prais and his colleagues at the National Institute of Economic and Social Research (NIESR), which look at the fit between the competencies of young entrants and the demands of specific jobs in specific industries (e.g. Prais and

Steedman, 1986). But even these studies raise difficult questions because they only focus on problems at the transition stage, that is new entrants from school or college. Of course lack of fit at this stage must cost business short term training costs but we do not have data about the long term performance of individuals who enter with certain competencies. For example, it is perfectly possible to construct an argument which suggests that if a young person entered employment with an excellent grasp of fundamental scientific concepts and good communication skills but no applied knowledge, then the short term training costs of this person would be high, and employers may well complain of their inability to immediately perform job-related tasks; but the long term productivity of this individual might be very good.

There are other ways of looking at subsystem articulation that by considering the satisfaction levels of employers. Most economists, for example, would want to examine the hiring policies of employers as indicators of their ability to discriminate between the qualities of new entrants. This method would not seem to produce any more satisfactory results, at least in the UK, than its sociological counterpart.[1] There are three obvious problems. In the first place there is the well known problem of hiring human capital as against (say) capital machinery. Human capital is purchased with only a perfunctory view as to its capacity. What employers do in such circumstances is to try and use some proxy measures of future potential like race, gender, class, type of school/college etc. Unfortunately, most evidence suggests that these measures seem more like indicators of social comfort than productivity. Now that some 90 per cent of the UK population attend comprehensive schools, employers cannot use school type as a reliable indicator for recruitment purposes. Furthermore, if one considers the youth labour market, which is the focus for debate about education–economic congruence, then one of the essential features of such a market is that it tends to be local; this means that employers effectively have a restricted choice in terms of type of school from which to recruit. Only when we get to graduate recruitment is there something like a national labour market where employers have a significant choice of graduates. There is some indication here that employers exercise some choice in favour of those with relevant competencies; for example those students who have undertaken significant work experience during their degree are more employable. But even in this market the social prestige of the institution and academic ability still seem to be the best indicators of employability, and it is by no means clear that these factors are related to individual performance inside the employing organization.

I have attempted to establish in what has gone before that it is difficult to rely on employers' views or behaviour about the performance of the education system when considering the question of the congruence of the education system with the needs of the economy, effectively the needs of the business sector. One complicating factor is the fact of increasing economic and industrial change. In a paradoxical way this has made some of the discussion easier because it has forced observers to see that there are a range of alternatives available on both sides of the equation, particularly the industrial side. Most of these models begin with the economy, or more specifically with the characteristics of businesses operating within the economy. These characterizations tend to specify the tasks or jobs which need to be accomplished. The human requirements for successful task completion are then delineated and these requirements are then projected back on to the school system in terms of a set of economic needs or requirements. In the crudest model, schools are expected to mirror these requirements in what they do (cf. Jamieson *et al.* 1988). Educationally this argument translates into a focus on curriculum with some emphasis on the organization of learning and pedagogy. There are interesting assumptions about the problem of transference here: in its clearest formulation that doing x at school, or an analogue of x, will transfer to competent performance of an x-like task in a specific context.

Models of Education–Business Articulation

It is possible, following Turner *et al.* (1994) to identify three main models which specify education–business linkages. The *traditional model* is based on Fordist conceptions of working. In this model most firms are seen as small to medium sized, essentially operating in a local or regional economy. The majority of tasks in the company are relatively routine with low to medium skill level requirements. Workers are traditionally trained in one skill and are not expected or required to undertake a wider range of tasks. The fundamental requirements of these workers are that they are compliant. As the economy has shifted more towards the service sector, and increasingly jobs in these companies require contact with the customer rather than the machine, then a greater emphasis has been placed on employees having the 'right' attitude. When these requirements are translated into the requirements of schooling then the curriculum focus is little more than a good grounding in the basic requirements of numeracy and literacy with perhaps some rudimentary information technology skills. However, in addition the schools need to instil in these proto-workers good discipline and a respect for authority. Some form of student profiling is thought to be useful to give employers some potential insight into the important personal qualities of young people. Finally, the schools are encouraged to undertake some transition education, that is education which gives students some knowledge and experience of the world of work. The classic example of transition education is work experience.

The next model has been termed the *excellence model* and is based not on what the majority of companies are doing, but rather on the practices of 'excellent' companies (cf. Peters and Waterman, 1982). These leading edge firms are held out as models for others to follow, and in the increasingly competitive world economy, as firms which others must follow if they are to survive. These firms have witnessed a decline in the number of unskilled tasks within them and a rise in the number of jobs requiring high level scientific and technical skills. Although these companies do recruit locally, they are organizations which are essentially in both national and international markets and their recruitment policies reflect this. The educational projection of this model is a curriculum focus on high level mathematics, science and technology skills placed in a framework of high levels of competence in communication skills. Schools are encouraged to meet high standards in traditional subjects with a traditional pedagogy, and to encourage as many of their students as possible to go on to higher education.

The final model is termed the *post-Fordist model* and its focus is on a very small number of high profile companies which are regarded as prototypical in terms of the way they organize work and deploy human capital. While companies in the post-Fordist model accept the importance of science and technology in production, their distinguishing characteristic is in their emphasis on new working practices. These working practices require great flexibility in terms of their workforce; the majority of workers are expected to have polyvalent skills which allow them to undertake a wide variety of jobs. The workers tend to work with far less supervision; they work in teams with a heavy emphasis on cooperation; they are required to solve complex problems and to learn new procedures quickly.

The educational reflection of this model represents something of a break from traditional models of schooling. Whereas science and technology are still important, there is a renewed emphasis on skills like information technology. Even more important than subject emphasis, however, is a new focus on modes of organizing work and pedagogy. Schools are expected to place more emphasis on activities like project work, team work and self-directed study. From the perspective of pedagogy teachers are expected to behave more like facilitators of learning; use more variation in the contexts of learning to promote transferable skills; and to make more use of constructivist techniques to promote meta-cognitive learning skills in students.

Although the three models discussed above are clearly ideal-typical constructs and the reality of the economy is far more complex, they do have the merit of showing that whatever model of the economy is portrayed or whatever its assumed trajectory there are clear implications for teaching and learning in the schools. It is possible to show that as the view of the economy shifts, so the nature of education–business relations itself changes. For example, the emphasis in education–business dialogue can be shown to change according to the state of the youth labour market. When there is a surplus of youth labour, the focus tends to be on a curriculum which stresses relevance to employment, for example the application of academic subjects; relevant experiences, for example work experience; and more generally on acquiring skills which make young people more employable. The argument here is that if only the education of young people was more focused on employer needs then employers would be more likely to take them on instead of substituting them for other employees, such as married women, or substituting capital for their labour. By contrast, when there is a shortage of youth labour, the education–business relationship tends to focus on schemes and projects which attempt to persuade young people that industrial employment is worthwhile. The two obvious examples are: the institution of Compact arrangements, which in their first incarnation offered jobs to young people if certain school performance criteria were met (Wellington, 1993); and work shadowing which aimed to show that the world of industry and commerce had lots of exciting jobs (Watts, 1986).

The rhetoric of education–business relations has usually taken the form of arguing that if the economy exhibits certain features and therefore has certain needs, then it follows that the schools must react in a certain way. The fact that this does not automatically happen produces the education–business movement which I have argued elsewhere is a loose collection of government agencies, business organizations, charitable trusts and specially constructed projects designed to improve the articulation between the two systems (Jamieson, 1986). Although schools are cast by the rhetoric in a passive, reactive mode, the reality is often quite different; as semi-autonomous institutions they have significant choice in how to react. Their role as active agents of choice is aided by the fact that there are now several versions of the economy available on which to model their response. The 'traditional', 'excellence' and 'post-Fordist' models of the economy clearly exist side by side of each other giving schools considerable scope to domesticate one or the other. The irony is that many schools in the UK seem to hold a more progressive version of the economy than a great many companies, particularly companies local to the school. It may even be the case that those teachers who have been influenced by developments in cognitivism (cf. Resnick, 1986; Berryman and Bailey, 1992), have found a model of the economy in post-Fordism which acts as a legitimation of their practice. The argument is however, that almost any practice in school can be legitimated by one version or another of the economy.

The curriculum focus of the education–business movement in the UK is in something of a contrast to other OECD countries (OECD 1992). In the US in more recent times at least, the curriculum has not been a focus for education–business relationships. Partnership arrangements, as they are called, were more likely to be concerned with assisting the school fulfil its own purposes. Business help tended to be financial, or the provision of 'in kind' services. Where companies 'adopted' a school it was largely to give it this form of help, although mentoring programmes, particularly for at risk students were also common. In summary, the focus was on supporting institutions in the local community within a philanthropic rather than an economic context.

The US picture changed dramatically in 1983 with the publication of *A Nation at Risk*, which argued that the nation's schools were failing the American economy (National Commission on Excellence in Education, 1983). The report heralded significant attempts at system reform, in particular to improve the articulation between the economic and education systems. In one sense the report went back to an older tradition of thinking about US schools, a tradition which argued that in order to be successful schools needed to be managed on business-like lines (Callahan, 1962).

The immediate outcome of such an approach included the emergence of the 'for profit' schools movement, whereby business organizations specifically took over the running of schools and were paid on the basis of the performance of the students. Underlying this particular strategy was a more general argument which suggests that part of the problem of poor school performance is poor management. Good quality management, so the argument continued, is largely to be found in private business. This is because only business organizations are both complex and have the discipline of the market place which forces them to be efficient.

This 'business knows best' argument clearly has its counterpart in the UK, and it can be argued that it is perfectly consonant with the tradition which suggests that schools must conform to the needs of the economy (business). The argument is not without its detractors and the counter-arguments are worth recording. First it is argued, managing schools in the public sector is quite different from managing business in the market sector, so one must question the relevance of many private sector managerial practices (Al-Khalifa, 1986; Keep, 1992). The second argument is that it is a perversion to view education as merely producing a product to fit the needs of the economy. Education must support various subsystems including the polity and the family, as well as the economic system. Third, it is not at all clear that we have clear models of successful business management to follow. Management, like education, is a somewhat uncertain science with a bewildering variety of claims and counter-claims about successful practice. Finally, it is possible to question the wisdom, in social engineering terms, of such a one-sided relationship where one partner wishes to unilaterally change the behaviour of the other.

A New Agenda

In the final section of this chapter I will be concerned to argue that a certain confluence of policy changes, structural changes and changing analyses are beginning to construct a quite different pattern of relations between education and business, particularly in the UK. The most significant change is the attempt to create some sort of a market in schooling. If this marketization process becomes successful then schools will find themselves in a territory that has been the historic domain of private business. They would then be in a position to share many common problems and potential solutions.

Whether education has been marketized is of course subject to significant debate. On the one hand one can point to open enrolment and inter-school competition for pupils; the attempts to publish 'consumer' information about schools, for example exam results and truancy data, in order to convince students and parents that they have choice in the market place; the devolution of budgets, and significant managerial autonomy to the level of the school. On the other hand it is easy to demonstrate that the model that has been created is, at best, a quasi-market (Le Grand, 1990). Parents do not pay directly for schooling; schools do not determine the price of places; in many areas of the country there is no significant choice of schools, and even where there is, most parents and students do not apparently view schooling in these terms (Ball, 1993).

This is a complex debate which cannot be further resolved in this chapter; however, it will be helpful to remind ourselves of two things. First, markets always exist in imperfect forms, the world of the perfect market is an ideal–typical construct of the economics textbook. Second, people's *beliefs* about the situation are very often at least as important as any analytical description of that situation because people act on the basis of those beliefs and perceptions. It is my contention that very many teachers, and particularly teachers who are part of the senior management teams of schools, believe that secondary schooling now operates in some sort of a market place and that there are significant similarities between running a business and running a school. This argument has increasing force when one considers that the ranks of local businesses have been joined by hospitals and health care trusts and the privatized utilities which have a long and recent history of operating in the public sector.[2]

The marketization of education is probably one of the reasons for the remarkable growth in the popularity of teacher placements in business, although traditional curriculum related purposes are still the most important reason offered by teachers for accepting a placement. The national Teacher Placement Service places about 8 per cent of teachers per year in industry, and in 1993 this amounted to 100,000 teachers (Teacher Placement Service, nd). Over one-third of these teachers were in a 'managerial' position (head of department or above) and six months after the placement some 40 per cent of these teachers had developed some form of reciprocal link with industry. Neil *et al.* (1994), in a randomly selected study of one in eight secondary schools, showed that over 95 per cent of respondents knew of a teacher who had been on place-ment and that 90 per cent of schools sampled were involved in some sort of education–business link. Furthermore, both of the above studies reported that teachers felt that the placements and links were both useful and important. These studies do indicate the very significant amount of interchange between the two systems, so that teachers should be in a good position to evaluate any claims that there are increasing similarities between schools and business.

If it is the case that many teachers now view schools as having a great deal in common with businesses then this has the potential to generate a significantly different agenda for education–business cooperation. This argu-ment gathers force if one accepts the view that the operation of the national curriculum in England and Wales has made it increasingly difficult for the traditional curriculum focus of education–business work to be sustained.[3]

The final cause of this shift in emphasis in education–business partner-ships has been a certain refocusing on local areas/regions in terms of social and economic regeneration. The British government, influenced by develop-ments in the United States, particularly the Private Industry Councils (PICs), devolved much of the task of social and economic regeneration to its Training and Enterprise Councils (TECs) (Bennett, 1994). This policy move has been reinforced by the devolution of some of the powers and finances of key government departments to integrated regional offices. The theory is that a multiplicity of significant forces need to be marshalled – like transport, environment, employment, education and training, and industry – so that both the local climate and infrastructure can be transformed to bring about social and economic change. While it is the case that the Department for Education is not part of this structure, the TECs are charged with a very significant education and training function. While the creation of national targets for education and training was a national initiative, the responsibility for attaining these targets locally is primarily the responsibility of the TECs.

These developments are beginning to give the schools and colleges a new role, or more accurately, they are beginning to reveal and highlight a role that secondary schools have always had, if only by default, in the local community. In other words, the role of education in the local socioeconomic infrastructure is being increasingly recognized. This role may be an economic one in the narrow sense of producing employees with certain skills to work in the local economy, or increasingly, there might be a wider economic role. This wider role springs from two factors which we have already discussed. First, as schools enter the local market place they begin to re-evaluate their assets and see what services they can trade. Many schools find, sometimes to their surprise, that much of what they can offer is in significant demand. To some extent these services are a volume extension of what they already offer, for example, opening up their buildings for sporting and recreational purposes. Schools and colleges are beginning to benefit from the significant growth in this sector of the local economy *per se*. It also has the effect of making the local community a more attractive place in which to transact business and so potentially attract inward investment. Less traditionally, schools and colleges are beginning to realize that they have relevant expertise which can be readily traded.

Three examples can be given to indicate the range of these activities. Teachers have skills which are often in demand in the local economy to help businesses. These include key skills like modern foreign languages and information technology (IT) which are likely to become ever more significant. Not only do many schools possess far more sophisticated skills in these fields than many small to medium sized local businesses, but they also increasingly possess significant equipment which can be used either to train employees or to assist the business (language laboratories; IT equipment). Our second example focuses on the distinctive ethos which schools and colleges usually try and generate for their own students – one that has traditionally embraced a pastoral or caring function. This makes schools excellent potential sites for cognate activities like drop-in centres for the young and post-retirement population; crèches, mother and toddler groups, etc. The final example acknowledges the fact that schools and colleges are significant organizations in their own right. A large comprehensive school can have a turnover in excess of

£2 million, an all-graduate teaching staff and extensive buildings occupying a large site in the local community. This makes it a much more significant undertaking to manage than all but the largest local firms. All other things being equal, the managers of such institutions are likely to have significant managerial know-how which can be shared with other members of the community. They are likely to have particular strengths in areas like human resource development, including training and staff development.

Several other developments are relevant to the transformation of the education–business relationship which are both a cause and a consequence of that relationship. The first develops the point we have just made about the management of schools. If one was to chart the development of serious books on educational management, particularly the management of schools, one would see the following pattern. In the first period we would find that the volumes drew heavily on the better developed business management literature. The second period reflects something of a rejection of this approach and we have books which claim that managing educational institutions is distinctly different. The current period illustrates something of the thesis of this chapter. In this period educational management rediscovers business management, both because of the marketization of education and because business management and some of the writing about it has itself undergone something of a transformation. This transformation is something of a reflection of the fact that certain features of the business world and its management have themselves been perceived to have drawn closer to the world of education. The inexorable rise of Japan and the countries of the Pacific rim have focused increasing attention on the world of eastern rather than western business. The eastern business model places much greater stress on the softer, process factors of business management like culture, vision, cooperative ways of working, and the importance of the group. These processes models are easier to transfer to educational contexts than some of the western stresses on factors like performance ratios and structures. Modern business management has now resigned itself to the idea that change and turbulent environments are a permanent feature of organizational contexts and the managerial prescriptions reflect this new state of affairs. School managers dealing with constant educational change in the new educational market place provide a ready market for this material. Finally, management books have paid increasing attention to the importance of knowing and understanding markets and this again resonates with education's new sense of the market place with parents and pupils as consumers.

One can see all this come together in the great success of books like Peters and Waterman's *In Search of Excellence* and the ready way in which the eight 'principles for success' were quickly and easily translated into educational management precepts (cf. Everard and Morris, 1990); or the way in which the ideas of the 'learning company' (Burgoyne, 1992) rapidly found their way into the educational management literature. The idea of learning in the sense of organizations learning to 'read' their customers and the contexts within which they work has perhaps become one of the central themes of the literature which spans both education and business management. Other themes include the importance of quality and culture to organizational performance. Some leading education management books, like Murgatroyd and Morgan (1993) take a significant number of their ideas from the business management literature, although they also draw on the effective schools tradition (Scheerens, 1992). It is significant that the major precepts about effective schooling look remarkably similar to the precepts about effective business. These develop- ments are celebrated by the arrival of the MBA in Educational Management, with its clear recognition of the similarities between education and business management.

There has been a general recognition in many OECD countries that the social structural differentiation which occurred through the process of indus- trialization, and which in many cases has led to social fragmentation and dis- integration, needs to be re-engineered. There are many movements and forces at work here but nearly all of them have strong, positive implications for work on the new education–business agenda. One of the most striking statements comes from the Confederation of British Industry (CBI 1994), which declares that 'The CBI's vision for links assumes the growth of "learning communities" in which employees as well as students continuously learn to improve their employability and quality of life'. Many other movements place education at the centre and many go back a long way; a clear example is the idea of community schooling which attempts to break down the barriers between the school and the community. More modern versions of this have tried to stress the potential importance of the school as a local economic or enterprise unit (Shuttleworth, 1993). Communitarianism, a movement spreading from the US (Bell, 1993) tends to stress the role of education in the social rather than the economic regeneration of local communities. It is probably fair to argue that most people see economic regeneration as the key to much social regenera- tion, as the Commission on Social Justice (1994) puts it, there is a 'need to build linkages between the economic, human and social capital investments required to achieve sustainable regeneration'. The most 'economic' version of this work is seen in the emergence of the economic district. Here local busi- nesses and their communities, often working in specialized fields, cooperate closely together in certain joint activities like education, training, quality cer- tification, public relations, while at the same time competing for business. Most of the good examples of this practice are to be found in continental Europe, for example the Emiligia-Romana region of Italy with its flexible manufactur- ing networks (Hatch, 1986).

Conclusion

The education–business agenda is a continuously shifting one. It is influenced by a variety of economic, social and educational forces. This chapter has at- tempted to chart some of the more recent vicissitudes of that agenda, arguing that it has been strongly influenced by the behaviour of the economy, particularly the youth labour market, and by theoretical models of the economy. The combination of the marketization of education, concern about social and economic regeneration, and significant shifts in models of successful business practice have had a profound influence on the education–business agenda. They have shifted it away from its traditional British focus on the curriculum towards a much greater emphasis on the role of schooling in local social and economic restructuring.

Such a shift has profound implications for our model of the school which has proved so resistant to change. Schools are now being enjoined not only to take an active and conscious role in local social and economic restructuring, but also to provide models for other organizations. If as organizations for learning for the whole community they can fashion themselves into learning organizations with flat structures and highly permeable boundaries, committed to staff training, and making extensive use of information technology services for teaching, learning and information access, then not only will they have revolutionized their own goals and structure, but they will have the power to regenerate and revolutionize their local communities. None of this can happen as long as schools are seen and see themselves as passive partners in an education–business relationship. The marketization of education has the power to transform that agenda by recognizing the business role of education.

Notes

1   The US evidence does suggest that employers are capable of some discrimination, cf. Stern *et al*, 1995.
2   The NHS operates an internal market which is not quite the same as the market place for private firms.
3   This assertion needs explanation. The national curriculum makes mention of cross-curricular themes, of which economic and industrial understanding (EIU) is one. However, the original implementation was dominated by the statutory core and foundation subject curriculum and those cross-curricular themes which depended on colonizing the time of many subjects suffered significantly because of their non-statutory nature. The activity of work experience was an initial exception to this because it was held in place by the contractual obligations imposed by TVEI and its extension. As TVEI works its way out of the system even this looked under threat (Jamieson, 1993). The Dearing Review (1993) of the national curriculum, which in principle creates more space in the 14–16 curriculum, and the rise of GNVQ might re-establish a curriculum focus to education–business partnerships.

References

AL-KHALIFA, E. (1986) 'Can educational management learn from industry?', in HOYLE, E. and MCMAHON, A. (eds) *World Yearbook of Education 1986: The Management of Schools*, London, Kogan Page.

BALL, S.J. (1993) 'Education markets, choice and social class: The market as a class strategy in the UK and the USA', *British Journal of Sociology of Education*, **14**, 1, pp. 3–19.

BELL, D. (ed) (1993) *Communitarianism and its Critics*, Oxford, Clarendon Press.

BENNETT, R.J. (1994) 'PICs, TECs and LECs: Lessons to be learnt from the differences between the USA private industry councils and Britain's training and enterprise councils', *British Journal of Education and Work*, **7**, 3, pp. 63–85.

BERRYMAN, S.E. and BAILEY, T.R. (1992) *The Double Helix of Education and the Economy*, The Institute of Education and the Economy, Teachers College, Columbia University, New York.

BURGOYNE, J. (1992) 'Creating a learning organisation', *RSA Journal*, **CXL**, 5428, pp. 321–30.

CALLAHAN, R.E. (1962) *Education and the Cult of Efficiency*, Chicago, University of Chicago Press.

COMMISSION ON SOCIAL JUSTICE (1994) *Social Justice: Strategies for National Renewal*, London, Vintage.

CONFEDERATION OF BRITISH INDUSTRY (CBI) (1994) *Creating a Learning Community: A CBI Review of Education–Business Links*, London, CBI.

DEARING, R. (1993) *The National Curriculum and its Assessment: Final Report*, London, School Curriculum and Assessment Authority.

EVERARD, K.B. and MORRIS, G. (1990) *Effective School Management*, London, Paul Chapman.

JAMIESON, I.M. (1986) 'Corporate hegemony or pedagogic liberation? The schools industry movement in England and Wales', in DALE, R. (ed) *Education and Training and Employment: Towards a New Vocationalism*, Cambridge, Pergamon Press.

JAMIESON, I.M., MILLER, A. and WATTS, A.G. (1988) *Mirrors of Work*, London, Falmer Press.

KEEP, E. (1992) 'Schools in the market place? Some problems with private sector models', *British Journal of Education and Work*, **5**, 2, pp. 43–56.

LE GRAND, J. (1990) *Quasi-Markets and Social Policy*, Studies in Decentralisation and Social Policy, SAUS, Bristol, University of Bristol.

MANPOWER SERVICES COMMISSION (MSC) (1981) *A New Training Initiative: A Consultative Document*, London: MSC.

MURGATROYD, S. and MORGAN, C. (1993) *Total Quality Management and the School*, Buckingham, Open University Press.

NATIONAL COMMISSION ON EXCELLENCE IN EDUCATION (1983) *A Nation at Risk*, Washington, DC, Government Printing Office.

NEILL, S.R.St.J., ABBOTT, I. and CAMPBELL, R.J. (1994) *Teachers' Views on Increasing Links between Education and Industry*, Department of Education, University of Warwick (mimeo).

ORGANIZATION FOR ECONOMIC COOPERATION AND DEVELOPMENT (OECD) (1992) *Schools and Business: A New Partnership*, Paris, OECD.

PETERS, P.J. and WATERMAN, R.H. (1982) *In Search of Excellence*, New York, Harper and Row.

PRAIS, S.J. and STEEDMAN, H. (1986) 'Vocational training in France and Britain: The building trades', *NIER Review*, May: pp. 45–55.

RESNICK, L. (1986) 'Constructing knowledge in school', in LIBEN, L.S. and FELDMAN, D.H. (eds) *Development and Learning: Conflict or Congruence?* Hillsdale, NJ, Erlbaum.

SCHEERENS, J. (1992) *Effective Schooling: Research, Theory and Practice*, London, Cassell.

SHUTTLEWORTH, D.E. (1993) *Enterprise Learning in Action: Education and Economic Renewal for the Twenty-First Century*, London, Routledge.

SKILBECK, M. CONNELL, H., LOWE, N. and TAIT, K. (1994) *The Vocational Quest: New Directions in Education and Training*, London, Routledge.

STERN, D., FINKELSTEIN, N., STONE, III, J.R., LATTING, J. and DORNSIFE, C. (1995) *School to Work: Research on Programs in the US*, London, Falmer.

TEACHER PLACEMENT SERVICE (nd) *Teacher Placement Works*, University of Warwick, Understanding British Industry.

TURNER, E., LLOYD, J., STRONACH, I. and WATERHOUSE, S. (1994) *Plotting Partnership: Education Business Links in Scotland*, Department of Education, University of Stirling (mimeo).

WATTS, A.G. (1986) *Work Shadowing*, York, Longman.

WELLINGTON, J.J. (1993) 'Restoring the implicit promise in schooling: Observations of compact in action', in WELLINGTON, J.J. (ed) *The Work Related Curriculum*, London, Kogan Page.

Chapter 3

Unsaleable Goods and the Education Market

Eric Blyth and Judith Milner

Introduction

This chapter examines the relationship between children and the market which has developed following the implementation of the Education Reform Act 1988. It is particularly concerned with the differing powers of consumers to effect the choices envisaged by the education reforms. For example, *Choice and Diversity* (DFE, 1992) is clear about the anticipated outcomes for consumers:

> By the next century we will have achieved a system characterised not by uniformity but by choice, underpinned by the spread of grant maintained schools. There will be a rich array of schools and colleges, all teaching the National Curriculum and playing to their strengths, allowing parents to choose the school best suited to their children's needs, and all enjoying parity of esteem. Our aim is a single tier of excellence.

However, markets derive their efficiency from the fact that there are winners and losers, risk takers and bankruptcies, entrepreneurs and uncertainty (Veljanovski, 1990). The most obvious losers in an education market are excluded children as both they and their parents are unable to exercise any sort of choice about school at all (for an overview see Blyth and Milner, 1996). As a quarter of excluded children may be lost to education altogether, we initially viewed the phenomenon in terms of civic exclusion and underclass ideology (Blyth and Milner, 1993, 1994) but a direct association between exclusion from school and the development of the education market was prompted by the remarks of a headteacher. He publicly referred to his own school's 'respectable' position in the recently-published league tables and the fact that this meant that his school had few pupils on 'free transfer'. We had long struggled with the fact that whatever the concept of the 'consumers' of education meant – parents, local industry, the 'country' etc. – it rarely seemed to include pupils themselves. Here was a stark admission that pupils were not simply the recipients of education or subjects of the educational process but were increasingly being seen as commodities in the new education market, some perceived as being of higher value than others. Indeed, some couldn't – it appears – even be given away.

The links between education and economic growth are not straightforward although as Ball (1993: 3) has pointed out:

> There is now in educational policy a well established, powerful and complex ideology of the market and a linked culture of choice which are underpinned by dangerous idealisations about the workings of the markets, the effects of parental choice and of 'profit' incentives in education.

It could be that education is a benefit bought from the profits of past growth as much as investment in future prosperity. It may also be that education simply acts as social selection for employment (Glennerster, 1993). Johnes (1993) argues that education does not enhance productivity directly, rather it acts as a means whereby unusually productive individuals are identified.

Certainly when job competition rather than flexibility of wages determines the allocation of jobs among workers, there is an inbuilt tendency to 'over-education' (Johnes, 1993). An analysis of academic inflation (Colton and Heath, 1994) demonstrates that lower level qualifications are of diminishing value in terms of obtaining employment. Thus the system is neither efficient (in terms of overeducation) nor equitable (in terms of job prospects for all).

Notions of social justice via education are exposed not only by recent concerns around efficiency in education but also by studies which show that even a good school can only have a marginal effect on pupils' life chances (Rutter *et al.*, 1979; Mortimore *et al.*, 1988). The breakdown in consensus about social justice has been further fuelled following the publication of a report into schools in inner cities which castigated schools for failing pupils (OFSTED, 1993) and the Secretary of State's threat to take over the first two schools to fail the new inspections. Disillusion with the welfare state plus its spiralling costs and the failure of socialism internationally means that the economic thinking behind Keynes and Beveridge as 'an unequivocal attempt to patch up capitalism' (Whynes, 1985) is no longer considered either tenable or desirable.

The drive for efficiency behind the Education Reform Act, 1988 and the Education Act, 1993 was, therefore, inevitable. While this legislation has become inexorably associated with the ascendency of New Right ideology, evidence of government and industry dissatisfaction with the British education system can be traced back at least to Jim Callaghan's Ruskin College speech, launching the so-called 'Great Education Debate'. However, the criticisms of the effects of the Act have neglected to consider whether or not efficiency has been achieved, tending to concentrate on issues of equity, particularly around selectivity, problems connected with the workings of a partial or quasi-market, and linking the interests of children and families as though they are necessarily identical. We will list some of these criticisms before suggesting that it may be more fruitful to examine how efficiency might be improved in a freer market; how there may be spin offs for equity when children are considered in terms of gender and race rather than *en bloc*; and how children can be viewed as consumers, actively participating in choices about their education.

The Effects of a Quasi-Market in Education

The advantages of a market system in education are generally considered to be twofold. First, consumers are able to express preferences about the type and quality of education they purchase and their choices will indicate the socially efficient quantity of each type of education. Second, competition will ensure that education is relevant and not wasteful. However there are problems in developing a free market in education because of tensions between the market and the state.

Ball (1993), for example, argues that the market is heavily constrained and singularly constructed by the government while Green (1993) maintains that a true market cannot exist under present reforms and that it can only do so if schools rely on payment from parents for their income. Somewhat earlier, Le Grand and Robinson (1984) cautioned that four conditions necessary for market allocation of commodity to be efficient are not met in education.

1   There is no chance of *perfect information* because children are not deemed to be able to exercise choice in their best interests. Choice, particularly in education up to further/higher education (FE/HE), is exercised by parents and education legislation enshrines the notion of parental choice. Yet, parents are not always able or willing to act in their children's best interests. One important function of education has been to protect children from their families and act as a secondary form of socialization. Recent research into parental choice and school effectiveness shows that while schools' responsiveness to competitiveness and parental choice has made schools keen to promote themselves, they are 'less likely to initiate ways of finding out how parents view the school' (Woods *et al.*, 1994) and parents' choices of schools are often determined by race and class divisions (Young, 1994).

2   The commodity does not *generate external benefits*. The problem here is one of measurement and definition and whether benefits are to be considered as private or social. The role of education in preparing children for work, parenthood and citizenship is particularly problematic in a society which has little work for school leavers and is concerned about almost every aspect of behaviour in late childhood from literacy to delinquency.

3   The commodity does not *generate external costs*. The failure to enable children to fulfil their potential via an education suited to their age,

aptitude and ability is not easily quantified but truancy and exclusion rates (and perhaps delinquency rates) are clear indications of potential public costs. Rowley (1978) comments that where an externality is complex and ambiguous, so that individuals do not know whether an activity is detrimental or beneficial to themselves, it is impossible to strike a bargain.

4　There should be no *monopolistic barriers* to competition in relevant markets. However economies of scale are such that monopolies are likely to develop. This is already evident with respect to popular schools and the use of busing which creates 'sink' schools. Spatial monopolies are also likely to develop in rural areas thus reducing choice.

Glennerster (1993), while spending much time on issues of equity, makes the interesting point that efficiency is lost under the new system because it is operating in a quasi, not a free, market. He says that the scheme for local management of schools (LMS) falls short of a full market solution for at least four reasons:

1　No money can escape to the private sector.
2　There is no mechanism to replicate free entry on the one hand, or bankruptcy on the other, to keep the market truly competitive.
3　Choice by parents is limited because of the requirements of the national curriculum.
4　Teachers' salaries, the largest slice of the school budget, are set by a Pay Review Board which excludes LEAs and governing bodies, limiting the freedom of school governing bodies to manage their budget.

We will return to the issue of money escaping to the private sector when we examine children's contributions later but will briefly challenge Glennerster's claims on the other three reasons.

Conservative vision of an education market place where schools wax and wane according to their popularity relies on substantial excess capacity in the system to guarantee parental choice. Not only are schools reluctant to expand once they have reached full capacity (Levacic, 1994) and, indeed, have limited capacity to expand (Bartlett, 1992) but this vision is inconsistent with another aim of the market – to significantly reduce the levels of surplus capacity by allowing parental choice to identify unpopular schools for closure. Winton School in Croydon closed suddenly due to safety fears and financial problems with the result that Croydon LEA had to accommodate up to 140 pupils at short notice. The burden of financial pressures fell on parents and teachers in Hertfordshire who raised £250,000 to rescue Manor Lodge Prep school from closure when the receivers were called in over debts amounting to £1.3 million (Preston, 1993). The exercising of choice by some parents diminishes the choice for others (Edwards and Witney, 1992).

This opening and closure under market conditions is already affecting efficiency as Education Welfare Services have been quick to realize that they cannot assume a consensus about the worthwhileness of their activities; they are examining their accountability and value for money via the development of performance indicators, marketing and competitive tendering. There is an emerging private service developing amongst redundant Education Welfare Officers (EWOs) or those taking early retirement and other educational specialists who are showing a readiness to undertake tasks as defined by the schools rather than those described by their professional dictates, such as escorts.

Green (1993: 1) argues that the education reforms were based on a consumerist view of parents as 'outsiders in judgement of schools rather than as co-partners in a long process of equipping their own children with the skills, knowledge and personal qualities necessary in a free, open and tolerant society'. While he sees that radical deregulation would help to re-energize teachers and reactivate dormant parental responsibility and commitment, the imposition of the national curriculum has forced the government to be dependent on teachers and exposed it to the risk of their unwillingness to cooperate – as, for example, in the case of testing. Green argues that this is a mistake and that the government should have dispensed real power to parents who could have forged genuine partnerships with schools. However, in a developing quasi-market, schools are more likely to

> interact with each other and take notice of other *institutions*, in preference for more difficult-to-reach individuals (parents) . . . This results in schools paying more attention to their feeders and other secondary schools. (Woods, 1993)

However large a proportion of costs teachers' salaries are though, they are not the only cost. Other costs are still rising; many schools are trapped by payments for improvement set in train in the 1980s; and repairs and non-essential expenses (delayed when the recession began to bite in the late 1980s) are becoming pressing. There has been a slackening in capital investment which cannot be offset by fixing teacher salaries at a lower level. The effect of market forces in the independent sector is unlikely to be altered significantly by teacher costs (a relatively fixed cost). There has been, perhaps predictably, a 'flight to quality' with a sharp rise in application rates over the last three years to Eton, for example, although many independent schools are desperately seeking customers in Malaysia and Hong Kong (Rae, 1993).

In the independent sector, market forces are ensuring high quality education for the rich and the prudent (insurance schemes are compulsory in some schools). In the state sector there is some evidence that teachers' salary costs are having some effects but not in a straightforward way. For example, Penney and Evans (1994) found that competition affected subject areas *within* schools:

our data showed the concept of 'winners' and 'losers' post-LMS needs to be considered in relation to both the schools as a whole, and its individual departments.

Should the government extend its reforms and decide to fund all schools from central funds, thus freeing up the market, Glennerster (1993) sees problems around both *efficiency* and *equity* issues, particularly the latter. For example, he makes the point that health care providers use their marketing and competition with other providers to ensure that only the minimum number of high cost patients are attracted and he envisages a similar situation with regard to education. Early effects would certainly support his view as there has been an enormous increase in the numbers of children excluded from school and a change in the reasons for exclusion – what was previously a rare event concerned with serious discipline problems has now become a relatively common occurrence in response to a constellation of negative attitude and behaviour problems on the part of some pupils.

Children's Contributions to the Economy

Children are marginalized in British society by the separation of work and home and by the high costs of childrearing – accentuated by the fact that their parents may be out of production during some childrearing years. Joshi (1992) has estimated that a woman on average earnings may forgo £202,500 in lost earnings over her lifetime as a result of having two children, while Oldfield and Yu (1993) estimate the weekly cost of a child under a modest-but-adequate budget at £62 for a 4-year-old child. Leach (1994) argues that society is actually hostile to children who are viewed as little more than an acceptable but expensive hobby. Certainly they are seen as a cost on the part of the increasing number of non-child households (Qvortrup, 1991).

Children contribute directly to the economy in a number of ways, however. Not only are they direct consumers of toys, clothing etc., they are increasingly obvious by their presence in advertisements for domestic products, and they exert a powerful influence on adults who might not otherwise bother to make sure that their clothes are sparklingly clean and fluffily soft! Children are also being directly targeted by supermarkets and other chain-stores to help financially hard-pressed schools. In the United States the phenomenon of 'teeny consumerism' has generated its own text, *Kids as Consumers* by James McNeal (cited in Durham, 1993).

Children as consumers are easily identified in this way but they are also employers. Childhood is a category constructed for 'us' in the child care business (Qvortrup, 1993) and they are the employers of an army of child welfare workers – psychologists, social workers, teachers, nursery nurses, academics etc. It is via the business of welfare that money is indeed escaping to the private sector.

The potential spending power of the secondary school pupil (approximately

£2000 per pupil per year) is proving an attractive factor in urban areas with large markets of high risk pupils. In several areas, for example, the traditional work of the Education Welfare Service in dealing with truancy is being re-shaped by the burger industry. Schools, industry and the police have joined forces so that pupils with good attendance are rewarded with milk shakes, chips and burgers. In Tower Hamlets, Burger King has opened its first school for truants.

While this movement of money into the private sector is at present only small, it is accompanied by reductions in the numbers of traditional welfare professionals. LMS funding which carefully circumscribes the percentage of money which can be spent on special services such as psychological assess-ments and social work support has meant that many LEA support services have been cut. There is a real possibility that the child care industry could become bankrupt.

Parental choice, already limited, is being eroded further. As children are viewed as potential high cost/low profit investments, as children become *pro-blems* for educators rather than children *with problems,* the evidence is that they are more likely to be excluded either formally or informally by pressure on parents. Such pupils are currently often lost to education (25 per cent of permanently excluded children are not in education at all; SHA, 1992). This is not necessarily an inevitable trend. Further education colleges faced with falling numbers are finding excluded adolescents an attractive proposition and are increasingly offering courses for such pupils, unconstrained by the requirements of the national curriculum.

It could well be in children's interests to be excluded from schools so that they can gain entrance to alternative forms of education. The slackening of national curriculum requirements is already well established by the official existence of Education Otherwise. It had been assumed that 'difficult' pupils would be educated in relatively expensive Pupil Referral Units but it may prove that the market can accommodate these pupils quite economically – without necessarily sacrificing either efficiency or equity.

The power of children to make choices in their own interests is also becoming apparent in another area. In an effort to attract low cost pupils to schools which had figured highly in school performance tables, there were some early competitive attempts to poach good pupils through advertising, busing etc. However, coeducational schools have realized that they already have potentially low cost/high yield pupils in their school populations – girls. School performance tables show that single-sex girls' schools figure promin-ently at the top of the table. Some schools have moved quickly to introduce single-sex teaching within schools. Between 1973 and 1993 one private boys-only school lost over 30 per cent of its older pupils and its academic reputation slumped as it scored only 460th place in the performance tables with 200 state schools above it. In line with the 200 public schools who have appointed development directors (Petre, 1994) it employed a new head and devised a radical plan to attack perceived weaknesses. The result was a decision to go coeducational (Tytler, 1993). That boys do well in the classroom at the expense of girls has been long established by research (Acker, 1981; Lees, 1986; Foster, 1988; Kelly, 1988; Tizard *et al.*, 1989) and has been the subject of much feminist lobbying. Yet it has taken the application of market forces to improve the quality of education for girls and, potentially, increase their choices. While children, *per se*, may not yet be complete employers in the mainstream economy (we return to children and the illegal economy later), certain groups of children have become more influential consumers.

Similarly, we can hypothesize that schools will begin to recognize the potential of black pupils as low cost, good investments. It is well established that black boys are as disruptive as white boys in schools and there is some evidence that they are disproportionally represented among both excluded pupils and those in units for pupils with emotional and behavioural difficulties (Cooper *et al.*, 1991), giving rise to the suspicion of racist practice which, like issues surrounding gender, has resisted attempts at eradication via costly, inefficient and cosmetic training efforts. However, it is equally well established that black children, while they may be anti-school, are not anti-education in the same way as white, disaffected male pupils are (Tizard *et al.*, 1989). Black children are only too aware of the need for qualifications if they are to succeed in a racist society (Duncan, 1988; Mac an Ghaill, 1988). Thus, it can be anticipated that a freer market will respond to the needs of black children much more positively. There is already one all black primary school in London (Channel Four, 1993).

In a freer market, it becomes irrelevant where the actual costs of educating a child are set. It matters little whether or not the state decides upon £2000 per child per annum, whether an independent day school charges twice this amount or whether alternative education is able to deliver the goods for substantially less. It will depend upon whether or not the child, the raw material, will provide a good yield for that particular investment. As Jamieson (1994) commented, we simply do not know what an education system that meets the needs of the economy would actually be like (see, also, Jamieson in this volume). The investment may be in producing children who can pass public examinations (not necessarily at the usual ages); it may be in producing well behaved, compliant children; it may be turning disruptive pupils into confident adults; it may be child minding while parents work. It matters little in a society that has no idea what it wants its future adults to be like but if the notion of playing out market forces encourages businesses (schools) to define the product then the role and purpose of education will become much clearer. For example, deregulation in East Harlem led to the proliferation of schools specializing in a wide variety of subjects and improving student performance (Chubb and Moe, 1990).

This, in turn, might make parental choice reality rather than myth, increasing efficiency and equity. The complexities of a freer market and some possibly unexpected benefits in terms of equity are outlined below in a hypothetical situation.

Four Hypothetical Schools

In this scenario we take four 'typical' schools and examine how their traditional outcomes might be moderated by market forces:

- *School A*: a medium sized comprehensive in a middle-class area which has lost some pupils due to demographic changes but has been little affected by this as it has been able to bus in pupils because of its respectable performance in the school league tables.
- *School B*: a large comprehensive in a working-class area hit by falling school rolls and unemployment. The catchment area is depressed with middle-class pupils decamping to 'better' schools causing the school to drift towards 'sink' status.
- *School C*: Burger King academy, initially started with a few truants; much publicity and high staff morale.
- *School D*: a traditional independent school with above average examination results which has been hit by the recession and spiralling costs. Attempts to compensate include introducing insurance and phased payments plus specialization.

The schools which would probably be most successful in adapting to the pressures of market forces would be schools A and C. School A would need to maintain its poaching of good pupils from other schools so would probably need to make further accommodations. These could include promotional endeavours with feeder schools and single-sex teaching but the most important aspect would be to exclude the disaffected white boys who are likely to depress league table performance. These pupils would go to School C.

School B is likely to sink rapidly with falling standards. As it becomes more inefficient it could decide to specialize in disruptive pupils. However, even disaffected pupils can spot a school with low morale and it is likely that they will use their streetwise skills to get themselves transferred to School C (see, for example, Garner, 1994).

School C has all the difficult pupils but is able to operate efficiently and get good results in the short term. If results become more elusive, it has the option of specializing in black male pupils.

School D finds that it has lost its traditional market and is soon in deep financial trouble. What it does not spot is that there is a potential market in low achieving, disruptive white male pupils – whom no one seems to want (Booth, 1996).

Overall, the system becomes more responsive to the needs of high achievers, girls and black pupils. Disaffected white boys are likely to be rejected by the system and receive either home tuition or disappear from the system altogether.

This hypothetical analysis demonstrates little more than that it is easier to effect change when it is in the economic interests of powerful groups. A right wing economic ideology lies exposed for the same reason as does any education ideology.

Problems Around the Definition and Measurement of Educational Effects

The problem of definition and measurement is particularly apparent in education where not only is it difficult to identify what the desirable end-product should be but also the ongoing adult costs of failure are almost impossible to gauge. We are particularly concerned with the public costs and benefits of a system which excludes children from the education process (however flawed or imprecise that process may be). The definition and measurement of the long term public costs of not investing in some children has not been attempted except in psychologically imprecise terms such as 'low self-esteem', 'depression' etc. We can hypothesize to some extent about these children in adult life. For example, we know that truants are less likely to find employment, suffer more ill health than average and figure more highly in suicide statistics, and that there is a strong relationship between educational attainment, employment, income and delinquency (Pyle, 1985). We also know that until recently, truants were more likely to lead solitary, depressed lives while disaffected pupils in schools were more likely to become involved in delinquency (Graham, 1988). As more disaffected children, particularly black children, are excluded from school then the two categories may merge and form the bulwark of what has been discussed as a burgeoning underclass, or they may, via delinquent behaviour, contribute to the illegal economy and/or become employers of police, probation officers etc. Excluded children's contributions to society as employers of adults, whether in the area of care or control, all remain significant while the state intervenes in the market.

Summary

While a freer market may be opening up educational opportunity on the one hand, it is being undermined by intense state intervention in the social and financial lives of young people, for example, draconian measures for New Age travellers, cuts in benefits etc. Debarred from participating in a freer market, except in the illegal economy, and being an increasing burden on the expenditure of the family, their options for an alternative lifestyle being eroded, we are left with what amounts virtually to an outlaw class of young people. It may be that the costs of their existence are substantially privately borne and that private misery is to be ignored, but there are probably substantial public costs in terms of social, health and legal services. We know, for example, that the costs of psychoses such as schizophrenia exceed £40 million per week, not including the costs of informal care and lost production (Kavanagh *et al.*, 1993). The long term costs and benefits of education need to be assessed before any education policy can be deemed to be either efficient or equitable; the economic equation has simply not been made explicit.

> In the domain of a behavioural science . . . the pertinent question becomes not whether economists should participate in policy making, not whether economic analysis could be useful in guiding policy decisions, not whether economists have helped shape the world. The question is rather why public policies exist in the way they do, and why they vary in different economic systems. (Burton, 1978: 67)

Acknowledgments

The authors would like to thank their colleagues Wendy Marshall and Bill Jordan for their assistance with earlier drafts of this paper and suggestions made by conference participants at the CEDAR conference where an earlier version of this paper was presented.

References

ACKER, S. (1981) 'Women and education', in HARTNETT, A. (ed) *The Social Sciences in Education*, London, Hutchinson, pp. 144–52.

BALL, S.J. (1993) 'Education markets, choice and social class: The market as a class strategem in the UK and USA', *British Journal of the Sociology of Education*, **14**, 1, pp. 3–19.

BARTLETT, W. (1992) *Quasi-Markets and Educational Reforms – A Case Study*, Studies in Decentralisation and Quasi-Markets, Bristol: SAUS, University of Bristol.

BLYTH, E. and MILNER, J. (1993) 'Exclusion from school: A first step in exclusion from society?' *Children and Society*, **7**, 3, pp. 255–68.

BLYTH, E. and MILNER, J. (1994) 'Exclusions from school and victim blaming', *Oxford Review of Education*, **20**, 3, pp. 293–306.

BLYTH, E. and MILNER, J. (eds) (1996) *Exclusions from School: Issues for Interagency Policy and Practice*, London, Routledge.

BOOTH, T. (1996) 'The way forward: Understanding exclusions in education', in BLYTH, E. and MILNER, J. (eds) *Exclusions from School: Issues for Interagency Policy and Practice*, London, Routledge.

BURTON, J. (1978) 'Conclusion', in CHEUNG, S.N.S. (ed) *The Myth of Social Cost: A Critique of Welfare Economics and the Implications for Public Policy*, London, Institute of Economic Affairs, pp. 90–91.

CHANNEL FOUR (1993) *Places for All*, 2nd March.

CHUBB, J. and MOE, T. (1990) *Politics, Markets and America's Schools*, Washington DC, Brookings Institute.

COLTON, M. and HEATH, A. (1994) 'Attainment and behaviour of children in care and at home', *Oxford Review of Education*, **20**, 3, pp. 317–28.

COOPER, P., UPTON, G. and SMITH, C. (1991) 'Ethnic minority and gender distribution among staff and pupils in facilities for pupils with emotional and behavioural difficulties in England and Wales', *British Journal of the Sociology of Education*, **12**, 1, pp. 77–94.

DEPARTMENT FOR EDUCATION (DFE) (1992) *Choice and Diversity: A New Framework for Schools*, London, HMSO.

DUNCAN, C. (1988) *Pastoral Care: An Anti-Racist/Multicultural Perspective*, Oxford Blackwell.

DURHAM, M. (1993) 'Chainstore vouchers tighten big business grip on schools', *The Independent on Sunday*, 11 July, p. 10.

EDWARDS, T. and WITNEY, G. (1992) 'Parental choice and the educational reform in Britain and the United States', *British Journal of Educational Studies*, **1**, 2, pp. 106–21.

FOSTER, E. (1988) 'Black girls and pastoral care', in DUNCAN, C. (ed) *Pastoral Care: An Anti-Racist/Multicultural Perspective*, Oxford, Blackwell, pp. 79–89.

GARNER, P. (1994) 'Exclusions from school: Towards a new agenda', *Pastoral Care in Education*, **12**, 4, pp. 3–9.

GLENNERSTER, H. (1993) 'The economics of education: Changing fortunes', in BARR, N. and WHYNES, D. (eds) *Current Issues in the Economics of Welfare*, Basingstoke, Macmillan, pp. 176–99.

GRAHAM, J. (1988) *Schools, Disruptive Behaviour and Delinquency: A Review of the Research*, Home Office Research Study No. 96, London, HMSO.

GREEN, D. (1993) *Reinventing Civil Society: The Rediscovery of Welfare Without Politics*, Choice in Welfare Series 17, London, IEA Health and Welfare Unit.

JAMIESON, I. (1994) 'Education as business', paper presented at Changing Educational Structures: Policy and Practice, Warwick, CEDAR, University of Warwick, 15–17 April.

JOHNES, G. (1993) *The Economics of Education*, Basingstoke, Macmillan.

JOSHI, H. (1992) 'The cost of caring', in GLENDINNING, C. and MILLER, J. (eds) *Women and Poverty in Britain, the 1990s*, London, Wheatsheaf.

KAVANAGH, S., KNAPP, S., BEECHAM, J. and OPIT, L. (1993) *The Costs of Schizophrenia Care in England*, London, PSSRU DP920.

KELLY, A. (1988) 'Ethnic differences in science choice, attitudes and achievement', *British Educational Research Journal*, **14**, 2, pp. 113–26.

LEACH, P. (1994) *Children First*, London, Michael Joseph.

LEES, S. (1986) *Losing Out: Sexuality and Adolescent Girls*, London, Hutchinson.

LE GRAND, J. and ROBINSON, R. (1984) *The Economics of Social Problems: The Market versus the State*, 2nd edn, Basingstoke, Macmillan.

LEVACIC, R. (1994) 'Evaluating the performance of quasi-markets in education', in BARTLETT, W. (ed) *Quasi-Markets in the Welfare State*, Bristol, SAUS, University of Bristol.

MAC AN GHAILL, M. (1988) *Young, Gifted and Black*, Milton Keynes, Open University Press.

MORTIMORE, P., SAMMONS, P., STOLL, L. and ECOB, R. (1988) *School Matters: The Junior Years*, London, Open Books.

OFSTED (1993) *Education for Disaffected Pupils: A Report from the Office of Her Majesty's Chief Inspector of Schools*, London, OFSTED.

OLDFIELD, N. and YU, A.C.S. (1993) *The Cost of a Child. Living Standards for the 1990s*, London, Child Poverty Action Group.

PENNEY, D. and EVANS, J. (1994) 'Changing structures: Changing rules: Implications for curriculum planning in schools', paper presented at Changing Educational Structures: Policy and Practice, Warwick, CEDAR, University of Warwick, 15–17 April.

PETRE, J. (1994) 'Schools tune in to benefits of promotion', *Sunday Telegraph*, 27 February, p. 7.

PRESTON, B. (1993) 'Parents and staff bail out school', *The Times*, 1 December, p. 6.

PYLE, D.J. (1985) *The Economics of Crime and Law Enforcement*, Basingstoke: Macmillan.

QVORTRUP, J. (1991) 'Childhood as a social phenomenon – An introduction to a series of national reports', *Eurosocial Reports 36*, European Centre for Social Welfare Policy and Research.

QVORTRUP J. (1993) 'New approaches to the sociological study of childhood', ESRC Seminar, Keele University, 24 March.

RAE, J. (1993) 'Eton's new man at the top', *The Times*, 6 December, p. 31.

ROWLEY, C.K. (1978) 'The problem of social cost', in CHEUNG, S.N.S. (ed) *The Myth of Social Cost*, London, Institute of Economic Affairs, pp. 11–17.

RUTTER, M., MAUGHAN, B., MORTIMORE, P. and OUSTON, J. (1979) *Fifteen Thousand Hours: Secondary Schools and their Effects on Children*, London, Open Books.

SECONDARY HEADS ASSOCIATION (SHA) (1992) *Excluded from School: A Survey of Secondary School Suspensions*, SHA.

TIZARD, B., BLATCHFORD, P., BURKE, J., FARQUHAR, C. and PLEWIS, I. (1989) *Young Children at School in the Inner City*, London, Lawrence Erlbaum.

TYTLER, D. (1993) 'Right on the competitive edge', *The Times*, 15 November, p. 31.

VELJANOVSKI, C. (1990) 'Foreword' to DE JASAY, A. (ed) *Market Socialism: A Scrutiny of 'The Square Circle'*, London, Insitute of Economic Affairs, p. 6.

WHYNES, D.K. (1985) 'Markets and Neo-liberal Political Economy', in BEAN, P.T., FERRIS, J.S. and WHYNES, D.K. (eds) *In Defence of Welfare*, London, Tavistock, pp. 99–121.

WOODS, P.A. (1993) 'Responding to the Consumer: Parental Choice and School Effectiveness', *School Effectiveness and School Improvement*, **4**, 3, pp. 205–29.

WOODS, P.A., BAGLEY, C. and GLATTER, R. (1994) 'Dynamics of competition – The effects of local competition arenas on schools', paper presented at Changing Educational Structures: Policy and Practice, Warwick, CEDAR, University of Warwick, 15–17 April.

YOUNG, S. (1994) 'Beware the Perils of Parent Power', *Times Educational Supplement*, **4062**, p. 7.

Part II

Changing School Governance

The School, the Parent, the Banker and the Local Politician: What Can We Learn from the English Experience of Involving Lay People in the Site Based Management of Schools?

Rosemary Deem

Introduction

In this chapter I review some of the wider policy implications and applicability of the findings of a four-year, Economic and Social Research Council-funded, multiple-site, case study which examined the impact of recent extensive UK-based school reforms on school governing bodies in England. This research was conducted by myself, Dr Kevin Brehony (project co-director), Suzanne Heath and Sue Hemmings, between 1988 and 1993 in two English local education authorities (LEAs). We were interested in exploring what aspects of school administration and management had been influenced or reshaped by greater lay participation at the school level, the processes by which school governance was accomplished, and the power relations thereby invoked (Deem, Brehony *et al.*, 1995). We also wanted to examine the experiences of school governors and the meanings that their activities in schools had for them in a period of extensive education reform. We carried out intensive qualitative fieldwork, including observation of meetings, interviews with key informants and analysis of documents, in 10 contrasting primary and secondary school governing bodies.

Though our findings are derived from the specific cultural context of two areas of England, they raise significant theoretical and practical issues about the role of the national and local state in education reform in general, and the participation of lay people in the running of schools in particular. These include the desirable balance between centralized and decentralized control over publicly funded schooling, whom constitute 'active citizens'; the political processes entailed in site based management of educational institutions, and finally whether requirements for efficiently run schools should take precedence over demands for local democracy in the administration of educational systems. These are not in themselves new questions. They have already been applied, for instance, to analyses of the USA school board system (Boyd, 1975). However what is more novel is their application to the governance of individual schools as opposed to school districts or locally based education authorities. Contemporary programmes of education reform in the UK, USA, Australia, New Zealand and several western European countries are seeking to reduce or abolish the powers of professional educational administration at the district/area level in favour of site (school) based systems. Our analysis also differs in two other crucial respects from some apparently similar studies undertaken in the past. First we have incorporated not just social class and occupational status but also gender and ethnicity into our account of the processes of school governance. Second, unlike some other attempts to analyse the lessons which might be learnt by those in other countries from UK school reform (Chubb and Moe, 1992), our conclusions are based firmly on systematic research data.

Educational Reform, School Efficiency and Enterprise Culture

Educational reform is widely reported to be occurring at the present time in many different societies, including the United States (Chubb and Moe, 1992), the UK (Simkins, Ellison *et al.*, 1992) and New Zealand (Gordon, 1993). We cannot assume that all contemporary processes of school reform, even those that seem similar, are identical in respect of their causes, mechanisms and effects (Dale, 1992). However, the argument that education reform often takes place in periods of economic crisis is one which cannot be ignored (Ginsburg, Cooper *et al.*, 1990).

Recent educational reforms in the countries already mentioned have given greater local control and autonomy to schools themselves, often exercised under the joint responsibility of headteachers or principals, in conjunction with lay people who are not themselves expected to possess significant amounts of educational expertise (Deem, 1994a). This decentralization, often called site based management, has usually been accompanied by two other changes. These are the removal or reduction in the powers of local or regional democratically elected bodies responsible for the planning and strategic development of education in an entire area, and the development of 'quasi-markets' (Le Grand and Bartlett, 1993). Quasi-markets is used because 'pure' markets are difficult to establish anywhere but particularly within the confines of a publicly funded education system. Under this, publicly funded schools are expected to compete for pupils rather than just recruit those living nearby, and parents are enabled to exercise choice over which educational establishment their offspring attend. It is also often claimed that these changes will provide a more efficient education service and higher educational standards.

In England, Wales and Northern Ireland, a further element of school reform has been the central control of curriculum and assessment.

Historically, as Boyd (1975) has noted for the USA, arguments about the shifting nature of values around government have often focused on issues about representativeness, ideas of politically neutral competence, and executive leadership. More recently, debates about efficiency have also come into the frame. All four of these notions are certainly key issues but ideas about citizenship are also becoming increasingly important (Turner, 1993). Liberal democracies are also becoming marked by an absence of participation in political decision-making (Brehony, 1992). Some of the more recent emphasis on citizenship is related to wider processes of globalization, since only in local contexts can individuals find some possibility of exercising citizen rights and voting preferences (Held, 1993). In addition, 'public choice' has risen to prominence, whereby citizens can make their needs known through the operation of a market system in the public sector provision of services. The shift to market systems is also a consequence of the questioning of levels of government spending on welfare services.

The juxtaposition of administrative and financial changes made to education and other public services, including healthcare and housing, in addition to changing patterns of citizenship in liberal democracies, are indicative not just of structural changes but are also underlain by particular clusters of ideological beliefs and values. These values question the notion that striving for some measure of equality of resource redistribution from privileged to non-privileged groups is worthwhile (Saunders, 1993). Notions of diversity have replaced those of equality (Yates, 1993). In the UK, USA, France, Australia and New Zealand, these ideological clusters can loosely be described as 'enterprise culture' which emphasizes entrepreneurialism, risk and the search for profit, and is thereby almost antithetical to the values typically found in non-profit-making organizations (Keat and Abercrombie, 1991). However the particular mix of values and ideas which comprise enterprise culture vary according to cultural context, as do the changes which arise; 'enterprise discourse is best conceived of as a rather diffuse set of changes' (Fairclough, 1991: 38).

So far as the reshaping of education is concerned, the invoking of enterprise culture appears to be an attempt at changing not only the administrative efficiency of education but also its cultures. The shift envisaged is from cultures concerned primarily with educational values about learning, skills, knowledge and nurturing, to those concerned with finance, competition, marketing and customer service. In England the shift has included new forms of schools such as city technology colleges, part state and part industry funded, and located in urban areas. Their establishment has been very controversial (Whitty, Edwards *et al.*, 1993). In California and elsewhere in the USA the idea of charter schools, not privately funded but nevertheless independent of local school boards and districts, has been floated (Wohlstetter and Odden, 1992). Other enterprise culture phenomena in education include the aggressive marketing and image projection of schools (Kenway, 1995), the increasing primacy in education of balancing budgets and fund-raising (Ball, 1994) and the emergence of a new educational discourse emphasizing terms like mission statements, contracts, quality assurance, cost centres, line managers and targets. Measurement of the effectivity of education through audit and the use of performance indicators comparing schools with each other are further enterprise culture elements. However we cannot yet be sure of the extent to which widespread enterprise culture discourses have replaced other discourses more traditionally associated with education.

Lay School Governors and Educational Reform

What role have English governing bodies played in recent educational reform? The origins of lay school governors go back before the nineteenth-century elementary school managers. For much of this century the task of the lay school governor was not exacting. Prior to 1980, the majority of non-teacher governors in state schools were political appointees of LEAs. The 1980 Education Act introduced parental representation into LEA maintained schools as of right. Coopted governors were also permitted. The 1986 no. 2 Education Act laid down more detailed requirements for cooptees, specifying that they should include those working in business.

Until the 1980s, governors' responsibilities were limited to generally overseeing the curriculum and school organization. The 1986 Act gave governors many new responsibilities. These included secular curriculum policy, sex education, involvement in headteacher appointments, monitoring political bias in the curriculum and producing an annual report to be discussed at a meeting open to the parents of all registered pupils.

The 1988 Education Reform Act added much more although ambiguity remains over the demarcation of decision-making boundaries between heads and governors. The 1988 Act gave governing bodies responsibility for delegated school budgets under local management of schools (LMS), *de facto* hiring and firing of staff, and overseeing the newly introduced national curriculum, national assessment system, collective worship and religious education. Other responsibilities included appeals against expulsion and non-admission, and control over the letting of school premises outside school hours. Governing bodies could also initiate the process whereby their school could apply, after a favourable parental ballot, to become directly funded by the government, and be called a grant maintained status (GMS) school.

In a 10 year period then, lay governors moved from being symbolic appointees with a range of ceremonial duties and a requirement to attend a termly meeting, to having a range of complex formal obligations. In all but one of our case study governing bodies, the enhanced workload necessitated the establishment of an array of subcommittees and working groups. At the same time, the advice and guidance available to governors from their LEAs decreased. Until the 1988 Education Reform Act, democratically elected LEAs had determined local policies and plans for their schools. In the early 1980s, LEAs had also been influential in shaping much of the culture and ethos of governing bodies (Kogan, Johnson *et al.*, 1984). The reforms swept away much of the democratic infrastructure of educational administration, replacing it with governing bodies only part of whose membership was elected, *and* a much more central government controlled curriculum, assessment and funding system.

Making Sense of Changes to School Governance

Can the changes to English education be regarded as an instance of 'mainstreaming' the administration of state funded education so that education becomes just another service with no special characteristics (Dale, 1992)? It is clear that in England the current education reforms have sought to eliminate the distinctive characteristics of education, including the role of educational experts in the formulation of policy, just as endeavours have been made to bring in managers of the health service who have no background in healthcare.

Are these changes being undertaken in the interests of capital accumulation, with the state seeking to secure the process, context and legitimation of this (Dale, 1989) or are the changes being pursued by government simply in order to develop more efficient schools and offer parents more choice unfettered by the bureaucratic activities of local politicians (Chubb and Moe, 1990, 1992)? In England site based management has been accompanied by a concomitant increase in the powers of central government, handing power to other politicians rather than parents or communities.

So we need to ask whether decentralization of schools is a democratic act. How representative of school populations and local areas do active citizens need to be? What kinds of qualities and expertise do they require in order to do the job? Should we be advocating that citizens utilize individual public choice (Chubb and Moe, 1992; Saunders, 1993), or should we invoke a notion of citizenship more akin to the classical model, whereby the exercise of individual market rights is insufficient evidence of citizenry and it is necessary also to engage in other forms of collective participation (Skinner, 1993)?

Participation as a concept may be interpreted in a number of different ways when applied to education. It may refer to market oriented individual participation as in school choice, a partnership between parents and educators or the instrumental benefits of participation such as better exam results (Woods, 1988). In our study we conceptualized participation as referring to the engagement of lay people in the political and administrative aspects of governing schools. We have also assumed that participation involves a political process because school governance involves decision-making, and decision-making involves the deployment of power.

We have defined active citizens as those people of any gender, class or ethnicity who engage in voluntary activities which benefit others in their community. However we suggest that problems may arise which get in the way of the participation of some individuals who wish to be active citizens. Many western notions of democracy and citizenship exclude women, both because of their sexual role in relation to men, and their capacity to give birth to children, which are seen as threats to rational decision-making (Pateman, 1989). Pateman's arguments are certainly applicable to school governance, where freedom from other commitments and a willingness to engage in a rational bureaucratic discourse are key domain assumptions surrounding school governance.

Finally, there is some evidence that the drive for school reform packages involving site based management arose through pressures to reduce bureaucracy in the administration of education, in the interests of efficiency and school effectivity (Chubb and Moe, 1990, 1992). However, in the USA, the reduction of bureaucracy in the restructuring of education has also often been understood as a means of *reducing* local democratic political involvement in education, while still retaining a large element of professional educator involvement in policy formulation at the school level (Strike, 1993). The latter may still inhibit the input which is made by lay people. Strike suggests that by combining a system of site based management at the school level, whereby lay people and professional educators have equal status, with a wider overseeing policy role for democratically elected local political institutions, we could ensure that both democracy and efficiency existed. This would combine Locke's notion of democratic accountability of public services to those who have helped fund them via the school board or other elected district authority (Locke, 1960) with Habermas' ideal speech community (Habermas, 1984, 1987). Those responsible for administering a school could freely express ideas, and the best ideas would be chosen rather than those which are most politically expedient or most skilfully presented. Strike suggests this would work best where there are shared core values. This is consistent with Boyd's (1975) hypothesis that citizens and school boards in socially homogeneous areas may have more influence over strategic policy decisions whereas in heterogeneous communities paid administrators may have more influence.

Governing Schools – Confusion and Ambiguity?

In our study experienced and new governors alike found the role of administering schools very demanding. It involved attendance at numerous meetings, the agreement of detailed budgets, and making decisions about hiring and firing of staff, as well as more mundane tasks. Many governors found their role confusing; what exactly were they supposed to be doing? Were they helping to run the school or just bystanders offering the occasional critical comment? In general they found it preferable to concentrate on those aspects of schools in which they had expertise (finance, the law, relationships with parents, building maintenance, school visits) rather than intervening in professional concerns such as teaching and learning where they had no expert knowledge.

This is consistent with the actual responsibilities of governors in Scotland and Catalunya (Deem, 1994a).

A range of individual motivations for pursuing voluntary work may not matter where volunteers carry out specific tasks such as serving in a charity shop or fund-raising. By contrast, what governors are expected to do is unclear. Legislation does not (nor could it) say how governors should enact their role nor what priority should be placed on different tasks. Personal interests play a key role in the ambiguity surrounding what governors do. It is likely that no volunteering is entirely altruistic but volunteering as a governor can have very direct benefits for the volunteer, especially if they are a parent or employer. However some of these supposed benefits may lie in precisely those areas, the nature of teaching and learning, where the governors we observed were reluctant to intervene.

Not only did governors shy away from decisions around teaching and learning, but it was also unclear to most of them what kind of relationship they ought to have with students and teachers in their school. In secondary schools governors who were not parents of current or ex-pupils seldom knew any staff other than the senior management team and teacher governors. What governors should do on their school visits was another difficulty; an initial visit might be used to find out how the school worked but the purpose of subsequent visits was unclear, since governors were unsure if they were a teacher's aide, visitor or inspector. Some teachers and governors regarded the school visit as a surveillance practice or 'governor gaze', viewing each other with mutual suspicion. Our evidence poses clearly the question of whether governors are supposed to be replacement, non-specialist bureaucrats, political actors making decisions about resources, or part of a group of equals taking shared decisions about the strategic operation of a school in which they all have an interest. This question applies equally to any contemporary education system and unless it is resolved, many of the ambiguities attached to school governance will remain. Perhaps these are among the unintended consequences which we must expect to flow from any social policy change?

Governor Diversity and Social Composition

Lay governors are from many different backgrounds, social groups and religious and political affiliations. However, it may be that a diverse mix, in conjunction with the political process, is crucial to the functioning of both governing bodies and their schools. This is particularly the case if schools are one of the few remaining areas in western globalized democracies where active citizenship can be exercised (Held, 1993). Pearce (1993), examining research on USA school boards (the equivalent of LEAs) suggests that diverse representation is important in ensuring effective operation of educational policy forming organizations. However whereas Pearce looked at occupational status only, we would also want to emphasize gender and ethnicity. National surveys of the reformed school governing bodies in England show that lay governors are recruited primarily from white, middle-class, highly educated sectors of the population, with women represented reasonably in all categories except amongst coopted governors (Keys and Fernandes, 1990).

Our case study research enables us to understand how social diversity may affect governance processes. This is discussed in more detail elsewhere (Deem, Brehony et al., 1995) but the important point for the argument made here is about the relationship between the social composition of governing bodies and those of the pupil intake of the school governed. Where these two were similar, however, we did not necessarily find particularly efficient or conflict-free governance; nevertheless in working-class schools and those with high minority ethnic group intakes, we did note a much greater awareness of issues of social inequality and its consequences for schooling (Brehony, 1995). We would thus suggest where, in schools drawing their pupils from disadvantaged neighbourhoods, there is a mismatch between the social characteristics of the pupils and the membership of the governing body, the pursuit of social justice and educational opportunities for all *may* be impaired (Deem, Brehony et al., 1994).

However, we can only suggest that this is the case from our evidence; we cannot make more extensive claims from case study research. Furthermore we are also cognizant of the difficulty of using social background alone as a firm indicator of the beliefs, values and practices of school governors. Thus, we did not find that female governors necessarily pursued issues of sexism, that governors with strong religious beliefs always favoured compulsory collective worship or that those governors who were members of the Conservative party always favoured reducing public expenditure on education. However we did note that black and Asian governors were frequently concerned with what they saw as issues of racism and with ensuring that black and Asian children got the best schooling possible. We also observed that in general gender, ethnicity and social class were significant aspects of the decision-making process engaged in by governors (Deem, Brehony et al., 1995).

The Politician, the Banker and the Parent

Although some proponents of site based management see it as removing political control over schools and giving power to parents and teachers (Chubb and Moe, 1992), this has not been the case in England where political appointees on governing bodies remain. Our study found that coopted and local education authority governors, regardless of political and religious affiliations (though gender *was* influential), played a key role in the politics of school governance (Deem, 1994c). Male business governors dominated the important finance subcommittees, and male LEA governors occupied the role of chairperson in seven out of our 10 case study governing bodies (Deem, 1989, 1991, 1994c).

How can we explain the continued prominence of LEA governors in the affairs of their governing bodies, despite efforts to reduce political dominance?

We found LEA governors were often locally powerful people with a network of external contacts which were useful for their schools (Deem, 1994c). These networks included local authority officers, Members of Parliament, community power holders, media representatives and those working at senior levels in other educational institutions. Such networks were only matched by those of male business governors in high status jobs but such governors often had little time for their voluntary work. Brehony has used the term 'urban gentry' to describe active LEA governors because of their wide involvement in public and community service, and concern to 'help others' (Brehony, 1992).

Active citizens may turn out to be recruited disproportionately from a narrow sector of society, namely those who have the time, money, cultural and political capital to enable them to assist others in a voluntary capacity. Does this matter? Although we were not endeavouring to discover the extent to which the urban gentry existed in governing bodies across England as a whole, we did note the consequences for schools. The urban gentry often possessed enormous appetite and enthusiasm for voluntary work and had considerable commitment to education. While not necessarily familiar at first-hand with the experiences of the less privileged, urban gentry had, on their own account, a notion of public good and welfare which influenced their activities as volunteers in a variety of contexts (Deem, 1994b). Their outlooks did not always seem to be consistent with notions that enterprise culture should shape the values and practices of schools. In a context of reshaping, the urban gentry may prove to be a force of resistance to change.

Excluding politicians from school governing bodies, as Strike (1993) advocates, may not necessarily be an effective way of ensuring that democratic practice pertains in schools, if the alternative is for governing bodies to contain only those with a direct interest in the school they govern. Despite Woods' (1988) contention that parents can act collectively through associations and groups, our observations suggested that this was often confined to fund-raising and social events rather than dealing with fundamental aspects of schooling. Parent governors were often knowledgeable about the school but this was a particularistic knowledge grounded in their own children's experiences, and did not always lend itself to informed debate about overall policies and principles. Our research evidence strongly supports the notion that a social mix of people, a blend of politicians and non-politicians, *and* representation of the school population are all important if there is to be genuine democratic debate over education at the site level. We accept that conflict is a vital part of the governance of education and that an ideal speech community as advocated by Habermas is not necessarily possible (Habermas, 1984, 1987).

Reshaping Education Through Lay Control?

We found unsupported the notion that lay governors could raise the standards of education *per se* rather than tinkering with the organizational and administrative parameters under which schools operated. Governing bodies in the schools we researched spent little time on issues of teaching and learning and as far as organizational and administrative issues were concerned, most energy was devoted to those affecting governors and governing bodies alone. So to what extent can lay governors be seen to be a means of re-shaping education? Though some political governors in our study specialized in complaints about exam results (Deem, Brehony *et al.*, 1994), there was little evidence that this strategy had any impact on the educational practices and standards of the schools concerned beyond lowering staff and student morale. Thus the notion that introducing lay people into the administration of schools results in those lay people having a significant impact on specifically educational issues, may itself be a casualty of the very processes and micro-politics implied in the school governance situation.

Yet one of the distinctive features of the 1980s education legislation in the UK was to encourage the cooption of governors from business and industry; this was re-emphasized in the 1993 Education Act which permitted LEA maintained and GMS schools to adopt 'sponsor governors' as well as cooptees from the business community. Partnerships between business and industry are commonplace in schools in many countries. However the explicit use as active participants in the *administration* of schools *at the site level*, of coopted, non-elected, business people *qua* business people, is something unique to England and Wales.

Indeed a frequently invoked argument for introducing non-specialists into educational administration is that they make school government more efficient by introducing the practices of the outside world; this is a micro-version of Dale's (1992) notion of mainstreaming by which processes and policies, publicly funded education is brought into the real world of business. There are two problems here though. Not all business governors are those with high level managerial and financial skills. Governors who work in the private sector comprise about one-third of all school governors in England and Wales. However as Thody (1993) has pointed out, the term business governor covers a very wide range of people, from shop floor operatives and routine administrators, to senior executives and managers. Many of those who are employed in business become governors on the basis of parental status or political party membership rather than because of their business credentials. Not all perceive themselves as business governors and they may indeed be parent or LEA governors rather than the cooptees who are supposed to reflect business and commerce. Such governors may not always want to impose business values and practices on schools. Those who did were affected by two things. First their experience did not always translate easily into the world of schooling. Second most of those who defined themselves as business governors explicitly coopted for that purpose did not have much spare time at their disposal and were sometimes dismayed to find out how much work was involved in being a governor. Both these factors were reasons for a relatively high turnover in coopted governors.

We found that governors with committee and management experience, whether derived from the private, public or voluntary sectors, were often quite skilled at making sure that the agenda items at meetings were discussed and the business dispatched speedily. However if efficiency is to move beyond the level of the governors' meetings and into the school itself, this is a rather different matter. We found no evidence that such a transfer had taken place and indeed the complex management structures of the secondary schools we studied were seldom matched by or paired with the structures found in their governing bodies. This was not surprising since we found relatively few governors in our secondary case sites who spent much time in school outside of formal meetings. Those who did spend such time in school were rarely those with extensive business connections.

Efficient Schools or Democratic Ones?

So far as democracy is concerned, the ideologies underlying recent English reforms of public policy as a whole display considerable ambivalence towards notions of democratic accountability in public life. This is particularly so in relation to debates about the role of non-elected quasi-governmental bodies or quangos (Barker, 1982; Stewart, Lewis *et al.*, 1992; Cohen and Weir, 1994; Hackett and Pyke, 1994; Weir and Hall, 1994; Deem, Brehony *et al.*, 1995). In addition, some critics of excessive bureaucratization and inefficiency of public services seem unable to separate these concerns from the fact that in western societies public services are still usually run with at least some democratic and political party involvement. Several UK and USA writers on site based management argue that bureaucracy and unnecessary intervention in schools caused by democratically elected local political bodies can be swept away without any great loss to education (Chubb and Moe, 1990; Davies and Anderson, 1992). Indeed these writers claim that there are significant advantages to standards of schooling if schools are run in a relatively autonomous manner. However, as Strike notes, democracy and bureaucracy do not have to be closely linked. He contends that it is possible to have democratic schools without necessarily also having bureaucratic and inefficient ones, especially if school boards are retained only as 'representatives of voice of the political community in the deliberations of the local school community' (Strike, 1993: 267).

The version of school governance that England currently has is not particularly close to the mix of Locke's notions of democratic sovereignty (Locke, 1960) and Habermas' 'ideal speech communities' (Habermas, 1984, 1987) which Strike (1993) advocates as a better solution to more democratic and effective schooling than simply setting schools adrift to make all their own decisions. The governing bodies of LEA maintained schools are a curious mix of democratic and undemocratic elements, of elected representation and corporatist arrangements (Brehony, 1994). Teacher and parent governors are elected from amongst the constituencies they represent in the relevant school. LEA nominees are unelected *qua* school governors; we found some LEA nominees who had no connection at all with the LEAs that had nominated them. However political party membership is often a criterion, with many LEAs choosing governors in proportion to the balance of political parties on that authority. Coopted governors are chosen by the other governors on their governing body; some governing bodies in our study selected on the basis of particular expertise (financial, legal etc.), while others opted for local community ties and/or evidence of a wish to join. The governing bodies of GMS schools have a majority of parents but only some of these need be elected; other foundation or first governors are chosen by the governing body. There are no LEA nominees on GMS governing bodies.

Both LEA and GMS school governing bodies are frequently referred to as forms of parent power, though in fact they are nothing of the sort, since they can only include a tiny fraction of parents from any given school and they also include non-parents. Gender, class and ethnicity are also important factors in shaping the extent to which actors can influence what happens in governing bodies. The English system at present is neither democratic nor efficient. It is increasingly a system which exists only at the level of the school and central government, with intermediary democratically elected layers of LEAs fast disappearing. It might have been possible to keep this intermediary layer, while still permitting schools day to day autonomy over their running, so that some accountability of schools to the wider community than their own parents and students was retained (Brehony and Deem 1993). So far however, little political enthusiasm for this idea has been shown. Although the National Commission on Education suggested that local (non-elected) Education and Training Boards should be set up to act as 'purchaser-providers' with a clear brief to be accountable as well as to undertake strategic planning and quality assurance, it was suggested that these were not to be directly elected (National Commission, 1993).

Conclusion

The power of the reformed English governing body, though frequently commented upon as though it were all-embracing, is in practice limited to a range of ill defined and excessively demanding functions which are not closely related to the core activities of the school, and only loosely connected to the efficiency of school administration, as opposed to that of the governing body itself. Furthermore, governor power and the system of site based management on which it is based, coexist with a massive concentration of power over curriculum, assessment, teacher conditions and the funding of education located not at the school or local level, but in the hands of central government.

The governing bodies we studied were neither particularly efficient nor democratic and some of them contained active citizens who were unrepresentative of the student and parent communities which they served. It would be possible to have representative and efficient governing bodies with a range of clearly delimited responsibilities rather than the current extensive range, and also possible to establish ways in which all participants are elected rather than some, as now, being nominated. We are more sceptical about whether it is also possible to ensure that all participants have a fair chance of influencing decision-making while structures of race, gender and class persist as significant social divisions.

However, neither the current composition of governing bodies in England, nor their organization and operation can be guaranteed or even expected to lead to more efficient or more democratic schools. The governing body and the school are, as we have demonstrated, different, though related, organizational entities. Democratic, representative, governing bodies that have a clear remit appropriate to the skills and knowledge of lay people, and that can operate effectively within that remit, with a local or regional democratically elected body presiding over issues about wider educational policy, are, we suggest, a necessary but not sufficient condition for the development of more effective and democratic schools. To achieve these in full requires an organizational and political change to educational policy and schools themselves, which in England at least seems to have been discouraged rather than encouraged by the 1980s and 1990s reforms. Hence fewer teachers are involved in school decision-making (Bowe, Ball *et al.*, 1992), the national curriculum has been riven by disputes about content, the form of national assessment is still a contested notion, and there is little or no time in schools for discussing questions of pedagogy or student learning.

Democratic schools may be difficult or even impossible to achieve in a political and cultural climate which values central control of education and the profit motive, enterprise culture, competition and the market above ideas about the nurturing and development of individual and collaborative potential through education. To this extent, the role of nation states in shaping the climate within which education exists is indeed a crucial one. In periods of global economic crisis and restructuring, the conditions for fostering a notion of education which goes beyond the assistance of the process, context and legitimation of capital accumulation are not much in evidence. Unless this changes, then the search for democracy in education is likely to continue to be subordinated to goals concerned with administrative efficiency and cost effectiveness, thinly disguised as concerns about educational standards and quality but with the result that students, parents, teachers, politicians and industrialists will all be the losers.

Acknowledgments

This chapter was originally presented to a symposium convened by David Halpin, Barry Troyna and Bill Boyd on 'Lessons in school reform from Great

Britain' at the American Educational Research Association Conference in New Orleans in April 1994. Thanks to Kevin Brehony, and the audience at the AERA symposium for their helpful comments on the original paper.

References

BALL, S. (1994) *Education Reform: A Critical and Post-Structuralist Approach*, Buckingham, Open University Press.

BARKER, A. (ed) (1982) *Quangos in Britain: Government and the Networks of Public Policy-Making*, London, Macmillan.

BOWE, R., BALL, S. *et al.* (1992) *Reforming Education and Changing Schools*, London, Routledge.

BOYD, W.L. (1975) 'School board administrative staff relationships', in CISTONE, P.J. (ed) *Understanding School Boards*, Boston, DC, Heath, pp. 103–29.

BREHONY, K.J. (1992) ' "Active citizens": The case of school governors', *International Studies in the Sociology of Education*, **2**, 2, pp. 199–217.

BREHONY, K.J. (1994) 'Interests, accountability and representation: A political analysis of governing bodies', in THODY, A. (ed) *School Governors: Leaders or Followers?* London, Longman, pp. 49–63.

BREHONY, K.J. (1995) ' "Race", ethnicity and racism in the governing of schools', in CRAFT, M. and TOMLINSON, S. (eds) *Ethnic Relations in Schools in the 1990s*, London, University College London Press.

BREHONY, K.J. and DEEM, R. (1993) 'Democratising school governance', paper presented to the Fabian Society Education Group, London, July.

CHUBB, J.E. and MOE, T.M. (1990) *Politics, Markets and America's Schools*, Washington DC, The Brookings Institute.

CHUBB, J.E. and MOE, T.M. (1992) *A Lesson in School Reform from Great Britain*, Washington DC, Brookings Institute.

COHEN, N. and WEIR, S. (1994) 'Welcome to Quangoland', *Independent on Sunday*, 22 May.

DALE, R. (1989) *The State and Educational Policy*, Milton Keynes, Open University Press.

DALE, R. (1992) 'National reform, economic crisis and "New Right" theory: A New Zealand perspective', paper presented to annual meeting of the American Educational Research Association, San Francisco, CA, April.

DAVIES, B. and ANDERSON, L. (eds) (1992) *Opting for Self Management*, London, Routledge.

DEEM, R. (1989) 'The new school governing bodies – Are race and gender on the agenda?', *Gender and Education*, **1**, 3, pp. 247–60.

DEEM, R. (1991) 'Governing by gender? school governing bodies after the Education Reform Act', in ABBOTT, P. and WALLACE, C. (eds) *Gender, Power and Sexuality*, London, Macmillan.

DEEM, R. (1994a) 'Free marketeers or good citizens? Education policy and lay participation in the adminstration of schools', *British Journal of Educational Studies*, **42**, 1, pp. 23–7.

DEEM, R. (1994b) 'School governing bodies – Public concerns or private interests?', in SCOTT, D. (ed) *Accountability and Control in Educational Settings*, London, Cassell.

DEEM, R. (1994c) 'Are you still coming to our meetings? Issues of power in a longitudinal study of school governing bodies', in WALFORD, G. (ed) *Researching the Powerful in Education*, London, University College London Press.

DEEM, R., BREHONY, K.J. *et al.* (1994) 'Governors, schools and the miasma of the market', *British Educational Research Journal*, **20**, 5, pp. 335–50.

DEEM, R., BREHONY, K.J. *et al.* (1995) *Active Citizenship and the Governing of Schools*, Buckingham, Open University Press.

FAIRCLOUGH, N. (1991) 'What might we mean by "enterprise discourse"?', in KEAT, R. and ABERCROMBIE, N. (eds) *Enterprise Culture*, London, Routledge, pp. 38–57.

GINSBURG, M., COOPER, S. *et al.* (1990) 'National and world system explanations of educational reform', *Comparative Education Review*, **34**, 4, 474–99.

GORDON, L. (1993) 'Who controls New Zealand schools? Decentralised management and the problem of agency', paper presented to British Educational Research Association conference, Liverpool, September.

HABERMAS, J. (1984) *The Theory of Communicative Action: Reason and Rationalization of Society*, London, Heinemann.

HABERMAS, J. (1987) *The Theory of Communicative Action: Lifeworld and System: A Critique of Functionalist Reason*, Cambridge, Polity Press.

HACKETT, G. and PYKE, N. (1994) 'Secrets of the quango tango', *Times Educational Supplement*, 22 April pp. 13–14.

HELD, D. (1993) 'By the people, for the people', *The Higher*, 22 January: 17–18.

KEAT, R. and ABERCROMBIE, N. (1991) *Enterprise Culture*, London, Routledge.

KENWAY, J. (ed) (1995) *Marketing Education: Some Critical Issues*, Geelong, Deakin University Press.

KEYS, W. and FERNANDES, C. (1990) *A Survey of School Governing Bodies*, Slough, National Foundation for Educational Research.

KOGAN, M., Johnson, D. *et al.* (1984) *School Governing Bodies*, London, Heinemann.

LE GRAND, J. and BARTLETT, W. (eds) (1993) *Quasi-Markets and Social Policy*, London, Macmillan.

LOCKE, J. (1960) *Two Treatises of Government*, Cambridge, Cambridge University Press.

NATIONAL COMMISSION ON EDUCATION (1993) *Learning to Succeed: A Radical Look at Education Today and a Strategy for the Future*, London, Heinemann.

PATEMAN, C. (1989) *The Disorder of Women: Democracy, Feminism and Political Theory*, Cambridge, Polity.

PEARCE, J. (1993) 'What type of director is best for your school?' *Management in Education*, **7**, 3, pp. 31–2.

SAUNDERS, P. (1993) 'Citizenship in a liberal society', in TURNER, B. (ed) *Citizenship and Social Theory*, London, Sage, pp. 57–90.

SIMKINS, T., ELLISON, L. *et al.* (eds) (1992) *Implementing Educational Reform: The Early Lessons*, British Educational Management and Administration Society, London, Longman.

SKINNER, Q. (1993) 'Classical and contemporary theories of citizenship', public lecture, Lancaster University, January.

STEWART, J., LEWIS, N. *et al.* (1992) *Accountability to the Public*, London: European Policy Forum for British and European Market Studies.

STRIKE, K.A. (1993) 'Professionalism, democracy and discursive communities: Normative reflections on restructuring', *American Educational Research Journal*, **30**, 3, pp. 255–75.

THODY, A. (1993) 'Practising democracy: Business community representatives in the control of English and Welsh schools', paper presented at a conference on School Governance and Democracy in the 1990s, University of Reading, October.

TURNER, B. (ed) (1993) *Citizenship and Social Theory*, London, Sage.

WEIR, S. and HALL, W. (1994) *Ego Trip: Extra governmental organisations in the UK and their accountability; the democratic audit of the UK*, London, Charter 88 Trust (pamphlet).

WHITTY, G., EDWARDS, T. *et al.* (1993) *Specialisation and Choice in Urban Education: The City Technology College Experiment*, London, Routledge.

WOHLSTETTER, P. and ODDEN, A. (1992) 'Rethinking school-based management policy and research', *Educational Administration Quarterly*, **28**, 4, pp. 529–49.

WOODS, P. (1988) 'A strategic view of parent participation', *Journal of Education Policy*, **3**, 4, pp. 323–34.

YATES, L. (1993) 'Feminism and Australian state policy: Some questions for the 1990s', in ARNOT, M. and WEILER, K. (ed) *Feminism and Social Justice in Education*, London, Falmer Press, pp. 167–85.

Chapter 5

School Governing Bodies in Northern Ireland: Responses to Local Management of Schools

Penny McKeown, Caitlin Donnelly and Bob Osborne

Following the Education Reform Act of 1988 for England and Wales, the government introduced the Education Reform (Northern Ireland) Order 1989 (ERO) to prescribe many of the same changes. These included formula-funding and local management of schools (LMS), open enrolment and a legislated curriculum with programmes of study and national assessment.

A key component of delegated management has been the extension of the powers and responsibilities of school governing bodies, so that the demands on governors, individually and collectively, have become much more wide-ranging. Equally, LMS has had implications for the role and functions of head-teachers, especially in their relationships with their governing bodies. While research in England and Wales (Golby, 1991; Deem and Brehony, 1993; Field, 1993) has investigated the impact of these changes on heads and governors, very little such research has been undertaken in Northern Ireland to date.

This chapter is based on two surveys of heads and governors of a sample of 60 Northern Ireland post-primary schools, undertaken at the beginning of the third year of LMS (in April and May, 1993) and on a small number of follow-up interviews of heads. It will investigate aspects of the changing role of school governing bodies in Northern Ireland under LMS. The survey was sent to a representative sample of schools according to management type, education and library board (ELB) area and school type (grammar or secondary intermediate). The term of office of the governors surveyed covered the period of transition from pre- to post-LMS. This cohort of governors was, therefore, in a position to make informed judgments about the extent and nature of changes which had confronted them.

The chapter describes the Northern Ireland education system and identifies the main areas in which the local reform package diverges from that of England and Wales. A second section will describe and analyse the evidence from the research in terms of a number of areas of interest. This will be followed by a discussion of the results.

The School System in Northern Ireland

ERO was imposed on a school system which already differed to a considerable extent from that of England and Wales. It was divided along religious lines, still operated selection for pupils at age 11, and was organized differently to reflect the historic divisions between the two main communities in Northern Ireland. Overall responsibility for the education system rests with the Department of Education for Northern Ireland (DENI) but since local government reform in 1973, local responsibility for most schools has been in the hands of five nominated authorities, the education and library boards.

Briefly: grant-aided schools are separated according to management type and according to the religious affiliation (Roman Catholic and Protestant) and academic attainment of pupils. The main sectors are:

- selective *voluntary grammar schools*, both Roman Catholic and Protestant;
- voluntary *maintained* schools, both primary and secondary intermediate (or comprehensive), attended almost entirely by Roman Catholic pupils;
- *controlled* schools, primary, secondary and grammar, attended mainly by Protestant pupils.

There are also very small numbers of schools in three other categories.

DENI figures (1992), show that 142,404 pupils were enrolled in 710 controlled schools, 139,241 in 580 maintained schools and 40,548 in 52 voluntary grammar schools. By mid-1992, approximately 2800 pupils were enrolled in the integrated sectors.

School Governance in Northern Ireland

Current arrangements for school governance in Northern Ireland date from the mid-1980s. By the mid-1970s a complicated, and often anomalous, set of management arrangements for Northern Ireland schools had emerged as a result of the historical accretion of education legislation. These reflected the religious divide in society as a whole and gave considerable influence on school management committees to representatives of the main churches. Following the Taylor Report of 1977, the Astin Committee (1979) recommended that every school should have a board of governors, identified with the school and its interests, which could contribute to the dialogue between the school and its publics. All governing bodies should have teacher and parent representatives and the number of church nominees should be reduced. Most of these recommendations were incorporated in new legislation (The Education and Libraries (Northern Ireland) Order 1984; The Education and Libraries (Northern Ireland) Order 1986).

A number of bodies and individuals are entitled to nominate or elect members to boards of governors of schools, depending on the management type of the school concerned. Briefly these are (DENI, 1993):

- *parents* (election; all schools);
- *teachers* (election; all schools);
- *ELBs* (nomination; to controlled, controlled integrated, maintained, and some voluntary grammar schools);
- *DENI* (nomination; to some controlled, most voluntary grammar, and all GMI schools);
- *Protestant churches* which transferred schools to the state (nomination; to controlled, and controlled integrated schools);
- *managers or trustees* (nomination; to maintained, controlled integrated, and voluntary grammar schools);
- *foundation governors* (nomination; to some voluntary grammar schools);

All grant-aided schools may, in addition, coopt up to three members of the local business community to serve as non-voting governors. Membership of the school governing body is completed by the headteacher, who is a member, but non-voting.

There are two main differences between this representation in Northern Ireland and that in England and Wales. The first lies in the absence of political appointees. While ELB nominees to governing bodies may be local councillors who are ELB members, they have no party political remit in that position. The second distinction lies in the extent to which the churches are formally represented on school governing bodies: the Protestant churches' representatives (transferors) have nomination rights to four-ninths of the membership of controlled schools, while the Catholic church nominates three-fifths of the members (trustees' representatives) of the boards of maintained schools. Both groups of churches have lesser nomination rights to controlled integrated schools (DENI, 1993). Such high levels of continuing denominational representation may be expected to replicate within and between schools the structural divisions within wider Northern Ireland society.

The Provisions of Education Reform

Education reform has made some significant changes to the system which operated before 1989. These are evident in three main areas: first, in the arrangements to fund schools and the delegation of management to school level, second, in the creation of new forms of school governance and third, in the intention to effect within the system real influence and choices for consumers. The Northern Ireland reforms vary in some important respects from those in England and Wales. These include a different curriculum (with differing assessment arrangements), a different timescale for the introduction of programmes of study, the promotion of an integrated school system, the creation of a Council for Catholic Maintained Schools (CCMS), and the non-availability, except for integrated schools, of opting out to grant maintained status (McKeown and Connolly, 1992).

Why Local Management of Schools?

As indicated by Wallace (1992: 2), the introduction into the UK school system of managerial and financial delegation through the LMS initiative, 'is not an isolated policy change but part of a comprehensive range of legislation designed to change the way schools work'. The motives which underpin the introduction of formula funding and LMS as elements of the broader reform package are varied and have been well documented (Thomas, 1988; Maclure, 1992). In particular they attempt to push decision-making in education as near as possible to its point of delivery as a spur to quality, to create a quasi-market in education, and to increase the accountability of schools to the community. Clearly the demands arising from these major new concerns are likely to generate new agendas and ways of working for school managers.

The Effects of Delegation on School Management

Under its LMS provisions, the 1989 Order required that full delegation was made to all controlled and maintained post-primary schools from 1 April 1991. Voluntary grammar schools have a tradition of largely autonomous management, so it seems likely that heads and governors of those schools will find less change of responsibilities arising from education reform.

DENI circular 1990/20 gave clear expression to the anticipated roles and relationships between school governors and headteachers. Governors' responsibilities were detailed (paras 6–13) and their relationships with the headteacher were spelled out in para. 11:

> The experience, knowledge and management expertise of the principal will be a major asset to the school in operating under LMS . . . DENI envisages that each Board of Governors . . . will delegate to the principal . . . the management of all or part of the school's delegated budget. In addition the principal will have a key role in helping . . . to formulate a management plan . . . and in securing its implementation . . . the Governors should ensure that the role of the principal . . . [is] clear to all concerned.

The first responses to LMS from school managers in Northern Ireland came from the early results of a Northern Ireland Council for Educational Research (NICER) study of the LMS pilot schools (Wells and McKibben, 1990a, 1990b, 1990c). While many principals have welcomed the increased autonomy and flexibility which LMS permits them, concerns included:

- anxieties about funding and a need for financial and administrative advice;
- a greatly increased managerial workload, which was 'distancing' principals from curricular concerns;
- the dominance of financial issues, rather than curriculum-led planning at governing bodies' meetings.

These findings have been supported by subsequent research in England and Wales, summarized by Wallace (1992: 167). She highlights three problematic areas identified by ongoing research:

- LMS is intended to devolve both power and accountability on to schools, but the powers are, in practice, limited and are outweighed by the enormous increase in workload associated with the demands of accountability;
- numbers-driven management substitutes for issues-driven management;
- governing bodies may be comprised of people who have little knowledge of schooling, or contact with the parents, teachers and pupils whose interests they are supposed to represent.

The Research in Northern Ireland

In examining the applicability of these findings to the first cohort of school governors in Northern Ireland to be confronted with the demands of full delegation under LMS, the research instruments asked questions in a number of areas. These included:

- personal details of age, gender, employment status, and earnings of governors;
- details of level of involvement in school governance;
- views about the extent and nature of governors' responsibilities in comparison to the period before LMS; those which were thought most onerous and how these were being coped with;
- training and support provided for governors;
- current procedures for dealing with aspects of governors' work, e.g. the annual report;
- wider links with the school in question.

In addition, heads were asked about the committee structure of their governing bodies, the level of vacancies, frequency and duration of governor meetings, the nature of their workload in connection with the governing body, the effect of the increase of governor responsibilities on their role as head and their general satisfaction with the role played by their board.

Who Responded to the Survey?

Access to individual governors was only obtainable through headteachers. Thirty-nine heads returned questionnaires, a response rate of 65 per cent, with no significant biases in non-respondents. Of the governors of those 39 schools, 62 per cent, (approximately 300), responded to the questionnaire. No governor responded from any school from which the head did not also respond, indicating probably that they did not receive the questionnaire. Among the respondents there was a spread of representation of the main categories of governor: 20 per cent were parents, 17 per cent ELB nominees, 16 per cent transferors, 16 per cent trustees, 11 per cent teachers, and 10 per cent DENI representatives.

Who Are School Governors in Northern Ireland?

In Northern Ireland, school governors are overwhelmingly male (71 per cent), middle-aged or older (90 per cent are over 40), in full time work (69 per cent) or retired (20 per cent) and earning more than £15,000 per annum (68 per cent). Except in respect of income levels, there are no large variations between governors from the various types of school. While over a third of maintained school governors earn less than £10,000 p.a., only 15 per cent of governors from voluntary grammar schools fall into this category. At the higher levels of income, the situation is reversed: less than a quarter of governors from the maintained sector earn more than £25,000, but over 40 per cent of those from voluntary grammar schools do. Controlled school governors' income pattern is closer to that of the voluntary grammar schools.

Governors, particularly those in the maintained sector, live close to the schools where they serve and they serve for extended periods (43 per cent have been governors for more than five years). Almost 50 per cent, but only 20 per cent of those from voluntary grammar schools, serve on more than one governing body. Their reasons for serving include a general interest in education (31 per cent), an interest in their own child's education (28 per cent), a wish to be involved in community service (20 per cent) or in connection with their paid work (14 per cent). Membership of more than one board was common with 92 per cent of the transferors' representatives and 53 per cent of trustees in this situation.

Heads did not report high levels of vacancies on governing bodies although levels were higher among transferors and trustees. However 69 per cent of schools indicated that there had been at least one governor resignation since 1990. Reasons given included professional or domestic commitments (32 per cent of resignations), moving out of the area (17 per cent), finding governor work too time consuming (19 per cent) or dissatisfaction with the new role of the governing body (8 per cent).

Governing Bodies: Structures and Workload

Most schools (83 per cent) had set up subcommittees of the board of governors since 1989. Most commonly these related to financial management (86 per cent), staff recruitment (67 per cent), school buildings and maintenance (31 per cent), staff discipline (36 per cent), pupil admissions (31 per cent), curriculum (25 per cent) and compiling and presenting the annual report (25 per cent). Other subcommittees included pupil discipline and exclusion, pastoral care, health and safety, marketing and the provision of information about the school. One school had a subcommittee to respond to DENI circulars!

On average, full boards of most schools met either monthly (36 per cent) or termly (36 per cent). A small number of schools reported a very high frequency of meetings, usually in connection with a forthcoming amalgamation or other extraordinary circumstance, but one school's board had not met since 1989. Almost 70 per cent of governors reported an increase in the frequency of meetings since the introduction of LMS, chiefly in controlled schools (81 per cent) while only half of governors from voluntary grammar schools reported this. Over a third of full board meetings lasted more than three hours, but in spite of this, 92 per cent of heads felt that the duration of meetings was 'about right'.

A large majority of heads (87 per cent) indicated that recent changes in the role of the boards of governors have resulted in a significant increase in the time they spend servicing the boards of governors with advice, support and information. This increased workload is due to the changed status and responsibilities of boards of governors in general and especially to issues arising from LMS. In broad terms, principals suggest that curriculum issues and policy (78 per cent), financial management (86 per cent), staff recruitment (69 per cent) and the compilation of an annual report (83 per cent) have required 'a great deal of extra work'. Principals also indicated a further range of issues which had required 'some' additional work including building and maintenance, admission of pupils, pastoral care and cross-community contacts.

The additional work reported by principals in relation to the boards of governors involves increased oral presentations and a significant increase in short and extended written contributions. They also record the increased involvement of specialist advice from ELBs, CCMS (where appropriate) and a significant amount of advice, especially on financial matters, from other experts. Principals also call on other members of the teaching staff in support of the boards of governors especially in relation to curriculum policy (89 per cent) and the preparation of the annual report (64 per cent).

Taking stock of this increased work, 75 per cent of heads suggest that it has resulted in an increase in 'work-related stress', and 69 per cent suggest they have less time for other work related to their functions as principal. Almost three-quarters suggest that as a result they have even less support for government education policy. On the other hand, almost two-thirds of principals agree that they have had the opportunity to acquire new skills and knowledge. However, the experience of working with boards of governors in the new arrangements means that only 55 per cent have increased their support for LMS.

Attendance by governors at meetings was patchy, according to the records. Attendance records from 16 of the schools recorded poor attendance (missing more than half of the full board meetings) by ELB nominees, by transferors (from nine schools) and by trustees (from six). Only in seven of the schools had all governors attended more than half of the meetings. It appears, therefore, that the clauses about removal of governors for non-attendance are largely being ignored by schools, perhaps in an attempt to sidestep an ensuing problem of vacancies on governing bodies.

The Role and Responsibilities of Governing Bodies

Governors demonstrated considerable agreement overall about the main areas of school activity in which they should be directly involved. Over 75 per cent identified staff recruitment (91 per cent), staff dismissal (77 per cent), pupil admissions and financial management (89 per cent), buildings and maintenance, health and safety, provision of information about the school (83 per cent) and accountability for the school (91 per cent). There was less general agreement about the curriculum (64 per cent), pupil expulsion (70 per cent) and pastoral care of pupils (57 per cent).

Business most frequently on the agenda reflected these areas. When asked to identify the three most frequent agenda items, governors responded as follows: financial matters (84 per cent), staff recruitment (66 per cent), buildings and maintenance (35 per cent). Curriculum was only reported by 12 per cent as a frequent matter for discussion. The three most onerous areas of responsibility were felt by governors to be financial management (61 per cent), staff recruitment (46 per cent) and curriculum (34 per cent).

Governor Skills and Governor Training

Governors agreed almost unanimously (96 per cent) that education reform has required them to develop new management knowledge and skills in a number of areas. However, in spite of these demands, 92 per cent of governors believed that they were coping well. In the main their sources of support had been the headteacher (97 per cent), the effective teamwork of the governing body (95 per cent), or their earlier experience of governor work (79 per cent).

More than 80 per cent identified a need, since 1989, for new knowledge – particularly of employment legislation, of interviewing, and of education policy. Between 70–80 per cent had had to develop skills in finance and curriculum. However only 23 per cent identified formal governor training as important in the development of these skills.

Attendance at governor training appears to have been patchy. Almost two-thirds (61 per cent) of governors had attended some training, but only 35 per cent of respondents from voluntary grammar schools had attended, compared with almost 90 per cent of those from the maintained sector. Of those who went, just over half attended only once or twice (but only 24 per cent from voluntary grammar schools). This consistently low level of attendance from the voluntary sector may be partly explained by a relative confidence about undertaking their responsibilities due to a longer experience of school autonomy and also a perceived lack of opportunity to attend (73 per cent were unaware of training opportunities).

Training was offered in financial management, employment legislation, accountability and general pupil matters, the provision of information to parents and the community, and the curriculum. Only a small proportion of respondents considered that the content of training courses had been inappropriate (23 per cent), but most of those who attended found them not very useful or inadequate.

Current Issues in Governor Work: Procedures Adopted

Governors were asked how their board had dealt with certain new responsibilities and what collective view, if any, the board had taken. The overwhelming majority (97 per cent) reported that the first annual parents' meeting had been held and 77 per cent of governors had actually attended. Two-thirds, however, were disappointed with the meeting, mainly due to the extremely low attendance of parents.

In dealing with the requirement for schools to devise and publish admissions criteria, governors reported that, mainly, this had been done collaboratively by governors and heads (82 per cent). However, in almost a fifth of schools, mainly in the controlled sector, heads alone had undertaken this task. Almost two-thirds (60 per cent) of governors (but only 43 per cent of those from voluntary grammar schools) believed that the criteria adopted had been 'very fair', while the rest felt that they were 'the best available in the circumstances' (56 per cent from voluntary grammars). The dissident view from the voluntary sector is likely to be a reflection of the rising pressure on admissions to selective schools.

Three-quarters of governors indicated that their board had discussed the publication of public examination results, but only two-thirds of maintained school governors had done so. Of those boards which had discussed the matter, governors reported that over a third totally disagreed with publication (over half in maintained schools). Almost two-thirds agreed with publication, but considered results to be of limited value without contextualization. Only 4 per cent of governors reported that their board agreed unreservedly with the publication of raw examination data.

Very few boards (12 per cent), mainly in controlled schools (almost 20 per cent), had discussed the publication of pupil attendance figures. More than half of these (almost 60 per cent) totally disagreed with publication. Almost all other governors felt that they were of limited value.

Governors' Wider Contacts with Their Schools

Two-thirds of governors had contacts with schools in connection with their governor work, other than at full board meetings. Over half had met school staff. Half (but 67 per cent of trustees' representatives) reported ad hoc meetings with the head. These governors are most likely to be those holding some office on the board or a subcommittee. Between a third and a half of governors had been to the school to inspect property.

Almost 90 per cent of those with wider governor contacts were satisfied with the level of contact with the school. Of the few who reported dissatisfaction, just over 40 per cent explained that this was because they felt the contact to be superficial.

Just over two-thirds of governors also had contact with the school outside their governor work. As might be anticipated, the highest levels were reported by teacher and parent governors. Other, most frequent, reasons for such contact were in connection with paid work (other than teaching) (almost 30 per cent of governors), or as a past pupil of the school (40 per cent of voluntary grammar school governors, compared with 7 per cent from maintained schools).

Who Governs and Who Should Govern?

Governors were asked to indicate the present role of the governing body and the role they would prefer. Just over a third of governors felt that they were in charge of the school, with half of voluntary grammar school governors in this category. A third of governors believed their current role to be as equal partners with the head in running the school, with a further 20 per cent believing that the head was in charge.

Responses from principals to two questions seeking views on how satisfied they were with the extent to which their board of governors had assumed their new responsibilities and how satisfied they were with the actual role played in the management of the school, were mixed. With the first question, almost two-thirds of heads were satisfied with how their boards of governors had assumed their new responsibilities, leaving a third who were not. Those who were dissatisfied were disproportionately principals of maintained secondary schools. In terms of satisfaction with the actual role being played in the management of the schools by boards, similar patterns were revealed. Once again the principals of maintained secondary schools were the most dissatisfied.

It is clear that principals are responding to the new situation *vis-à-vis* their boards of governors in different ways. A strong principal may resent the interference of lay members who are perceived as lacking the relevant professional expertise or experience. Thus:

> The board of governors do not have the information or experience to make any of the decisions required of them. (controlled secondary principal)

and more forcefully:

> Unfortunately, few members have any managerial skills and scant knowledge of the education system. (maintained secondary principal)

> It is tiresome to have to use the collective wisdom of governors. (controlled secondary principal)

In this context some principals see the members of boards of governors as acting as 'rubber stamps' for the decisions of the principal and the senior management team:

> A lot of hard work is done by the senior management team and then is 'rubber stamped' by the governors without any acknowledgment. (controlled grammar school principal)

Of course a 'leave it to the professionals' approach by a board of governors can be welcomed by a principal rather than seen as a source of complaint:

> Broadly, governors do not want to run the school at all and usually seek and follow guidance from the principal. I think I am very fortunate. (voluntary grammar principal)

Other issues included feelings that the increased bureaucratic burdens faced by schools had introduced sources of conflict between the governors and teachers particularly where teachers perceived their areas of professional competence being queried. Some heads drew attention to the multiple membership of boards of governors by individuals and indicated the potential for a conflict of interest, particularly where schools may become competitors with one another.

The disproportionately negative attitude of maintained school heads was explored further in the small number of follow-up interviews (five in total, including a voluntary grammar school, a controlled grammar school, a controlled boys' secondary school and two maintained schools, one coeducational and one for girls). All these heads described governing bodies which were highly committed to the schools and very supportive of the heads. However, both maintained school heads felt strongly that, apart from their chairmen (in both cases the local parish priest), their governors did not play the role envisaged by the legislation. One head indicated that,

> they didn't actually know what [education reform] was all about . . . they really aren't aware . . . still not aware, not at all. They very much look to the chairman for direction and leadership.

This principal felt that part of the explanation for the governors' reluctance to exercise their responsibilities more fully related to the inherited

> tradition [in the maintained sector] of what they called the old school manager and the school manager was the parish priest, and the parish priest and the principal ran the school and did absolutely everything.

For the future, 54 per cent of governors believed that they should be in control, but nearly a third still felt that they should act mainly as adviser to the head, with a higher proportion of these governors coming from the maintained sector.

Some heads also sought more involvement by the boards of governors but suggested that governors were unlikely to achieve this:

> Too much is expected from busy people without knowledge of how a school operates and no time to find out. (maintained secondary principal)

The maintained schools' principals who were interviewed both believed that, in due course, their governors would more fully exercise their responsibilities. They identified various factors which were likely to accelerate this process, including,

> CCMS, I think, have in fairness tried very hard to get the governors more involved . . . training them. The difficulty has been trying to get them . . . to see that the Church actually really does want them to play a bigger part in running the school . . . [and] CCMS [are] informing the trustees to bring people onto the boards of governors who can actually contribute.

the role of governors is much more in the public domain as an issue for discussion and debate.

the governors [have been taken] to the industrial tribunal by two teachers, so I think that might smarten them up a bit. They realize that they have to . . . go through all the procedures [now] . . . have to have t's crossed and i's dotted and all the rest.

In spite of such problems and others which heads anticipated, all those interviewed believed, for a number of mainly pragmatic reasons, that the proper involvement of governors was important to the school and likely to be beneficial for everyone:

I certainly get a fair bit of support . . . I mean, if there is a crisis, I know it's always there. (maintained school)

It makes for better decision-making, actually . . . first, because I'm not making them all myself, so I feel more comfortable with them. (voluntary grammar school)

I do find it useful . . . they are very, very committed to the school . . . to have outsiders, with a different viewpoint . . . is very, very useful. (controlled school)

The Satisfaction Levels of Governors

In an attempt to gauge how far governors had accepted their wider role and more onerous work load, they were asked whether they intended to serve again. Over two-thirds (70 per cent) replied that they did, with some variation between governors from controlled schools (just under two-thirds) and from voluntary grammars (three-quarters). Of the rest (who often gave more than one reason), approximately two-thirds were 'unhappy with government education policy', just over half felt the work was too time-consuming, just over a third felt that boards had been given too much responsibility, almost a quarter believed that they had not been properly advised by ELB or CCMS and 15 per cent were uncomfortable with important decisions taken by their board. Controlled school governors were disproportionately represented in some of these categories (governor work too time-consuming, with too much responsibility). These more negative views may well reflect the high numbers of transferors' representatives who serve on several governing bodies in the controlled sector.

As a postscript, 40 per cent of all governors (including more than half of those from controlled schools but very few from voluntary grammars), believed that they should be paid for their time.

Discussion and Conclusion

Central to ERO in Northern Ireland was the issue of accountability; the empowerment of the governing body is the means by which government is trying to ensure that schools, like other organizations, remain accountable to their users. A number of important issues in this area seem to be emerging from our investigation, many of which parallel those identified by research in England and Wales.

The governing body has (in theory at least) been given much freedom with regard to the management of schools. Matters which were originally the prerogative of the head or the ELB have now become, by law, the sole responsibility of the governing body. In an environment as complex as a school, the idea of shifting power from the producer to the consumer is likely to prove problematic, since it is difficult to guarantee the social and political affiliations and aspirations of governors (Flude and Hammer, 1990). These reforms are likely to demand a change in the culture and philosophy of the school, in particular by headteachers, but, as evidenced in the maintained school sector in Northern Ireland, also by governors accustomed to a more limited range of responsibilities. Findings show, for example, that the relationships and roles that have emerged since the reforms have already caused some 'dichotomy in thinking between principals and governing bodies' (Finlay, 1990), with considerable further potential for conflict.

As indicated above, a range of attitudes has been identified among heads with regard to their governors. These range between those who appear resentful of lay governors and who appear reluctant to allow them to fulfil their role, and those who favour governor involvement in schools and consider it to be a vital source of support. Thomas (1992) has emphasized the point that the ability of governors to get involved in management decisions of the school is contingent on such attitudes on both sides.

Nirmala Rao (1990) also supports this view and has suggested other important factors arising from the diversity of governing bodies; in the Northern Ireland context, it seems clear that the differing governing and management traditions of, for example, the maintained and voluntary grammar school sectors continue to be reflected in how they operate as well as in governors' attitudes on a range of issues.

Another key variable in the head–governor relationship is likely to be the nature and volume of information and advice that is passed on from the headteacher to the governors of the school. Evidence from England and Wales (Hellawell, 1990; Field, 1993) confirms our findings that the headteacher is typically the source of guidance for governors, either directly or as a gatekeeper for others. Heads with negative intentions may be either parsimonious with information or may assist their governors to drown in an information overload! Thomas (1992) has highlighted the need for an investigation of whether the head provides information in a non-partisan manner and if he or she is fully committed to the idea of public accountability. Our research only touched on this area, but, as recorded above, many governors indicated that they felt their contacts with school outside formal governor meetings to be superficial and therefore unsatisfactory. This may imply that more substantial contacts with a greater range of parents, pupils and teachers would be welcomed as giving governors greater opportunities to obtain information independently of the head.

Heads' responsibilities have of course also been increased under LMS and it is evident (Arnott *et al.*, 1992) that there are now more opportunities for them to choose areas for their activity or for delegation, and so maximize their influence. They are clearly in a good position to manipulate their governing body if they wish. Thus if governors (such as some of those in the maintained sector in Northern Ireland) are inclined to keep their distance, especially in professional educational matters, and allow themselves to be managed by the head then it seems likely that the current, apparently consensual, relationship is likely to continue, probably at the cost of governors failing to become fully involved in the exercise of their legal authority. It does appear, however, that in this kind of situation, some heads feel themselves to be overexposed as sole decision-makers and will encourage governors to be more proactive.

Marren and Levacic (1994) have found that some governors will be more likely than others to get involved in school decision-making; LMS is leading to a concentration of financial tasks within a select group of governors and senior managers, with governors frequently playing the subordinate role. The Northern Ireland findings also indicate that governors' areas of active concern are very limited; even the apparently more confident and experienced voluntary grammar school governors are reluctant to be directly involved in areas beyond finance, recruitment and maintenance. Governors' confidence and assertiveness is likely to be connected to their length of service. More practical support can be offered to the principal if the governing body has a thorough knowledge of the education system and a strong commitment to the philosophy of the school. Such knowledge requires extended service (Mortimore and Mortimore, 1990), so if there is a high governor turnover (or perhaps high levels of intermittent absenteeism), then the headteacher may dominate the relationship.

The research also indicates that some issues are more likely to generate friction between principals and governors than others; heads believe that conflict is more liable to occur over matters of educational practice (teaching methods, exam results and the curriculum), than issues like school building and maintenance.

Confusion surrounding relative authorities and accountability resulting from LMS needs also to be highlighted: Morgan *et al.*, (1993) suggest that it is natural for the participants to be unsure of their responsibilities in the initial period. However over time, if governors press for a more substantial role, it is unlikely that headteachers will be able to withstand such pressure and a more participative model of school management may emerge. The need for good quality training and a clearer delineation of roles for both headteachers and governors is then a priority if the role of governors is to have substance (see also Deem, 1993). Our findings however, suggest that governors have not, to date, found formal training to be either particularly relevant or useful. Effective management of change will hold the key to the success of the educational reforms, so a proficient and well trained headteacher and governing body working in partnership are necessary preconditions for improved accountability. This must be an issue for governor trainers, in particular the ELBs.

The head of a voluntary grammar school at interview very neatly expressed these contingencies which help to create the complex relationships between heads and governing bodies:

> I think that probably three strands . . . are important in terms of how governors and principals-with-governors work. One of them is what I would call what was the existing culture within a board, what kind of relationship existed . . . before education reform. There is also the impact of education reform, including LMS and all the rest of it in that. The third factor . . . is the nature, the kinds of people who have become governors as a result of elected representation, teachers and parents. These factors are going to vary significantly from school to school.

The imposition of delegated management to schools apparently presumed both a willingness and a capacity on the part of thousands of individual governors to undertake responsibility for those schools, accompanied by an ability of all those involved to develop effective working relationships in an entirely new situation. Apart from the findings of the pilot schemes in local financial management, which were not based on formula funding, there is little evidence available to suggest that these assumptions were tested in advance of the legislation. Thus although school managers welcome aspects of LMS (Arnott *et al.*, 1992), it is not surprising that many important issues have emerged during the early years of its implementation.

In January, 1994 there were reported crises in the relationships between headteachers and governors. Such conflict is not yet overt in Northern Ireland. Perhaps because the key players are still learning their way around the new system or because some key issues are being avoided, most heads seem satisfied with the role played by their governors. While some principals do express frustration and some resentment at the increased powers of their governors, as many report frustration due to the unwillingness of their governors to become fully involved in their joint undertaking.

Acknowledgment

The authors gratefully acknowledge the financial support of the Nuffield Foundation for the research reported in this chapter.

References

Arnott, M., Bullock, A. and Thomas, H. (1992) *The Impact of Local Management on Schools: The First Report on the 'Impact' Project*, Birmingham, University of Birmingham, for the National Association of Head Teachers.

Astin Report (1979) *Report of the Working Party on the Management of Schools on Northern Ireland*, Belfast, HMSO.

Deem, R. (1993) 'Education reform and school governing bodies in England 1986–1992: Old dogs new tricks or new dogs new tricks', in Preedy, M. (ed) *Managing the Effective School*, London, Chapman, pp. 204–19.

Deem, R. and Brehony, K. (1993) 'Consumers and education professionals in the organisation and administration of schools: Partnership or conflict?', *Educational Studies*, **19**, 3, pp. 339–55.

Department of Education for Northern Ireland (DENI) (1990) *Local Management of Schools. General Guidance on the Operation of LMS*, Bangor, Department of Education for Northern Ireland, Circular 1990/20, June.

Department of Education for Northern Ireland (DENI) (1992) *Pupils and Teachers in Grant-aided Schools*, Statistical Bulletin, 1/1992, Bangor, Department of Education for Northern Ireland.

Department of Education for Northern Ireland (DENI) (1993) *Educational Administration in Northern Ireland. A Consultative Document*, Bangor, Department of Education for Northern Ireland.

Field, L. (1993) 'School governing bodies: The lay–professional relationship', *School Organisation*, **13**, 2, pp. 165–74.

Finlay, R. (1990) 'The arrival of the LMS initiative: Current educational dimensions – Early management experiences of two pilot project schools', *Journal of Educational Research Network of Northern Ireland*, **4**, pp. 48–59.

Flude, M. and Hammer, M. (eds) (1990) *The Education Reform Act, 1988 – Its origins and Implications*, Basingstoke, Falmer Press.

Golby, M. (1991) *School Governors Research*, Exeter Papers in School Governorship, 3, Exeter, Fair Way Publications.

Hellawell, D. (1990) '"Head teachers" perceptions of the potential role of governors in their appraisal', *School Organisation*, **10**, 1, pp. 65–82.

McKeown, P. and Connolly, M. (1992) Education reform in Northern Ireland: Maintaining the distance? *Journal of Social Policy*, **21**, 2, pp. 211–32.

Maclure, S. (1992) *Education Reformed*, 3rd edn, London, Hodder and Stoughton.

Marren, E. and Levacic, R. (1994) 'Senior management, classroom teacher and governor responses to local management of schools', *Educational Management and Administration*, **22**, 1, pp. 39–53.

Morgan, V., Fraser, G., Dunn, S. and Cairns, E. (1993) 'A new order of cooperation and involvement? Relationships between parents and teachers in the integrated schools', *Educational Review*, **45**, 1, pp. 43–52.

Mortimore, P. and Mortimore, J. (1991) *The Secondary Head: Roles and Responsibilities*, London, Chapman.

Rao, N. (1990) *Educational Change and Local Government: The Impact of the Education Reform Act 1988*, York, Rowntree.

Taylor Report (1977) *A New Partnership for Our Schools*, London, HMSO.

Thomas, H. (1988) 'From local financial management to local management of schools', in FLUDE, M. and HAMMER, M. (eds) *The Education Reform Act 1988: Its Origins and Implications*, London, Falmer.

THOMAS, H. (1992) 'School governance and the limits of self-interest', *Educational Review*, **44**, 3, pp. 327–34.

TIPPLE, C. (1990) 'Parents and consumers' in MORRIS, R. (ed) *Central and Local Control of Education After the Education Reform Act 1988*, BEMAS.

WALLACE, G. (ed) (1992) *Local Management of Schools: Research and Experience*, BERA Dialogues, 6, Clevedon, Avon, Multilingual Matters.

WELLS, I. and McKIBBEN, T. (1990a) *First Experiences of LMS*, Summary Series, 12, Belfast, NICER.

WELLS, I. and McKIBBEN, T. (1990b) *Local Management of Schools: Questionnaire from the Pilot Schools*, Belfast, NICER.

WELLS, I. and McKIBBEN, T. (1990c) *Local Management of Schools: Information from Interviews with Teachers and School Governors*, Belfast, NICER.

Chapter 6

Devolved Management: Variations of Response in Scottish School Boards

Margaret Arnott, Charles Raab and Pamela Munn

Introduction

Devolved management of schools is a key element in the Conservative government's education policy in Britain. It promises major changes in the structures and processes of educational decision-making, finance and management. It also both presupposes and reinforces an ethos that situates schools more firmly in a competitive market for pupils, resources and public esteem. Further important elements of this ethos are parental choice of school, and the ability of schools to opt out of local education authority control and receive their funding directly from central government. Devolved management thus plays a large part in a reformed education system that has important implications for the roles and relationships of local education authorities, for headteachers and school staff, for parents and pupils, and for central government itself.

Government policy embodies devolved management in specific schemes: local management of schools (LMS) in England and Wales, and devolved school management (DSM) in Scotland. While they differ in detail, the main features of LMS and DSM are similar. They include the formula-funding of schools, and delegation of decision-making on finance and staffing. Change has gone further in LMS than in DSM, which dates only from April 1994. For several years, however, Strathclyde Region – the largest education authority in the United Kingdom – has innovated its own, relatively modest, form of devolved management of resources (DMR). In this chapter, we report some preliminary Scottish findings of a comparative, cross-national research project (Adler *et al.*, 1991) that investigates the effects of devolved management of schools upon parents, secondary schools and local education authorities in three areas: Strathclyde and Lothian Regions (Scotland), and Newcastle-upon-Tyne (England).[1] The key issue addressed in the project is the likelihood of achievement of the aims of policies that promote devolved management and its associated objectives. The latter include lay participation, professionals' accountability to parents, and the creation of a (quasi-) market in schooling. Using governing bodies and school boards as our main research sites, we are interested in the consequences that these policy initiatives have for roles, relationships, and

Margaret Arnott, Charles Raab and Pamela Munn

decisions in secondary schools and other levels of the system of educational governance.

There are three main methods of investigation. The first one is observation of at least three meetings of the governing body of four schools in Newcastle and of four school boards in each of the two Scottish Region, in some cases supplemented by observations of committees or subcommittees of these bodies. The second is interviews with selected members of the governing bodies and boards and of the schools' staffs, and with key local education officers and civil servants in the respective education departments of central government. The third method is a telephone survey of a sample of parents at each school.

The present chapter considers only a small part of the larger topic, based upon data gathered through observations of meetings of Scottish school boards. To help maintain confidentiality, the schools have been given fictitious names. We analyse the way in which they have begun to comprehend and respond to the market and their schools' place in it; how they have handled information in the context of meetings at which members discuss issues and contemplate action requiring collective decisions; and how they interact with an outside world of organizations and persons whom they seek to influence or whose activities are relevant for the operations of the board and the school. Understanding these aspects of boards' work, and explaining differences and similarities, is important in assessing the boards' exercise of powers, responsibilities and initiative in the emerging system.

Even a first attempt to analyse observational data throws up relevant comparisons and contrasts that may be explained by the different governance characteristics of the two education-authority settings or of the schools. Concerning the education authorities, the four Strathclyde schools were in the first phase of the Region's DMR, thus providing an opportunity to observe decision-making, roles and relationships under a form of devolved management. In contrast, the four Lothian schools functioned in a more centralized system of local educational management. However, during the year 1993–4 in which we observed school boards in operation, the imminence of DSM throughout Scotland influenced all schools to one degree or another as regions devised implementation schemes and put them to boards and schools for comment.

The Scottish and Regional Contexts

Scottish schools had no equivalent to English and Welsh governing bodies until school boards were introduced under the 1988 School Boards Act. Parents, teachers and coopted members sit on these boards; headteachers have advisory status and therefore attend but cannot vote. In contrast to the composition of governing bodies, parents have a majority on Scottish boards. However, boards' statutory responsibilities are far fewer than those of governing bodies as set out in the 1986 Education (No. 2) Act and the 1988 Education

Reform Act. Governors' responsibilities include the school's adherence to the national curriculum, the provision of sex education, discipline policy, financial control and staffing appointments and dismissals. In contrast, certain significant decision-making areas remain outwith the remit of school boards. Responsibility for the curriculum, admission policies, assessment, and minimum staffing levels lies with the Scottish Office Education and Industry Department (SOEID) and local authorities. Boards have very limited financial powers, the principal one being the ability to review the school's per capita allocation. They have no direct involvement in the school's curriculum, and have limited say in staffing matters; they may add names to the short list for senior teaching appointments and are represented on interview panels. The purpose of boards is less to involve parents directly in school management than to give boards the right to request information, and to make representation about, a variety of matters.

Macbeth (1991) argues that the fact that boards have very limited statutory responsibilities has enabled them, to a large extent, to set their own priorities and purposes; they may discuss and thus influence most aspects of the school. However, available evidence suggests that boards have not been eager to extend their role. Although boards can apply for increased powers in certain fields, to date no boards have done so, and only two schools have opted out under the Self-Governing Schools etc., (Scotland) Act 1989. Boards' apparent reluctance to become involved in 'professional' areas (Munn and Holroyd, 1989; Arney *et al.,* 1992; MVA Consultancy, 1992) may help to explain why they have not sought greater powers; thus DSM is being introduced against a background of general parental unwillingness to extend their role in schools beyond that of consultation.

As with LMS, the stated objectives of DSM imply a radical change in function for education authorities and for their relationship with and funding of schools (SOED, 1993). The government believes that DSM will offer schools greater flexibility and increase their efficiency and effectiveness. While there are important similarities between DSM and LMS, such as the principle that schools should be funded predominantly on the basis of pupil numbers, there are significant differences. First, the Scottish policy clearly enhances the position of headteachers by delegating budgeting decisions to them, whereas LMS strengthens the position of the governing body. School boards have a purely consultative role in financial delegation and are only involved in appointments, other than those for senior promoted teaching staff, if they so wish. Second, Scottish education authorities have more flexibility in devising their schemes than their English counterparts. While the government has stipulated the percentage of an education authority's budget which must be devolved to school level, it has not specified a figure which authorities must use when devising the pupil-driven component of a school's budget. Moreover, authorities can vary their schemes for schools of different categories or in different areas, and can fund schools on the basis of actual rather than average staffing costs.

Differences within Scotland may reflect regions' ability to draw up their own DSM schemes, and the schools' varied social, historical and political position in the market. Lothian schools had no experience of operating devolved budgets. However, in pre-empting DSM with DMR, Strathclyde initially delegated limited funds, excluding staff costs, to one secondary school and its associated primaries in each of its six divisions, representing different social and geographical contexts.

Analysis of School Boards

To study devolved management in a variety of circumstances, four schools each in Lothian and Strathclyde Regions were chosen to reflect different socio-economic areas (see Table 6.1). These areas include an area of high socio-economic deprivation (Campbell, Rankin); an affluent area of predominantly owner-occupied housing (Bennett, McMaster); a 'mixed' catchment area (Lochside, Corbett); and a traditional working-class area (Thomson, Muirland). The most important variable used was the percentage of pupils entitled to free school meals, a good indicator of social deprivation. In order to simplify comparative analysis, all schools chosen were state, non-denominational secondaries. In this section, the eight Scottish school boards are considered in terms of the three main dimensions mentioned in the introduction. In a few instances the analysis is enhanced by information gained through preliminary discussions with the headteacher or through official minutes of meetings that were not attended.

The first dimension, response to the market, concerns the reflection of the school's market position in the board's awareness, in its handling of issues, and in any ensuing action. The second concerns the way the board dealt with information that it had from various sources; this dimension provides insights into relationships between the board and the headteacher, and into the way it arrived at decisions. The third dimension, links to the outside world, involves the resources available to the board through its connections beyond the school itself, and thus indicates the board's cultural capital and its political resourcefulness.

Response to the Market

Boards' responses to issues that raised market questions or that had implications for the school's position varied. In some cases, the board was only the passive recipient of the head's response, particularly in matters which were his prerogative (all the Scottish schools in this study had male headteachers). In this section, we consider *what* was done, *why* it was done, and *who* was the main protagonist of the discussion or decision. Regarding *what* was done,

Table 6.1 Main Characteristics of School Boards in Study

LOTHIAN:

SCHOOL	NATURE OF CATCHMENT AREA	SIZE OF SCHOOL AUG.1993 (ROUNDED)	% ELIGIBLE FOR FREE SCHOOL MEALS AUG.1993	NET LOSSES/GAINS AUG.1993	SIGNIFICANT CHANGES IN COMPOSITION OF BOARDS DURING OBSERVATIONS	OTHER REMARKS
BENNETT	Situated in residential suburb. Local housing is predominantly owner-occupied.	810	1.9	(+) 55	1 new teacher member 2 new parent members new chair	Community school. Acting head was in post for part of the observation period.
LOCHSIDE	Public housing stock predominates although some houses are owner-occupied in this recently built up area. The school is on the outskirts of the city.	750	21.2	(–) 26	2 new parent members 1 new co-opted member	School undergoing major refurbishment.
THOMSON	The catchment area is varied in a 'traditional' working-class part of the city	940	21.5	(+) 29	2 new parent members	
CAMPBELL	This school serves an area of socioeconomic deprivation, where the housing stock is almost all provided by the council.	340	60.1	(–) 49	No significant changes	Community school which was recently under threat of closure. Recently appointed head.

Table 6.1 Cont'd

STRATHCLYDE:

SCHOOL	NATURE OF CATCHMENT AREA	SIZE OF SCHOOL AUG.1993 (ROUNDED)	% ELIGIBLE FOR FREE SCHOOL MEALS AUG.1993	NET LOSSES/GAINS AUG.1993	SIGNIFICANT CHANGES IN COMPOSITION OF BOARDS DURING OBSERVATIONS	OTHER REMARKS
McMASTER	Situated on the outskirts of the city in the leafy suburbs. Housing is predominantly owner-occupied.	880	3.5	(+) 30	1 new teacher member	
CORBETT	Situated in a peripheral part of a new town. The area is characterized by lack of pupil movement.	680	10.7	(−) 7	2 new staff members 1 new coopted member 2 new parent members	Recently appointed headteacher.
MUIRLAND	School is situated in a 'traditional' working-class area of a town.	1100	17.1	(−) 9	3 new parent members	
RANKIN	The school serves an area of high socioeconomic deprivation on the outskirts of a city.	460	53.2	(−) 8	Board dissolved after 2 observations	Recently under threat of closure

boards' deliberations over possible action were often inconclusive. In explaining *why*, we mainly report overt reasons and explanations offered by members and heads during meetings. In describing *who* took the lead, we consider the respective roles of the head and of the board as a whole.

The use of the term 'market' requires explanation. Broadly, this refers to the school's position in relation to others with which it perceives itself to be in competition for pupils and therefore for resources. The school's image, its performance as judged by published examination results or by inspection reports, and its relations with local or wider communities may all be of concern to the board insofar as they may affect the school's ability to increase or maintain its intake of pupils, of 'the right kind' of pupils, or of other users of school facilities.

Increasing or maintaining pupil numbers, and therefore resources, was of central concern. Six boards acted in direct response to the market issue. The most frequent mode of response was the desire to enhance or maintain the school's image amongst parents of current or prospective pupils, and in the wider community. The action they contemplated varied as between increased school discipline, greater emphasis on publicity and communications, and modifying the curriculum. Discipline and the cultivation of a particular ethos was important to Bennett, for example. To counteract the infiltration of a denim/drug/baseball-cap culture, the board strongly supported the head's promulgation of a mandatory dress policy, although they did not simply endorse the precise details of his first proposal. They were also concerned about the bad influence of certain 'undesirable' kinds of post-leaving age pupils re-entering education at Bennett. The board tried to deal with this through the school's 16–21 admissions policy, although this went against the Region's rules. An exchange of letters with the education authority resulted in a stand-off.

Publicity efforts, another type of response, were seen by four boards as important to their image, although proposals varied between the ad hoc and the strategic. They targeted parents, the local press, and other constituencies. McMaster worried about parental ignorance of the board's activities, and also wished to disseminate a favourable inspectors' report. Anticipating this inspection, the board had surveyed parents' attitudes towards the school. Because contact with parents played a part in the inspectorate's qualitative performance indicators, this board hoped to involve more parents, and considered several strategies including an open house and homework- and curriculum-related meetings. Most members as well as the head spoke at meetings, agreeing to keep the publicity question on the agenda, and perhaps to learn from parents what kind of information they wanted.

Sometimes prompted by its head, Lochside's board also considered publicity to offset a 'rough school' image. Its approach involved better leafleting about parents' evenings, promoting the School Development Plan as the school's 'vision', publicity about lettings, and a glossier brochure. Minutes of previous meetings suggested that the level of parents' interest had given cause for concern that increased information and publicity could counteract. The board had agreed to give parents a positive statement about the published examination results, which had ostensibly deteriorated; senior staff had reported to the board on ways of improving results. Also, the head and staff had deplored press coverage of a pupils' demonstration. Muirland's publicity-related efforts were unique among the eight schools. They wished to acquaint local business and industry with the school, its employment-oriented emphasis, and its academic achievements. Led by the headteacher, the board considered an open day for businesses.

The fourth publicity-minded school was Bennett. The head thought publicity 'a double-edged sword', and feared raising unrealistic parental expectations, even though – like McMaster – it enjoyed a reputation as a 'good' school with excellent examination results and buoyant pupil numbers. Apart from tightening up discipline, the board wanted more favourable articles in the community newspaper. There appeared to be little parental apathy that publicity needed to overcome, but they wanted to advertise sporting and artistic activities celebrating the school's tenth anniversary. As a relatively new school without deep local roots, and despite its formal status as a community school, all felt that publicity could help to promote its image. The board hoped to sell gift items and to give them to visitors in future. Worries about the 'drug culture' and about 'undesirable' pupils can, of course, be seen as a desire to avoid image-damaging unfavourable publicity.

It seems plausible to assume, for most if not all schools, that image may have been less an end in itself than a means to other market and resource ends, especially as parental choice, fluctuations of pupil numbers, and devolved, formula-derived budgets kept rolls and resources high on agendas. Thus discipline was observed to be important to Campbell, as publicity was to Lochside, both of which *did* have worries about the size of their pupil intakes. In addition, publicity in a more specific, industrially-oriented way, was salient to Muirland, whose numbers were not particularly threatened but for which local industry was seen as a source for enriching curriculum resources.

Four boards approached the question of pupil numbers and the consequent resources more directly. Lochside's consideration of the school's position in the first year of DSM evinced concern about maintaining staffing levels in the face of declining numbers, caused by a drift to other schools and by falling rolls at its feeder primaries. Closer links were therefore established with the primaries in a programme that included Lochside teachers visiting them and the involvement of upper-primary pupils in technical projects. Along with publicity to parents, this was seen as a way of countering the competition and keeping numbers up when the pupils would enter secondary schooling. Campbell is a small secondary school with a declining roll; under its previous head, it successfully campaigned against closure. That head then produced a development plan to promote the school, although the board took no part in its drafting. The new head shared with the board his worry about the school's poor image. His concern about poor examination performance was probably prompted by a perceived need to arrest further decline in the roll. He regarded the school as 'statistically challenged', and a working group was set up with heads of similar schools to identify common strategies that included an emphasis on literacy, thinking skills, behaviour management and partnership with parents. Urban Aid funding was being sought.

Thomson's roll was not falling, but there was concern about the composition of its pupil body. Both the head and the board were very aware of the market, and several meetings were preoccupied with curricular provision for 'high achievers'. The main case was made in terms of the market: the need as 'a fact of life' to attract more middle-class pupils, to present Thomson as a credible alternative to other 'good' schools, and to sustain an academic ethos. Examination results were seen as closely related to the prospects of retaining the middle class, who could easily choose other schools with more obvious and long-standing academic reputations. The board well understood the relationship between pupils and DSM funding, as articulated by the head. In Corbett, pupil numbers also engaged the board's attention, but in a much less striking way. Members were aware of the market, and to some extent of the link between numbers and funding which the previous head had taken pains to explain. However, they did not feel vulnerable to the vagaries of parental choice because this was not frequently exercised in Corbett's part of town, for the Region 'zoned' the primaries for each secondary. At stake, however, was whether a proposed new primary would be 'zoned' for Corbett, for which the previous head had lobbied the region.

Pupil numbers are not the only key to resources; some boards directly approached the resource question. Muirland's interest in school/industry links was illustrative. Led by the head, but with the enthusiastic participation and initiative of some members, discussion centred on setting up a liaison committee with local businesses through which activities could be organized: practical school courses made available to firms' employees; language pupils translating letters for firms; firms donating technical magazines and materials, thus enhancing its practical and scientific curriculum. Bennett exemplified another direct approach. The board and the head, with guidance from a community education official attached to the school, frequently discussed their relative underfinancing and underappreciation as a community school. The main worry was that Bennett might enter devolved management with a low baseline of community–school resources. While the school had convinced the Region to accept a more favourable basis for calculating funding, Bennett now disputed the way in which the Region applied this. A working group was set up, including the head and the former chair.

Rankin has not yet figured in this section. Although its position was very unfavourable as a small, declining school in a severely deprived area, no activity seemed to be undertaken or discussed by its board in response to this adversity. While it used some of its devolved resources to improve the appearance of the school's interior, this did not appear to be motivated by market-related 'image' reasons, nor were there deliberations about publicity, improvements to its enrolment, or resources. It was as if the school, although aware of its market position, felt unable to affect it.

Information, Discussion and Action

There were also similarities and differences in both the extent to which boards requested information from the head and in the way they dealt with what they got. One of the boards' main powers is to request information on a wide range of issues, and heads must respond. However, in some cases, boards seemed not to exercise this right; rather, the head decided what information they should have. For example, Rankin's head appeared to draft the agenda for board meetings, drawing members' attention to policy developments and issues which he thought it should note. Not only did he seem to be their only source of information, but the board did not observably request it. They were generally very reluctant to become involved in educational issues, and at no time did they challenge him. In other schools, boards also looked to the head for advice and information on school matters and national policy developments. Thomson's head was asked for information on finance, school board elections, contacts with local primaries and attendance panels. At Bennett, the acting head was asked to do 'some homework for the next meeting' about the board's applying for additional powers. The board requested information on the curriculum, finance, discipline and links with the local community. However, the head did not shy away from drawing their attention to particular issues and supplying information on these. For example, he gave fairly detailed reports about the funding of the school's community education programme. This resulted in their active support of his attempts to secure additional money.

Boards also appeared to differ in the way they handled information they received (Figure 6.1). Excepting Rankin, all boards discussed information to different degrees. The other boards towards the left hand side of the continuum had a varying but low level of awareness of developments within education and mainly seemed to 'rubber-stamp' the head's decisions with relatively little discussion. Generally, these boards were passive and deferential to 'professionals'. They also tended not to act upon their information. At

Figure 6.1   How Boards Handled Information

received	received/discussed	received/discussed/decision taken
• Rankin	• Lochside	• McMaster
• Corbett	• Thomson	• Bennett
• Campbell		
• Muirland		

Corbett, Campbell and Muirland, the head was the main source of information on almost all educational matters. These boards rarely, if ever, questioned his reports. For example, despite the head's drawing attention to league tables and examination results, neither of the Corbett or Campbell boards discussed them. However their heads did not dominate the meetings to the same extent as did Rankin's.

On occasion, members raised points on issues which were of interest to them, leading to discussions in which they were able to elicit information from the head. Thus the Campbell board was well aware of the school's community-education status, and initiated discussions, which included the head, about community-oriented issues including the school's local reputation and better access for disabled pupils. At Corbett, members discussed necessary repairs in some detail. This was true to a lesser extent of the boards at Thomson and Lochside. When Thomson's board discussed special provision for 'high achievers', the head was restrained during these lengthy discussions and intervened only occasionally to try to promote consensus when the debate became heated. At Lochside, members likewise deliberated over information they received concerning, for example, issues such as DSM, declining rolls, and Lochside's image in the local community. However, the board did not take any subsequent decisions.

This behaviour is in sharp contrast to those boards located at the right of the continuum. The Bennett and McMaster boards were very active almost as pressure groups working with the head. They appeared to enjoy a close working relationship with him, and while they looked to him for information, he was not their only source, and information was shared. Long discussions were not uncommon. Bennett's head sought the board's support on a number of issues including funding, discipline, staffing levels, enrolment policy, links with feeder primaries, and maintenance. Action tended to result from these discussions, including writing to the education authority, helping the head to formulate strategies on issues, consulting parents through a questionnaire or organizing public meetings. McMaster's board supported the head's request to the education authority that he should be free to appoint his choice of candidate for unpromoted teaching posts. The board invited an Assistant Director of Education to one of its meetings to justify the Region's policy. Like other boards, while members frequently sought clarification of the head's position, neither of these schools' boards challenged him, accepting instead his professional judgment although not, on the whole, displaying a deferential attitude.

Links with the Outside World

A main policy objective of DSM is to enhance the participation in schools of parents and other lay persons. This assumes that they have the necessary skills and political sophistication. Those boards which were well connected to the

Figure 6.2   Boards' Links with the Outside World

weak	moderate	strong
• Corbett	• Thomson	• McMaster
• Rankin	• Lochside	• Bennett
• Campbell	• Muirland	

outside world tended to adopt a more active role and to be less deferential to the head. Boards appeared to differ in the degree to which they, or individual members, had these links. By the outside world we mean significant influential groups, organizations or persons in the educational, business or political worlds beyond the school. The performance of the board's role, particularly its relation to the head, seems to be partly influenced by the extent of its external networks and more generally by the resources or cultural capital it, or its members, could call upon in 'working the system'. Cultural capital refers to the non-material resources enjoyed by boards and members, including their knowledge of educational developments and of how to exert influence, and their self-confidence in deliberations and decisions.

The eight boards seemed to divide into three broad categories (see Figure 6.2). Three were insular and lacked much cultural capital, apparently having few external educational contacts and weak local links. At Rankin the board, and parent members especially, could mobilize very few connections as an educational resource, and the head did not act as their channel to the outside world. One member recognized that the area's housing problems meant that, for parents seeking involvement, there was 'more glory in the Housing Association' than in the board. Members tended to lack self-confidence in their role on the board. Commenting on parental involvement in the appointment of teaching staff, one member stated that she

> wouldn't know how to interview. I'm not capable of saying who is better at the job . . . I'm scared of making a mistake in case I look like a right dumpling.

Another felt it necessary to ask the head's permission to leave the meeting a few minutes early. Campbell's board also had weak external links, but members generally were more conscious than were Rankin's of the school's place in the local community. Hence the board frequently discussed issues which related to the community stature of the school, but they appeared to be poorly connected except through the head. Another factor that these boards had in common was that their links with parents seemed intermittent or non-existent. It was the head rather than the board who communicated, to varying degrees, with parents.

Boards with weak connections tended not to act as supportive pressure groups for their heads, who may have perceived little gain in securing their support. These boards were not seen to be questioning or challenging the region on the head's behalf, or generally trying to mobilize networks of influence. Those boards with moderate links – Thomson, Lochside and Muirland – were somewhat insular and lacking in self-confidence and knowledge, but showed signs of developing external ties. The Thomson board responded to an initiative from a local primary school to improve links, resulting in an informal meeting of board members and PTAs for associated primaries. However, the board asked the head to draft their response to DSM proposals, and the chair asked him about the desirability of a member's attendance at a conference on opting out, remarking, 'I didn't even realize you could [opt out] in Scotland.' In their ventures, these boards relied heavily on the head and on teachers' representatives for information. Generally, parent members appeared to have less knowledge than did the others of school matters or national policy developments.

It was in those boards with well-established outside networks that heads were seen to be seeking their help as a pressure group. They had the necessary resources or accumulated expertise to pursue the school's interests actively. At Bennett, especially, the head tapped the board's expertise in 'working the system' to support him in disputes with the authority. Members were very well plugged into the local community and into the education system. In one meeting, the chair reported that he had phoned a senior official at the Scottish Office for advice and 'was surprised I got to speak to him. [Bennett] must be a magic word.' At meetings, the head would skilfully present his case and usually suggest a course of action, sometimes involving external activity.

For example, the head was unhappy with the quality of cleaning Bennett received under its contract with the authority. Believing that cleanliness was crucial to the school's ethos, he suggested that the board should consider applying formally to assume responsibility for cleaning and ground maintenance: 'the feeling round the table is that we should not, then that will close off one option to us.' Had the board agreed, it would have been the first one in Scotland to have applied for additional powers. Over two meetings, they debated the advantages and disadvantages, during which the head's position changed, and he came to doubt the value of seeking additional powers in this case. However, he wanted the board to complain to the Director of Education about the unsatisfactory contract. The board deferred to his judgment about additional powers and wrote as he had suggested. Thus, while they worked with him to consider strategies, there seemed to be some reluctance, even in a board with substantial cultural capital, to challenge the head. Both the Bennett and McMaster boards have considered their and the school's relations with primary schools and parents in general, in part perhaps as an element in an image-management strategy. Whilst McMaster's board was keen to have parents see the positive HMI inspection report, the low level of parental attendance at certain functions was seen as a weakness in its own outside connections.

Conclusions and Speculations

Firm conclusions cannot yet be drawn about the consequences of the market, and more specifically of DSM, for roles, relationships and decisions in Scottish school boards. However, one interim finding is that those boards weakly linked to the outside world also tended simply to receive information, without discussion or decision, whereas those boards with strong ties were more active. This is perhaps not surprising given that well-connected boards may be better placed to follow decisions through, and are better endowed with the cultural capital that is necessary for dealing with information, persons and organizations in the external educational world. The association between these relative capabilities and the socioeconomic position of the school, and possibly of its board members, cannot be confidently asserted from the evidence so far, although it is at least plausible. On the other hand, the relationship between the variables concerning information-handling and external links, on the one hand, and market-related perceptions and actions, on the other, is far less clear for most of these boards; any differences here may be more in the mode of response than on any quantitative dimension, and there appears to be no obvious relation to socioeconomic factors.

It is too early to say whether the boards' overriding aim was the maintenance or improvement of the school's market or resource position. Certainly, many discussions and conclusions were explicitly focused on these objectives, or can be plausibly interpreted as ultimately about pupil numbers or money. But it would be an oversimplification to argue that preoccupation with discipline, contact with parents, and the like only had meaning, to members or heads, in terms of market position, and that the ethos or achievements of the school and its pupils as such counted for little in the world of professional or lay values. That said, and in view of the fact that the main planks of current education policy include DSM, promoting accountability at school level and enhancing lay influence in decision-making, what do the data suggest? Three main points are worth highlighting, although they lead to speculations beyond the observations and analysis to date.

First, all boards, regardless of the size of school, its catchment area, or time in post of headteacher, deferred to the head's judgment and advice. Some boards discussed and debated issues more than others but the board overruled the head in only one observed instance, and that was more a matter of detail than of principle. This was an important exception, for it concerned discipline, a key area of school life. Boards may generally believe that heads will act in their schools' best interests and that their professional knowledge, enterprise and competence should not be challenged. This suggests that, rather than enhancing lay participation in decision-making, DSM is likely to enhance the political and presentational skills of heads *vis-à-vis* boards in particular and parents in general. We may note that acquiescence in professional leadership is a deeply-rooted feature of Scottish educational culture (McPherson and Raab 1988; Arnott 1993).

Second, the prospect of DSM, linked to formula funding and parental choice, has heightened awareness of the relationship between pupil numbers and the size of budgets. The eight schools have reacted in different ways to this. One seemingly capitulated, with both the board and the head believing that they were powerless to increase the school roll. Another attempted to retain its buoyant market position by making sure that parents and the local community knew about its various activities. Indeed raising awareness about the school seems a fairly common element in most schools' strategies. This may be construed as a desire to go beyond the key performance criteria in league tables to draw attention to other features. At one level, then, market responses could be characterized as more cosmetic, concerned with image management, than substantive, affecting the educational process itself. In only two schools have heads considered making specific modifications to teaching and learning as part of a marketing strategy. For instance, Thomson's decision to make special provision for more able pupils was a marketing ploy to attract more middle-class pupils to the school. Here the school was less concerned with increasing the number of pupils than with changing the kind of pupil.

Third, and most speculatively, schools' relationships with each other are likely to change. There are three main aspects to this. One is that there may be more arduous cultivation of lay links with primary schools by secondary schools as part of an image management strategy, going beyond informal meetings between secondary boards and the boards or PTAs of their associated primaries. Further, the average cost of educating pupils at particular schools is becoming more transparent. Therefore, as heads and boards become aware of, for example, the degree of protection afforded to schools in disadvantaged areas, there may be debate about the extent and justification of such protection, and arguments about redistributing resources. This may be especially likely in schools where staffing costs are on the agenda. Glimmers of this are just becoming visible in some Lothian schools. Finally, and to some extent a corollary of the above, particular kinds of school may band together to defend or protect their position in the market. In Lothian, schools at the bottom of the league table have already formed a group. Although this is confined to headteachers and staff, it might well extend to boards and others. Schools that are particularly advantaged or disadvantaged under new funding arrangements might likewise look to each other for support. There is thus a prospect of the development of new networks, or subgroups within existing networks, as a consequence of devolved management. The impact of such developments on the Scottish tradition of a collective welfare orientation remains to be seen and is a key area of research interest.

Note

1   This chapter is based on an earlier paper presented at the 1994 CEDAR conference. We wish to acknowledge Carole Moore's contribution to that paper, Lucy Bailey's critical comments on this chapter, and Michael Adler's role in the ESRC project.

Margaret Arnott, Charles Raab and Pamela Munn

References

ADLER, M., MUNN, P. and RAAB, C. (1991) *Devolved School Management,* Economic and Social Research Council Grant No. R00233653.

ADLER, M., PETCH, A. and TWEEDIE, J. (1989) *Parental Choice and Educational Policy,* Edinburgh, Edinburgh University Press.

ARNEY, N., MUNN, P. and HOLROYD, C. (1992) *The Provisions and Take-up of School Board Training,* Edinburgh, Scottish Council for Research in Education.

ARNOTT, M. (1993) 'Thatcherism in Scotland: An Exploration of Education Policy in the Secondary Sector', unpublished PhD thesis, University of Strathclyde.

MACBETH, A. (1991) *School Boards: From Purpose to Practice,* Edinburgh, Scottish Academic Press.

McPHERSON, A. and RAAB, C. (1988) *Governing Education: A Sociology of Policy Since 1945,* Edinburgh, Edinburgh University Press.

MUNN, P. and HOLROYD, C. (1989) *Pilot School Boards: Experiences and Achievements,* Edinburgh, Scottish Council for Research in Education.

MVA Consultancy (1992) *Study of the Work of School Boards: First Interim Report,* Edinburgh, MVA Consultancy.

SCOTTISH OFFICE EDUCATION DEPARTMENT (SOED) (1993) *Devolved School Management: Guidelines for Schemes,* Edinburgh, SOED.

Chapter 7

The Grant Maintained Schools Policy: The English Experience of Educational Self-Governance

Sally Power, David Halpin and John Fitz

Introduction

The devolution of financial and administrative responsibility to schools has been a prominent feature of recent education policy, both in England and elsewhere. In England, the drive towards such independence is most clearly embodied in the grant maintained (GM) schools policy, which enables schools to opt out of their local education authority (LEA) and become autonomously incorporated institutions.[1] The policy has not only become the flagship of government strategies designed to restructure the education system along market lines, it is also heralded in other countries as a shining example of radical innovation (e.g. Chubb and Moe, 1992).

This chapter outlines some of the key findings of our research on the implementation and short-term consequences of this radical innovation.[2] It argues that, thus far, there is little to suggest that the policy is fulfilling the objectives of its advocates. Indeed, it suggests that in some cases the effects would seem to run counter to the intentions of the policymakers. However, the chapter also considers whether these outcomes arise from the detail of the policy or the context in which it is implemented.

Exploration of the English experience of self-governance is important on two related counts. First, it has implications for understanding and evaluating the outcomes of similar policies implemented in different contexts. Second, comparative analysis is not only central for evaluating and predicting policy effects elsewhere, it is also a means by which we can begin to find out more about ourselves (Dale, 1992). In Britain, we are surely ideally placed to begin such a comparative task – having within our boundaries four nations with similar, yet distinctive, educational systems.

Sally Power, David Halpin and John Fitz

The GM Schools Policy – Purpose and Progress

The 1988 Education Reform Act allows schools to opt out of LEA control and become grant maintained. Although only one policy amongst many, opting out subsequently became increasingly central to the government's overall strategy for reform. In the 1993 Education Act, for instance, the overwhelming majority of clauses relate to the GM schools policy.

The process of opting out is initiated by the school's governors, or a parents' petition. There is then a secret postal ballot of all parents with children at the school, the outcome of which determines whether the school can apply to the Secretary of State for GM status. When a school is granted GM status it has opted out of its local education authority and obtains its funding directly from central government. Like other maintained schools, it is run by a governing body although this no longer contains any local government appointees. In addition, it gains increased powers in relation to admissions, finance and staffing and can directly petition the Secretary of State for a change in its character. The expansion of the policy is apparent in changes which have meant that all schools are eligible to opt out. There are now provisions to enable the creation of new GM schools, as well as allowing existing private schools to opt in.

The first GM schools opened in September 1989. Since then, over 1000 schools have opted out. These figures fall far short of Margaret Thatcher's confident prediction that most schools would hurry to opt out. However, while the GM sector includes only a small proportion of all maintained schools (currently less than 5 per cent), its significance should not be underestimated. Uptake within secondary provision in particular has been quite considerable, if geographically patchy. Although only about 2 per cent of all primary schools have achieved GM status, 16 per cent of secondary schools have. While the pace of opting out has slowed considerably over recent months, the GM sector provides an important exemplar of more thoroughgoing institutional autonomy.

Although the objectives of the GM schools policy have undergone alteration and its uptake has been patchy, the policy has been driven by a consistent conviction that the LEA monopoly of state education has contributed to a system which is insufficiently responsive to the needs of its users. GM schools, it was argued, would bypass top-down control and enhance parental voice through allowing them to determine future school governance (e.g. Baker, 1988; Centre for Policy Studies 1988). Furthermore, the creation of a new kind of school would diversify education provision and further extend parental empowerment through the creation of new choices (e.g. MacGregor, 1990; DFE, 1992). This chapter begins by looking at the extent to which GM schools have realized these objectives. In doing so, it draws upon extensive research[2] within GM secondary schools and neighbouring LEA and private schools. Thirty headteachers, over 200 parents and 400 pupils were interviewed in the early stages of the policy. Headteachers and pupils were then revisited two years later.

Policy Effects

GM Status and Parental Voice

One of the ways in which the GM schools policy is supposed to empower parents is through giving them the right to take their children's school out of LEA control. Most of our parent respondents did take part in the ballot and most voted for GM status, which might be taken to indicate popular support for the policy – although more recent figures (e.g. DFE, 1995) suggest that such popularity appears to be waning.

We also gained the impression from our sample of 'pro-GM' parents that their support for opting out was more a reflection of loyalty to the headteacher, rather than the result of deliberation on issues surrounding opting out. In schools where the headteacher was heavily involved in promoting GM status, our data would support Roger's (1992) argument that parents often constitute little more than 'ballot-fodder'.

It is also difficult to claim that the right to vote in an opting out ballot represents a significant devolution of power. While the policy's advocates argue that these ballots are often more democratic than local authority elections inasmuch as the percentage turnout tends to be higher, only parents with children at the school at the time of the ballot are able to vote. Second, there is no corresponding mechanism through which parents might subsequently elect that their school be returned to local authority control.

In common with other research on GM schools (*cf.* Bush *et al.*, 1993), we also have little to suggest that opting out has led to any greater degree of grass roots influence in the running of schools. Only very few parents felt that their involvement in the ballot had given them an increased sense of ownership of the school. Even here, it is hard to see how this feeling will extend through their child's school career, and, perhaps more crucially, through into the next generations of parents.

Parents in our sample of GM schools did not report increased levels of involvement. In fact, more parents from LEA schools claimed to be involved with their child's schools. In terms of parent representation through governors, there appears to be little clear correlation between school type and familiarity with the governing body. The experience of parent governors of GM schools is little different from that of LEA schools. There is certainly nothing to suggest that opting out has resulted in a reformulation of teacher–parent relations. Teachers, and particularly headteachers, still devalue, marginalize and, in many cases, channel lay participation into non-controversial areas, such as fundraising. Indeed, in some GM schools even this minimal level of participation is diminishing as their more generous funding does away with the need for such activities.

Far from empowering parents through eliminating existing forms of producer control, our research suggests that GM status might paradoxically create a new variety in the form of headteacher control (Halpin *et al.*, 1993). There is certainly little to suggest that GM status is empowering parents across the board in any significant way.

GM Status and Parental Choice

Advocates of the policy often claim that the principal mechanism for augmenting parent power will be through the exercise of choice rather than voice. GM schools, it is argued, will contribute to a system based on diversity rather than uniformity, a system in which equal but different schools will vie with each other for parental approval. Even here, though, our research indicates that GM schools have, thus far, been ineffective.

We have no evidence to show that opting out has made any great difference to the nature or range of school provision that is available. GM schools were certainly not perceived by parents as anything different, and heads usually felt that opting out had enabled them to continue as they were. Pupils similarly gave us no indications of any changes relating to the curriculum or pedagogy. Indeed, if anything, GM schools would appear to be contributing to curricular and pedagogic conservatism. The vast majority of GM schools exhibit a reinvigorated traditionalism which is as likely to lead to uniformity as to foster innovative diversity.

There is certainly little to suggest that the GM sector will significantly contribute to curricular specialization. Despite receiving extra money to develop their technology curriculum, not one of our sample of GM schools was willing to emphasize this dimension or market their schools along technological lines. DfE, progress reports (1995) reveal that, as of 1995, only 10 of the 633 secondary schools which have opted out incorporate the terms 'technical' or 'technology' within their name.

While even more new funds, some would say 'bribes' (Whitty and Edwards, 1993), are now available to GM schools, to become 'specialist' schools, the most frequent form of specialization being sought is academic selectivity. Several schools have already successfully applied for grammar school status with more expressing similar intentions. Furthermore, many schools are in the process of becoming partially selective, i.e. selecting a proportion of their intake on the basis of academic ability in order to create fast tracks within comprehensive schools. GM secondary schools are also keen to establish sixth forms (GMSC, 1994) – yet another reflection of the desire of many GM schools to model themselves along traditional lines.

The profile of the GM secondary sector (which already contained a disproportionate number of single-sex 11–18 grammar schools) together with more vigorous reputation management, might enable GM schools to foster an image of themselves as the hallmark of good state schooling. Such impressions are likely to be further endorsed through formal between-sector comparisons made on the basis of published examination results (GMSC, 1993, 1994). Opting out is therefore more likely to consolidate school hierarchies rather than to contribute to an education system based on diversity with parity of esteem.

GM Status – Pattern and Locality

The summary of the findings outlined above would suggest that the GM schools policy has failed to achieve its objectives. Indeed, it suggests that it might produce outcomes which run counter to its stated intentions. Far from empowering parents, GM schools might actually be diminishing parental involvement both currently and in the future. Similarly, such little diversification as is apparent appears more likely to lead to a consolidation of hierarchies rather than their diminution through the establishment of a range of schools which are equal but different.

There is, however, another feature evident in our research findings. One of the main frustrations with analysing the data has been the difficulty of tracing any clear pattern. Although it is possible to discern overall tendencies, these are less marked than the profusion of variation where contrasts between localities appear more pronounced than common features. In many cases the differences within each sector are greater than the differences between sectors. In some GM schools, for instance, opting out does appear to have been used as a vehicle to facilitate parental involvement, while in others such involvement has been diminished. Similarly, in terms of the creation of hierarchies between sectors, there is no simple pattern. In some areas, the GM school is at the apex of the informal hierarchy. In others, LEA schools remain more prestigious and attractive to parents.

This complexity, however, should not be seen as interference but as a significant outcome in itself. It is the increasing complexity and situationally specific nature of the impact of opting out which is perhaps one of our key findings. While not suggesting that patterns of school provision have ever been simple, it would appear that opting out has contributed to an even greater fragmentation of provision. Moreover, such 'localization' (Johnson, 1989) is more than just a finding, it is also an explanation. Although the implications of increasing localization will necessarily be complex, there can be little doubt that '[l]ocal peculiarities have provided further differences which privilege has been able to colonize' (Johnson, 1989: 100).

Explanations and Implications

Does the failure of opting out stem from the administrative detail of the legislation, or is it more to do with the context within which it has been implemented? If so, are the peculiarities of the English education system (e.g. Green, 1991) of greater significance than the more deep-rooted structural features which are likely to be more generic? As Johnson (1989) hypothesizes, are the problems of English schooling the product of English exceptionalism or state education itself?

The sociologically proper answer is to say that the outcomes of any particular intervention are the unique articulation of all three elements – policy, context and structure. Nevertheless, for the purposes of comparison, it is useful to try to disentangle each dimension analytically. The next section, therefore, explores the dimensions of policy, context and structure with reference to the failure of GM schools either to enhance parental voice or to expand parental choice through diversifying provision.

Policy, Context or Structure?

Despite government claims to the contrary, the GM schools policy is remarkably constrained. In terms of empowering parents, for instance, it is quite clear that government strategies concentrate on what Hirschmann (1970) refers to as 'exit' rather than 'voice'. In addition, the government's notion of empowerment is fairly unfocused and sloganistic; 'meaningless, beyond a superficial level, merely offering a symbolic gloss of popular democracy, and freedom from (usually local) state bureaucracy' (Vincent, 1993: 374). Although opting out might give parents a one-off decision-making role, it is very limited. Even where parents are given more voice in the running of the school through governing bodies, it is narrowly conceived as merely 'another economic function, that of management' (Johnson, 1989: 116). Parents are certainly a long way from being given majority control as in some American reforms (Hess, 1992). Furthermore, the case of Stratford School, Newham, where the head and her chair of governors came into direct conflict (Anonymous, 1992) provides an illustration of the way in which central government intervenes when parental/community involvement is seen to overstep the mark.

On the other hand, these policy limitations are not sufficient in themselves to account for the inability of the GM schools policy to mobilize parental participation more effectively than in the past. The parents we spoke to did not appear to be using even the limited power which they had to be particularly directive in school management. There is no reason why they should not be involved in a wide range of issues concerning the curriculum, teaching activities and teachers themselves (Raywid, 1985). Such a level of involvement, though, is not considered. Even those parents mandated to govern schools do not seem to be very directive. In GM schools, as in other governing bodies, it would appear that parents are the least participative members (Golby and Brigley, 1989) with women, working-class and black governors being 'at best ignored and at worst interrupted' (Brehony, 1992: 210).

Is the limited and uneven nature of involvement to which we have alluded peculiarly English, however? There is evidence to suggest that in England, many parents defer unquestioningly to the authority of the teacher rather than monitor or challenge their activities, although the authority invested in education professionals is hardly situationally specific.

This dominance is likely to be in part a product of the relative class location of groups of parents and teachers. While the prestige accorded the profession may vary from one country to another, teachers are undoubtedly middle-class in destination, if not origin (Reid, 1980). It could also be argued that the rise of the professional middle class is in itself related to the subordination of disadvantaged groups (Lowe, 1988). More systematically, however, teachers are made powerful through their location as distributors of future opportunities. The teaching profession 'has a vested interest in the examinations industry and the status hierarchies which go with it' (Batten, 1987: 48). This interest stems as much from the tenets of meritocracy as from any particular cultural investment in teachers' intellectual prowess or professional practice.

It would also seem likely that policies which remove forms of local government in favour of site based management not only might be ineffective at empowering parents, but may further marginalize the already disadvantaged. As Jonathan (1993: 9) argues, 'to increase the rights of children's proxies is to ensure that winning or losing is even less a result of characteristics inherent to the child than it has been up to now'. It is therefore inevitable that such policies will result in a 'ratcheting of the spiral of cumulative advantage which passes from one generation to the next' wherever they are implemented.

In terms of the inability of GM schools to diversify education provision significantly, the case for laying the blame at the door of the policy might be more convincing. There is plenty within the policy itself to suggest that it is aimed at preservation rather than innovation. For instance, all GM schools originally had to be up and running institutions. They were not only already established, but had to be viable in terms of pupil recruitment in order to obtain the Secretary of State's approval. Such schools were therefore under little pressure from market forces to change. The 1993 Education Act does offer more radical possibilities by allowing the creation of new GM schools, as well as enabling existing private schools to opt in. Although several schools, mostly religious, have made applications, prospective recruits can hardly have been encouraged by the Secretary of State's refusal to give voluntary status to an Islamic primary school in London (Pyke, 1993). The lack of diversity could also be explained in terms of the constraints of other government policies, particularly the imposition of the national curriculum which GM schools, like their LEA counterparts, have to teach.

Such constraints, however, are again not the whole story and cannot entirely explain GM schools' resistance to diversify. The national curriculum, for instance, is undoubtedly prescriptive, but it is not necessarily the straitjacket that it is often made out to be. Furthermore, subsequent modifications (Dearing, 1993) have given schools greater room for manoeuvre.

Moreover, GM schools, as we have seen, are now being actively encouraged to specialize. They are able to select a minority of pupils on the basis of ability and aptitude. Along with the now familiar drive to promote technology, with technology colleges being established to supplement existing technology schools and CTCs, other curricular specializations are being urged. Schools are being invited to specialize through selecting pupils with particular aptitudes in languages, music or sport. Yet only very few are pursuing these options. The most frequent form of specialization relates to the revival of academic selectivity rather than curricular diversity.

The reinvigorated traditionalism of GM schools does not stem straight-forwardly from the policy, or indeed, the government's expressed intentions. Although some might say such schools are following the government's implicit perception of 'good practice', there is nothing within the terms of the legisla-tion to prevent them from modelling themselves along alternative lines.

Arguments emphasizing the nationally specific nature of such conservat-ism are quite compelling. The resistance to curricular specialization and diver-sification has to be viewed within the English context where 'educational innovation has persistently failed when it has diverged too sharply from the academic model firmly entrenched in the high status private sector and in the more favoured public schools' (Edwards and Whitty, 1992: 113). That equal but different alternatives to traditional modes of schooling are unlikely to de-velop can be seen from the low profile of GM technology schools. It is worth noting that seven of the 10 specialist schools alluded to earlier are located in areas which still operate a strong selective system. Such niche marketing is therefore as much a response to firmly entrenched hierarchies as a challenge to them. Indeed, in contexts where diversification operates to compensate for formally stratified provision, it is likely to endorse, rather than diminish, the perceived superiority of the academic model.

If, as Johnson argues, 'there is a strong case for regarding differentiation as the hallmark of English education' (1989: 97), then one might anticipate that similar reforms would have different consequences in other countries. It would therefore be interesting to consider the degree of differentiation and élitism within Northern Ireland and Scotland.

There is some evidence of greater diversity in countries such as the United States (e.g. Chubb and Moe, 1990; Hess, 1992), but even here it is hard to imagine that these schools all enjoy parity of esteem. That hierarchy will develop must surely be a generic, systemic process rather than the product of situation-ally specific features. It results from the relationship between schooling and society. Unlike many other 'commodities', education is not an 'absolute', but a 'positional' good (Hirsch, 1977; Miliband, 1991), the value of which is deter-mined by its scarcity. The attractiveness or desirability of one particular school and the kind of 'goods' it offers is not dependent on its actual qualities, but on its relative position to other forms of provision. Although at times stratification may be more pronounced within schools rather then simply between them, such differentiation is an inevitable consequence of the linkage between edu-cation and a stratified socioeconomic structure.

Education has long been an area through which it was important for parents to take and preserve the leading edge. In England, the middle classes have always been able to manipulate and colonize educational opportunities, be it the tripartite system (e.g. Jackson and Marsden, 1967), comprehensivization (Ford, 1969), or even specifically targeted policies such as the assisted places scheme (Edwards *et al.*, 1989). Furthermore, policies such as opting out provide even greater scope for colonization through increasing 'opportunities for divisions and exclusiveness' (Johnson, 1989). It seems unlikely that the same processes would not be at work elsewhere.

However, while such tendencies might be universally evident, it could be argued that they are particularly pronounced in England. Johnson (1989: 96), for instance, claims that 'in no other country in the world has it proved possible to commence to deconstruct an established system of public education'. If localization exacerbates existing inequalities, are Wales, Northern Ireland and Scotland better placed to resist such processes?

It is certainly the case despite claims of 'dull uniformity' (e.g. Patten, 1994) there has never been a common system of secondary schooling in England. As well as the extensive and prestigious private sector and the state-maintained but religiously controlled voluntary schools, which account for one-fifth of state provision, there are innumerable local variations where the legacies of past systems are still evident. The comprehensive system of secondary schooling has always been 'a revolution postponed' (Lowe, 1988). At the time of the 1988 Education Reform Act, one-quarter of English LEAs retained some form of selective secondary education. Kent, for instance, has a system which includes grammar, wide ability, bilateral and high schools. In just one town in Devon (Torquay), there are grammar, comprehensive, bilateral and secondary modern schools. Surely it is unsurprising, given the local variation and stratification between schools, that any measures which further fragment provision would result in the polarization rather than the diminution of hierarchies.

Conclusion

What can Northern Ireland, Wales and Scotland learn about the English experience of opting out? At an empirical level, the GM schools policy shows little signs of achieving its objectives. In fact, research suggests that its outcomes may even run counter to its stated intentions. Far from empowering parents, GM schools might actually diminish parental involvement both currently and in the future. Similarly, such little diversification as is apparent appears more likely to lead to a consolidation of hierarchies rather than their diminution. In both cases, it is the further localization of educational provision and governance which appears to be significant.

Whether similar effects are likely to be reproduced in the other countries of the United Kingdom is of course impossible to determine given the unique articulation between policy, locality and structure. However, this chapter has tried to argue that contextual features are at least as important as the clauses of the policy. Of these contextual features, systemic properties are no less significant than national specificities. Policies that contribute to increasing localization of provision provide new opportunities for the preservation and magnification of inequalities. Although the nature of the opportunities and the degree of magnification will vary according to context, they are likely to be variations on a theme.

Notes

1 Although the legislation also applies to Wales there are significant differences. For instance, the policy is overseen by the Welsh Office rather than the Department for Education. The research from which this chapter draws is based, therefore, on the English experience.
2 The research upon which this chapter is based was supported by two grants from the Economic and Social Research Council (Award Nos R00231899 and R00023391501).

References

ANONYMOUS (1992) 'Preventing school fiefdoms', *Independent*, 22 February.

BAKER, K. (1988) 'Parliamentary debates', *Proceedings of the House of Commons*, 23 March, Column 453.

BATTEN, E. (1987) 'Attainment, environment and education', in BASTIANI, J. (ed) *Parents and Teachers Vol 1*, Windsor, NFER-Nelson.

BREHONY, K.J. (1992) ' "Active Citizens": The case of school governors', *International Studies in Sociology of Education*, **2**, 2, pp. 199–217.

BUSH, T., COLEMAN, M. and GLOVER, D. (1993) *Managing Autonomous Schools: The Grant-Maintained Experience*, London, Paul Chapman.

CENTRE FOR POLICY STUDIES (1988) 'Advice to the education secretary', in HAVILAND, J. (ed) *Take Care Mr Baker!*, London, Fourth Estate.

CHUBB, J.E. and MOE, T.M. (1990) *Politics, Markets and America's Schools*, Washington DC, Brookings Institution.

CHUBB, J.E. and MOE, T.M. (1992) *A Lesson in School Management from Great Britain*, Washington DC, The Brookings Institution.

DALE, R. (1992) 'What do they know of England who don't know they've been speaking prose', paper presented at ESRC Research Seminar, Methodological and Ethical Issues Associated with Research into the 1988 Education Reform Act, University of Warwick, 29 April.

DEARING, R. (1993) *The National Curriculum and Its Assessment: The Final Report*, London, Schools Curriculum and Assessment Authority.

DEPARTMENT FOR EDUCATION (DFE) (1992) *Choice and Diversity – A New Framework for Schools*, London, Department for Education.

DEPARTMENT FOR EDUCATION (DFE) (1995) *GM Schools General Progress Report*, Statistical Memorandum, London, Department for Education, January.

EDWARDS, T., FITZ, J. and WHITTY, G. (1989) *The State and Private Education: An Evaluation of the Assisted Places Scheme*, London, The Falmer Press.

EDWARDS, T. and WHITTY, G. (1992) 'Parental Choice and Educational Reform in Britain and the United States', *British Journal of Educational Studies*, **50**, 2, pp. 101–17.

FORD, J. (1969) *Social Class and the Comprehensive School*, London, Routledge & Kegan Paul.

GOLBY, M. and BRIGLEY, S. (1989) *Parents as School Governors*, Tiverton, Fair Way Publications.

GRANT-MAINTAINED SCHOOLS CENTRE (GMSC) (1993) *Annual Report*, High Wycombe, Grant-Maintained Schools Centre.

GRANT-MAINTAINED SCHOOLS CENTRE (GMSC) (1994) *Annual Report*, High Wycombe, Grant-Maintained Schools Centre.

GREEN, A. (1991) 'The peculiarities of English education', in Education Group II (ed) *Education Limited: Schooling and Training and the New Right*, London, Unwin Hyman.

HALPIN, D., POWER, S. and FITZ, J. (1993) 'Opting into state control?: Headteachers and the paradoxes of grant-maintained status', *International Studies in Sociology of Education*, **3**, 1, pp. 3–23.

HESS, G.A. (1992) 'Chicago and Britain: Experiments in empowering parents', *Journal of Education Policy*, **7**, 2, pp. 155–71.

HIRSCH, F. (1977) *Social Limits to Growth*, London, Routledge & Kegan Paul.

HIRSCHMANN, A. (1970) *Exit, Voice and Loyalty*, Cambridge, MA, Harvard University Press.

JACKSON, B. and MARSDEN, D. (1967) *Education and the Working Class*, London, Routledge & Kegan Paul.

JOHNSON, R. (1989) 'Thatcherism and English education: Breaking the mould, or confirming the pattern?' *History of Education*, **18**, 2, pp. 91–121.

JONATHAN, R. (1993) 'Parental rights in schooling', in MUNN, P. (ed) *Parents and Schools: Customers, Managers or Partners?* London, Routledge.

LOWE, R. (1988) *Education in the Post-War Years: A Social History*, London, Routledge.

MACGREGOR, J. (1990) *Conservative Party Conference News*, London, Conservative Party, 10 October.

MILIBAND, D. (1991) *Markets, Politics and Education: Beyond the Education Reform Act*, London, Institute for Public Policy Research.

PATTEN, J. (1994) Speech given to the Conservative Local Government Conference, London, March.

PYKE, N. (1993) 'New slight for Muslims', *Times Educational Supplement*, 27 August: 1.

RAYWID, M.A. (1985) 'Family choice arrangements in public schools: A review of the literature', *Review of Educational Research*, **55**, pp. 435–67.

REID, I. (1980) 'Teachers and social class', *Westminster Studies in Education*, **3**, p. 86.

ROGERS, M. (1992) *Opting Out: Choice and the Future of Schools*, London: Lawrence & Wishart.

VINCENT, C. (1993) 'Education for the community', *British Journal of Educational Studies*, **41**, 4, pp. 366–80.

WHITTY, G. and EDWARDS, T. (1993) 'And now, a word from our sponsors', *Times Educational Supplement*, October 22.

Part III

Experiencing Local Management

The New Headteacher: Budgetary Devolution and the Work Culture of Secondary Headship

Julia Evetts

Changes to the headteacher role have been a common theme in sociological and educational research (Peters, 1976; Earley and Weindling, 1987). It is recognized that the role of the head is becoming increasingly diverse and complex (Fullan, 1992). The expansion of managerial and executive tasks and a reduction in educational leadership aspects have been recognized and were documented by Morgan *et al.* (1983). Such changes have been magnified, however, and accelerated as a result of the implementation of the 1988 Education Reform Act. This chapter will argue that budgetary devolution, local management of schools (LMS), the option of grant maintained status (GMS), and increased competition between schools for pupils, have dramatically altered the work culture of headship. Headteachers' work is now far removed from the professional activity of educational leadership. Their work now focuses on financial management and on the managerialist activities found most commonly in industrial and commercial organizations. Hierarchical forms of management seem to be an inevitable consequence of the increased complexity of school organization following budgetary devolution. Heads are no longer educational leaders; the gulf between heads and their teacher colleagues is growing. Increasingly they are finance managers. Heads are feeling more isolated within their schools, as a result of their separation from teaching staff (other than senior management colleagues).

Some preliminary explanation is required of the term work culture of headship. In general work culture is the daily work routines and practices that are involved in *being* a headteacher. It consists of heads' work tasks and responsibilities, their manner of dealing with such tasks, how work time is distributed between jobs, their relations with colleagues, parents and pupils, officials and other professionals in schools. In addition it consists of heads' own experiences of their work and how they interpret the constraints and opportunities that influence their working lives. Studies of the occupational cultures of particular work groups have mostly been a product of interactionist theoretical perspectives (Woods, 1983) and of ethnographic methods. Reports of aspects of teachers' classroom and staffroom work cultures were common in the 1980s (Hargreaves, 1980; Woods, 1980; Hargreaves and Woods, 1984; Pollard, 1985; Nias, 1989). In general studies of the occupational culture of headship have been less common but there are some notable exceptions (Burgess, 1983, 1984; Hall *et al.*, 1986; Gillborn, 1989; Acker, 1990).

In the summer of 1990, one year into the transition to LMS, I interviewed 20 headteachers, 10 men and 10 women, from comprehensive schools in two Midlands educational authorities in England. The interviews were part of a research project on headteachers' career histories but, in addition, the heads were asked about their early experiences of educational change. The sample of 20 heads was unusual only in the fact that half were women. For the female heads, the sample of 10 was 66 per cent of the population of female heads of comprehensive schools in the two authorities. For the male heads, 10 represented a sample size of about 8 per cent. This overrepresentation of women was deliberate since the exploration of gender differences in career was one of the objectives of the research. In other respects the career history headteachers could be regarded as representative. Their schools varied in size from unit total group 8 to group 12 and the heads' lengths of time in headship posts had varied from one year to 20.

These headteachers were contacted again in the autumn of 1992. A questionnaire invited them to comment on particular aspects of their experiences of headship in the previous two years, since the original career history interviews. Of the 20 headteachers, 18 responded. In the interim period, three heads had retired, one prematurely as a result of a school closure. Other than these retirements, the heads' personal circumstances had not changed, except one (male) head was experiencing a period of 'second parenthood' with the birth of two baby sons. Changes to their schools were more common, however. One school had been closed. Two schools were at various stages of seeking grant maintained status. All schools had delegated powers and were receiving formula-funded budgets, some with historic funding supplements. Five schools were experiencing an increased pupil intake; one a reduction in pupil numbers as a result of parental choices of alternative schools.

It is these headteachers' accounts of their experiences of change that are used in this chapter. Two aspects of change will be examined. First new aspects of their day to day work activities and the focus on finance management will be demonstrated. Second, changes in work relationships in schools will be illustrated. It will be argued that changes in work activities necessitate more hierarchical forms of management in schools and create a growing gulf between headteachers and their staff.

Aspects of the New Work Culture of Headship

In the original interviews and in the follow-up questionnaire study, all the headteachers commented on the greatly increased work load involved in running their schools. This section will examine how some headteachers described their work. It will consider what the career history heads explained as being their main day to day work tasks and responsibilities.

The vastly increased amounts of paperwork involved in curricula changes, in incorporating national curriculum requirements and standard assessment testing (SAT) into schools (as well as TVEI initiatives and broadening the sixth form curriculum) were dramatic changes in themselves. The career history heads had dealt with these curricula changes in different ways but mostly these responsibilities had been passed down the line to heads of subject departments and to staff with particular, designated, whole-school responsibilities. Heads required that they were kept informed and some actively discussed the implementation of such changes. But the day to day responsibility for curricula change had effectively shifted from the headteachers' remit. Heads were now more concerned with other aspects. They were concerned with financial management, with planning cycles and with the coordination of the financial and administrative requirements of curricula provision.

> Then there is the curriculum planning cycle. The governors will determine how many teachers we are having. Now they can't determine that unless we know what the curriculum is, and you can't determine that until you know what the intake is, both at 11 and 16.
>
> I've got to know by December how many sixth formers we are going to get because that will need to go into budget estimates to put us on a legal budget by April. But to know how many sixth formers by December means that the sixth form curriculum and any changes, and the marketing, advertising and brochure, the parental interviews and the careers service all need sorting out by October. And that's just one curriculum area. (Mr Bennett)

Heads now had other work tasks. Three will be illustrated:

- control of maintenance and running costs;
- relations with governing bodies;
- income generation.

Control of Maintenance and Running Costs

An amount for the maintenance and running costs of school premises is included in formula funding thereby enabling heads and governing bodies to allocate such resources according to a school's priorities. One year into LMS, the career history heads were not entirely clear how this would work. In the follow-up questionnaire, the rules were becoming clearer. Heads were very much in favour of this change. They saw real advantages in getting work done when the school wanted it and could afford it but there was recognition that amounts were small thus giving little real choice. Mr Bennett's account illustrated the different arrangements under LMS compared with LEA controlled maintenance schemes:

> If you take painting as an example. The LEA would have said this is your painting programme; we have determined it on a budget owned and controlled by us and it's three classrooms a year and in March; which three classrooms do you want painting? I would look at their records at what was painted and when. I would note that room hasn't been painted for nine years and that one for nine years and that one for 10 years, so we'll have those three done. And then the following year they'd come again and say we'll do four this year, which four do you want? Oh the school hall has had a lot of wear and tear this last year, we'll do that. But now all those decisions are going to be the decisions of the governing body against a budget. That opens up all sorts of areas of argument and disagreement . . .
>
> There is no doubt in my mind that we are now into school development planning and as part of that we are heavily into planning cycles. If you take just premises, [all the decisions about maintenance] are the decisions of the governing body against a budget. So in terms of the up-keep of the premises you've got to have a five-year progressive planning cycle that says a set of classroom furniture has a five-year life; a set of tables and chairs is £1500; therefore to keep abreast of what we need, we need to be spending £6000 on the cycle of classroom furniture renewal (for one classroom). And that is just one planning cycle, there are many others. (Mr Bennett)

In general the increased control of maintenance and running costs afforded by LMS were welcomed by the career history heads. Two years later, in the follow-up study, this aspect of LMS was still very much appreciated. All the heads applauded the greater control, the flexibility and freedom, and the ability to prioritize. Heads and their governing bodies could more easily respond to their schools' needs and develop maintenance programmes to improve their school environments. The heads felt in control of institutional maintenance and upkeep. A few heads still commented about the underfunding and the time taken to put contracts out for tender. In general, however, this aspect of the principle of devolved management received widespread approval.

It did, however, represent a significant change in the way headteachers used their working time. Heads' time was now spent in seeking out suppliers and contractors and in developing planning cycles, in other words, in aspects of financial management.

Relations with Governing Bodies

Under the provisions of the 1988 Education Reform Act, the powers of governing bodies were increased substantially. Governors are required to take on management responsibilities. They manage a budget which will eventually cover more than 80 per cent of the total resources available to a school (100 per cent for a GMS school). They have staffing responsibilities; set strategic goals; approve the head and senior management's policies for achieving those goals; and consider reports on a school's performance (Levacic 1989). The role of governors in school management is more immediate and direct as they now have real resources to control and responsibilities for the selection and appointment (and dismissal) of staff (Coopers and Lybrand, 1989).

The career history heads' experiences with their newly empowered governing bodies were variable. Some reported their governors' willingness to accept unquestioningly the head's recommendations and a reluctance in querying the head's wishes. Other heads focused on the practical difficulties, in particular the extended timescale for getting decisions agreed. What was clear, however, was the increase in the amount of negotiation that was required in attempting to operationalize arrangements with the newly constituted and empowered governing bodies. What was also clear was the impact of budgetary constraints on all aspects of discussion and negotiation.

> The governors are finding now that they can't cope with the work. They have set up subcommittees so they can divide the work up through subcommittees. That's throwing a lot of strain on us because to service the working subcommittees demands a higher level of input from ourselves and that is far more frequent. I mean a governing body used to meet, what, once every two months and now it meets once every six weeks and there is a subcommittee meeting every week. I or my deputies or other senior staff are always attending a subcommittee, week in and week out. The committees quite rightly need promoting, they need guidance, knowledge. Basically they ask questions, they set up whole trains of information which they don't want divided from the meeting, which then has to be serviced. (Mr Oakes)

> All decisions are constrained by the budgetary implications. The financial consequences have to be the overriding consideration. (Mr Stevens)

Two years later the increased amount of negotiation was confirmed together with increased delegation to subcommittees and working parties. In general it was felt that decision-making was slower both because of the increased extent of negotiations over policies and because of the need to cross-check policy objectives and intermediate measures against constantly changing legal requirements, as well as against budgetary consequences and implications.

The chances of conflict in such negotiations were also increasing. In the follow-up questionnaire six heads were as yet unconcerned since they felt their advice and recommendations were usually followed. But four heads had commented on the emergence of certain tensions in their relations with their governing bodies. Sometimes the head's authority had been undermined; sometimes the interventionist stance of some governors was beginning to be felt. One head had commented on the number of in-quorate committee meetings which gave more opportunities for the Clerk of Governors to claim to represent the views of the governing body. Wherever heads and parent governors were united over policy matters (e.g. over the introduction of a school uniform which did not correspond with LEA policy) then the increased power of governing bodies was welcomed by the heads. The heads were becoming increasingly aware, however, that their recommendations would not always go unchallenged or that consensus would not always result.

Income Generation

Under LMS, formula-funded budgets for schools are based to a large extent on numbers of pupils and their ages (age-weighted pupil units). Some schools, particularly in the transition period, received extra allocations for special needs and historic differences. More important in the long term, however, is that extra resources can now be earned by schools as a result of income generating activities. Schools could always do this, but now this element has become an increasingly important part of devolved school budgets. Such activities can financially benefit a school directly. Heads, their senior management teams and governing bodies are having to think in commercial terms. They are increasingly engaging in negotiations with industrial and commercial organizations in order to expand their resources. They are renting their buildings and charging for services. They are seeking sponsorship from industry and local business for both capital expenditure and to meet running costs.

The career history heads' responses to this change were mixed. All recognized the necessity for such activities although some were reluctant to welcome such schemes. Others were actively seeking out and developing income-generating and self-help activities. Income generation, as well as finance management, had become an important task in headteachers' work.

> There's nothing in our estimates for capital development. What I'm saying to the governors is we can't have any capital development on a budget like this and County Hall doesn't allow for that. We've got to find sponsorship and I'll handle that with my contacts in the business world. And it's not a one-off thing; I'm looking for about £30,000 every year minimum because I don't see how we can develop without it because money isn't going to come from anywhere else. That's got to be a major part of my effort I think, because otherwise we won't get new suites of rooms, the place will run down, we won't be able to afford to refurbish the theatre, we'll never restock the library. We're lucky in that we've had the information technology project from county

but we won't be able to keep it up if we don't get that sort of money from outside. So I think it's madness to ignore that. Already we've done quite well, we've got something approaching £30,000 sponsorship from DTI; it's for a very specific project, a bar-coding project, a stock control project. I mean there are lots of other benefits, links with industry and so on. We've raised several hundred pounds from an all-night disco specifically for school funds. We do something which I suspect is quite illegal and ask them to give a donation when they join. I suppose I might get away with it again. A local firm donated the new econet cable for the computer system. You just have to be always on the look-out for things. We're investing in equipment that is high cost but is a more effective use of labour in the ancillary staff; so we bought a fax machine, we bought an improved reprographics facility. We're trying to do things that speed things up, make things run more smoothly and more effectively. I think we have to look at those sort of ways of saving labour, glass washing machines in science, all those sort of things you have to be aware of and look at.

We do a lot of self-help repairs, a lot of self-help redecorating, inside even, and I think we've got to do more of that. We had an environment week and cleaned the whole site of litter. It's a very vulnerable site with rights of way through it and the Sports Centre open all the time; nice pleasant place to walk your dog. But we got the whole place cleaned up, a self-help generated campaign just before half-term. I think you can't let up on any of those sort of things if you want the sort of environment that children deserve to be educated in. (Mrs Peters)

This section has considered three new aspects of the day to day work activities of being a headteacher. In respect of the control of maintenance and running costs, relations with governing bodies, and income generation in schools, the occupational culture of headship had changed significantly. At the same time control of curriculum change itself played a less important part in their work experience since this responsibility had been delegated to other senior managers in schools. The consequences of such changes for headteachers' relations with their teaching colleagues will be examined next.

Changing Work Relations in Schools

Headteachers' relations with their teacher colleagues in schools (classroom teachers and other middle and senior managers) is another aspect of the work culture of headship. One consequence of the changing orientations of headship which have been illustrated, is that hierarchical forms of management are being institutionalized and becoming inevitable in schools. Another is that a gulf is developing between heads and their staffs. The finance work of headteachers is becoming far removed from the teaching work of their colleagues in classrooms.

Where management is hierarchical, then authority is based on 'office' and orders are passed down through the layers and levels of management in the hierarchy to be operationalized. Job descriptions specify areas and extent of responsibilities and everybody knows what they are required to do, who they accept orders from, and give orders to. In a hierarchical management system in schools, a high degree of authority is vested in the headteacher and is transmitted through heads of departments/years to the classroom teacher. In the case of schools an alternative ideal-type model, a collegial system, is usually preferred. In schools some elements of collegiality (where professional equals govern their affairs by democratic procedures) are usually assumed.

According to the career history headteachers, however, many of the recent changes in education were necessitating and endorsing hierarchical management in schools.

I am now having to plan the year and look at the cycle of events for the year and the management processes within the school. And alongside that I am looking at a budgetary cycle as well and tying it in with LMS. Then at the same time a series of committees is being set up that work with the governors and the governors are part of those committees . . .

I have become more of an administrator and a manager. I think maybe now I am more like a managing director with a board of directors but behind that there is the governing body as well . . .

I would argue that we have a sophisticated management structure in the school. My responsibility is the more senior staff, encouraging them, whereas the more junior staff should be encouraged by the heads of departments. My deputies and senior teachers are encouraging the middle managers and I'm encouraging the senior team. (Mr Hall)

In addition, the work of these headteachers was becoming increasingly different to and differentiated from the work of other teachers in their schools.

I'm becoming a computer buff. I didn't think that's what headship involved. (Mr Oakes)

Running LMS is putting a gulf between me and the school. (Mrs Grainger)

It's a waste of a deputy head's and headteacher's time and educational skills. (Miss Hollis)

I'm experiencing a growing feeling of isolation. (Mr Stevens)

In terms of day to day work activities, headteachers were more completely managers and administrators. Their financial management tasks, their need to forward plan for their separate individual schools, to keep up with the mountains of paperwork and the need to match up calendar, financial and academic considerations, meant that they were more completely office-bound. Contact with pupils was becoming minimal (other than for serious disciplinary offences and exclusion meetings) and contact with teaching colleagues, other than senior management, was considerably reduced. Heads were becoming isolated; a gulf was growing between manager-heads and the school organizations they were administering.

A new headteacher was required, one who could maintain boundaries around what were appropriate financial managerial work tasks and what were not, what was involved in corporate management and what was peripheral. In the past headteachers had been generalists in their educational leadership roles, displaying a collegial/managerialist concern for students and staff colleagues. Currently, however, heads are increasingly required to become finance and strategic planning specialists, in other words, managers of an organization. The work culture involved in *being* a secondary headteacher was changing fundamentally.

The New Headteacher

This chapter has argued that in respect of the day to day work activities required in being a headteacher, and in the work relationships involved in running schools, the occupational culture of headship has changed fundamentally, and that budgetary concerns and finance management are the primary work tasks.

It is also important, however, to consider some of the wider consequences of the narrower focus on *financial* management by headteachers in schools. What has actually been devolved to schools is a range of management tasks and responsibility for their budgets. The choices this gives to schools are very limited, however. Educational decisions (such as over curricula and to an extent pedagogy), are more strongly controlled from the centre with national curriculum requirements, SATs and proposals for teacher appraisal. These aspects do not involve choice. They are devolved to senior management in schools for operationalization only, and school results are compiled and compared in school league tables.

Other aspects of educational choice, such as about educational policy and delivery, about the nature and purpose of schooling, about local needs and responsibilities, are all secondary to and constrained by budgetary considerations. The political rhetoric might emphasize autonomy, choice and school responsiveness to perceived needs. The reality of budgetary devolution is rather that schools, and particularly headteachers, are now responsible for managing cutbacks and financial constraints.

Educational management is becoming increasingly complex as more budgetary powers are devolved to self-managing schools. This examination of the work culture of headship has demonstrated that budgetary devolution is likely to decrease (not increase) the responsiveness of schools to the needs of pupils and their communities. Finance managers are necessarily separated, even distanced, from their staff, pupils and communities. Community representatives, in the form of school governors, must spend most of their time on school budgets and the costs of any decision or proposal. Educational choice is necessarily constrained by budgetary considerations.

Other researchers have argued that the role change for headteachers has been less than that of many of the other participants in educational administration such as governors and LEA officials (Hill *et al.*, 1990: 66). This chapter has argued that, nevertheless, in respect of both the work culture of headship and the relations between heads and others in schools, the changes have been far-reaching and fundamental. The new headteacher is a finance manager first; aspects of educational leadership have diminished dramatically in the work culture of headship.

References

ACKER, S. (1990) 'Managing the drama: The headteacher's work in an urban primary school', *Sociological Review*, **38**, 2, pp. 239–63.

BURGESS, R.G. (1983) *Experiencing Comprehensive Education: A Study of Bishop McGregor School*, London, Methuen.

BURGESS, R.G. (1984) 'Headship: Freedom or constraint?' in BALL, S.J (ed) *Comprehensive Schooling: A Reader*, London, Falmer Press.

COOPERS and LYBRAND (1989) 'Local management of schools', in LEVACIC, R. (ed) *Financial Management in Education*, Milton Keynes, Open University Press.

EARLEY, P. and WEINDLING, D. (1987) *Secondary Headship: The First Years*, Windsor, NFER-Nelson.

FULLAN, M. (1992) *What's Worth Fighting for in Headship?* Buckingham, Open University Press.

GILLBORN, D.A. (1989) 'Talking heads: Reflections on secondary headship at a time of rapid educational change', *School Organisation*, **9**, 1, pp. 65–83.

HALL, V., MACKAY, H. and MORGAN, C. (1986) *Headteachers at Work*, Milton Keynes, Open University Press.

HARGREAVES, A. and WOODS, P. (eds) (1984) *Classrooms and Staffrooms*, Milton Keynes, Open University Press.

HARGREAVES, D. (1980) 'The occupational culture of teachers', in WOODS, P. (ed) *Teacher Strategies*, London, Croom Helm, pp. 125–48.

HILL, D., OAKLEY SMITH, B. and SPINKS, J. (1990) *Local Management of Schools*, London, Paul Chapman Publishing.

LEVACIC, R. (ed) (1989) *Financial Management in Education*, Milton Keynes, Open University Press.

MORGAN, C., HALL, V. and MACKAY, H. (1983) *The Selection of Secondary School Headteachers*, Milton Keynes, Open University Press.

NIAS, J. (1989) *Primary Teachers Talking*, London, Routledge.

PETERS, R.S. (ed) (1976) *The Role of the Head*, London, Routledge and Kegan Paul.

POLLARD, A. (1985) *The Social World of the Primary School*, Eastbourne, Holt, Rinehart and Winston.

WOODS, P. (1980) *Teacher Strategies*, London, Croom Helm.

WOODS, P. (1983) *Sociology and the School: An Interactionist Viewpoint*, London, Routledge and Kegan Paul.

Chapter 9

A Question of Costs: Budget Management in Secondary Schools

Lynda Huckman and John Fletcher

Introduction

This chapter is based on the findings of a two-year study of the support and resource needs at two LMS secondary schools and the processes by which decisions were made. In accordance with the rationale on which recent changes in the English and Welsh education system is predicated, heads and governors are being urged to adopt more systematic and rational approaches to planning, resource allocation and decision-making in order to maximize effectiveness and efficiency. This chapter begins with a review of some of the possibilities for using cost effective exercises to improve the quality of decision-making and discusses the implications of these for school organizations. An analysis of the schools' budgets provides a financial backdrop against which resourcing decisions were made, while data gathered from interviews with heads and financial administrators establishes the context for a discussion of the options for decision-making which were available to headteachers confronted with the task of formulating and administrating their budgets.

Cost Analysis in Education

A major aim of the Education Reform Act (1988) was to expose schools to the effects of market forces in a belief that this would have a beneficial effect upon the quality of the service provided. Local management of schools (LMS) entailed the devolution of over 90 per cent of budget management to schools based on the assumption that budgets would be more effectively and efficiently managed by the resource users.

However, efficiency, in terms of achieving value for money, is a comparatively new phenomenon in education, especially at school level. This could be the result of earlier lack of information on educational finance generally (Knight, 1983). It could also reflect a generic lack of interest among the majority of teachers in issues that relate to administration and finance, unless those issues directly affect their classroom situations (Nias, 1980; Dennison, 1984). Attitudes change either when resources are scarce and competition for them fierce or when resource level and usage is taken as a measure of effective management and of increased educational opportunities for children (Dennison, 1990).

Giving schools greater control over their budgets also creates the right conditions for a greater interest to be taken in how resources are funded and distributed. The change, devolving the level at which allocation decisions are taken, is assumed to lead to outcomes which more closely match client needs. However, Simkins's (1987: 228) study found that a systematic consideration of alternative choices was absent from the decision-making processes of the teachers he interviewed:

> The interview material suggests that alternatives were not really considered. Those making the decision were confident that, given their budget and their 'choice-influencing' views about its in-built commitments, theirs was the only choice open . . . the only other item on the agenda of alternatives was to have made no change at all from the given budget.

The advantages of exercises in which a variety of programmes are examined according to an analysis of relative costs and benefits was not considered relevant to situations that existed, if they were considered at all. It could be of course that such an analysis was considered too time-consuming, and budgets too small to warrant such attention.

A full analysis in terms of costs will include the use of cost effective analysis, which is a way of studying the relationship between the costs of inputs and the achievement of objectives measured in terms of achievement tests, exam results etc. If two types of education produce the same level of output, then the most cost effective is the one which achieves this output at least cost. If output varies, then cost effective analysis can show which alternative achieves the highest level of output at a given cost. However, in both cases of cost effective analysis, it is necessary to measure both costs and effectiveness in quantitative terms.

Knight (1983) notes a distinction between cost efficiency and cost effective analysis. Cost effectiveness relates output to longer term objectives. He quotes the example of a school's attempts to reduce losses of books from the school library which he describes as cost efficiency. If as a result of the measures taken, pupils are discouraged from using the library, then this would result in a loss of cost effectiveness. Thus efficiency can be equated with value for money and effectiveness with educational benefit.

While accepting the fact that there are imponderable difficulties involved in attempting to establish a causal relationship between school inputs and educational outcomes, (see the school effectiveness literature, e.g. Gray, 1980; Fullan, 1985; Reynolds, 1985; Reynolds and Cuttance 1992, for a comprehensive discussion of these problems) the question still remains whether any form of cost analysis can be useful to educational practitioners as a means of planning and then evaluating the efficiency of ways of meeting educational objectives.

The International Institute for Educational Planning (IIEP, 1972) undertook a research project in 1968 to examine various ways of using cost analysis in education in developed and developing countries. Among the many possibilities of cost analysis, the following seem to be the most relevant to the use of cost analysis in schools:

- estimating the cost of alternative policies, (a consideration of 'opportunity costs');
- comparing alternative ways of achieving the same objectives so that the most efficient or economic can be selected;
- improving the efficiency of resource utilization.

Coombs and Hallak (1972, 1985: 253) support these findings and criticize the arguments against the use of cost analysis in schools as being 'pessimistic'. Their study includes some suggestions for school-based cost analysis and recommends an action research approach.

In a pioneering study of school costs in 1977, Knight devised a breakdown of an individual school's costs over a number of headings which were then allocated to main teaching subjects. From this, he was able to calculate and compare different items of expenditure, for example, the cost of a subject, or the cost of a pupil period. Although Hough (1981) criticized the basic assumptions upon which the original headings were calculated, the study was nevertheless the first to deal with cost analysis at school level and in a meaningful way. Knight's study also included a list of 'tactical options' (1977: 13–23) which were aimed at improving standards and increasing efficiency and value for money. Each area of the school budget was examined for the possibility of reducing expenditure without losing effectiveness. Significantly, teachers' salaries were described as being 'the heart of the problem' as a major unavoidable expenditure. Knight's (1983) work included Coombe and Hallak's suggestions for using cost analysis. It proposed the notion of the school as a cost centre in which the monthly budget print-outs and cost audits acted as facilitators of analysis to provide the means for a comparison of costs between schools on a per-pupil basis and as the foundation of future efficiency.

Unsurprisingly, the devolution of financial decision-making to individual schools via LMS and grant maintained status (GMS) has accelerated interest in the subject of school finance and resourcing. Writers offer managers of schools rational plans which involve a series of easily identifiable steps along which to organize their resourcing strategies. Having first defined their objectives and identified what resources are needed, managers are required to oversee the implementation of plans and evaluate the results (Caldwell and Spinks 1988, 1992; Brockmann, 1989; Davies and Braund, 1989; Davies and Anderson, 1992).

Rational planning strategies such as these are ways in which the quality and standards of the service provided can be monitored and as such, they are in keeping with the notion of education as a commodity to be evaluated and chosen by consumers. Questions of effectiveness and efficiency are more easily judged in quantifiable terms, and so the consumer assesses the 'products' via league tables of examination results, or whether budgets balance (Maclure, 1988). The type of rational thinking described above is meant to provide a means of conceptualizing both problems and solutions. Objectives and the means of implementation and evaluation are written as statements of intent into the schools' development plan, and should be reflected in budget formulation, a process which Strain (1990: 17) describes as the *objectification* process which has the aim of facilitating prediction:

> operations where inputs and the necessary mix are known and linked definably to particular outcomes lend themselves most readily to this conceptualisation of the resource task.

As Strain (1990) also observes, however, information based on costs may be readily quantifiable but such information can describe only volume and type; it does not provide indications of whether resources have been deployed to maximum advantage. Similarly, from the consumer view of parents, it is more likely that their preferences will be based on narrow judgments provided by league table assessments which represent outcomes that are easily identifiable.

Imposing business objectives and discipline on education also fails to take account of the professional status of the employees, and the diffuse nature of educational goals and runs the danger of viewing educational outcomes in terms of a production-function only. The problems of applying hyperrational and commercial models to education have been argued elsewhere (Huckman, 1994; Huckman and Hill, 1994).

Simkins (1987: 228) has no difficulty in viewing schools as units of production; what he considers necessary is an approach which also recognizes the differences that exist between schools and commercial organizations:

> What is needed is certainly a view of the school as a unit of production because that is central to an understanding of the principle of autonomy, but it must also be a theory which recognizes uncertainty about production requirements, relative prices and alternative production possibilities, and which is sceptical about the knowledge and interests of educational managers and sensitive to the ways in which particular circumstances affect judgements about perceived opportunities or resources.

Simkins (1994) reviewed research into LMS and concluded that effectiveness which entails the matching of outputs to some objective function raises certain questions that need to be addressed, for example, what assumptions about production efficiency guide choices in the allocation of resources to and within schools? How do those within schools choose to deploy resources towards objectives that must balance the demands of the national curriculum, of parents, of other clients' expectations and their own values and concerns (Simkins, 1994: 16)? A deeper understanding of the relationship between resourcing and educational outcomes for children may only be provided by those involved in the processes of educating. As Strain (1990: 29) suggests:

> Knowledge of the necessary conditions for pupil learning, of the requisite material resources and how they can be utilized: skill to control and influence the quality of classroom interactions, to establish an enabling relationship based on trust, mutual respect and self-discipline; judgement in the allocation and prioritization of available time for particular learning projects. All these remain in the hands of teachers themselves.

The research on which this chapter is based attempts to answer these questions by providing some insights into the rationale that governs the choices made by schools.

The Research: 1993–95

The Schools

Allyn High (pseudonym)

Allyn was a 11–18 comprehensive school with 807 pupils enrolled in January 1993 and a full-time staff of 56 including the headteacher and two special needs teachers. Eight hundred and twenty-nine pupils were forecasted for January 1994 assuming that the school would be able to recruit 60 students into year 12 and 160 into year 7. (There were 54 students in year 12 in January 1993.) By 1994 the numbers of pupils on roll had fallen and staff numbers had been reduced to 52. Allyn was situated on the perimeter of the city serving a residential area consisting of a large council estate built between the wars. From this estate the school drew the majority of its pupils who entered the school from three associate primary schools.

In the mid-1970s the school had been designated as a social priority school. At the time of the 1981 census, the school catchmant area had the greatest incidence of unemployment in the city at 18.8 per cent and it stood at 15.5 per cent in 1990 (1991 Census of Employment: GB regions prepared by the Government Statistical Service). The census data also revealed a high incidence of one-parent families (15.9 per cent) and large families of three or more children (25.8 per cent). In September 1990, 34 per cent of the new intake of pupils was diagnosed as having a reading age two or more years below their chronological age, while 30 per cent were entitled to free school meals. Pupils of high academic ability were few in number, while those with learning difficulties were numerous. According to standard verbal reasoning quotients, very few pupils in a year group scored more than 110, and the majority scored between 90 and 100. As HMI observed in 1985: 'Since its establishment the school has faced an uphill educational task . . . staff are not discouraged by an apparent lack of parental support for their efforts.'

A notable feature of the teaching staff was its stability. Forty-seven staff had served in the school for three or more years and a significant number for more than 10 years. In spite of the obvious difficulties, staff were loyal and committed to the school and were anxious to improve the situation at Allyn, but held differing views as to possible solutions and chances of success.

Penlyn High (pseudonym)

Penlyn was a 11–18 secondary school which served a catchment area described by respondents as being 'mixed' and 'truly comprehensive' in its intake. New middle-class housing had joined longer established council estates around the old village centre providing a pupil intake which was mixed socially and by ability. The school enjoyed a high standing in the community and was very popular. The school roll in January 1993 was 1432 and 1441 in September 1993, which the head felt was 'edging towards absolute physical capacity'. The first year intake was 252 in September 1992 and 223 in September 1993. An increase of pupils in the sixth form meant that, with a 60 per cent 'stay on rate', A-level numbers were close to three figures instead of averaging 70+ as they did in the past. In 1993 there were 85 full-time teachers, a slight reduction from the position in 1992 when the school had 87 full-time teachers. The pupil–teacher ratio had risen from 16.3:1 in 1992 to 16.9:1 in 1993. Seventy-eight children were recorded as having free school meals. The school had a partial hearing unit which met the needs of 10 children and the educational welfare officer reported that Penlyn did not have any special problems with regards to pupil attendance. Penlyn was in the top third of the league table of results at GCSE and A-level examinations for the area, whereas Allyn was at the bottom.

A Summary of the Schools' Budgets

Tables 9.1a and 9.1b show the indicative budget allocation provided by the LEA for the school's guidance for the number of teachers including relief staff, premises costs and teaching materials costs. The percentages of these budget elements over the total net expenditure for the school is also shown. For 1993/94, the staff salary budget at 76.15 per cent was above the national average (72 per cent) and the teaching materials budget at 2.97 per cent, way below the 6.5 per cent recorded by the Audit Commission 1993.

Table 9.1a   Allyn High Budgets 1990–95 (LEA Indicative Formula)

	1990/91	1991/92	1992/93	1993/94	1994/95
Teachers	£1 097 693	£1 192 040	£1 284 759	£1 256 417	£1 253 179
Premises	£191 365	£216 786	£218 921	£231 966	£233 282
Teaching materials	£41 633	£48 042	£50 012	£48 108	£47 262
Net expenditure	£1 439 677	£1 557 457	£1 673 217	£1 649 759	£1 645 849

Table 9.1b   Percentages of Net Expenditure (Total Allocation by Formula)

	1990/91	1991/92	1992/93	1993/94	1994/95
Teachers	76.24%	76.53%	76.78%	76.15%	76.14%
Premises	13.29%	13.91%	13.08%	14.06%	14.17%
Teaching materials	2.89%	3.08%	2.98%	2.97%	2.87 %

However, the LEA indicative budget did not account for the deficits sustained by the school. For example, the revised planned budget formulated by the school managers in 1993/94 had to take account of a deficit of £81,702 on the total employees budget. This deficit resulted from differences between the average salaries for staff provided for in the LEA formula and the actual salary costs incurred. To counteract this deficit, £6596 was vired into the salary budget heading from the premises budget and £20,728 was transferred from monies allocated for teaching materials. A carry-over sum from the previous year 1992/93 reduced the deficit by a further £28,207, but £26,087 had still to be found by the next budget formulation in March 1994. The carry-over sum of £28,207 represents Allyn's end of year balance from the previous year 1992/93. At 1.87 per cent of the total net expenditure for that year, it was below the average end of year balance for secondary schools which the Audit Commission (1993) recorded as being 3.5 per cent.

Penlyn High school also suffered from deficits, which the headteacher described as resulting from LEA formula calculations that had been based on historic costs that did not account for the rapid growth of the school since 1985. In the headteacher's estimation, the catchment area of the school had become 'more middle-class' and did not enjoy the extra funding provided for inner city schools on formula funding. He had been unable to discover exactly why his school did less well than other schools in better areas:

> We find it hard to understand as a school why other schools in better catchment areas get more funding than we do per capita – I think it's the historic basis – the fact that we've grown very rapidly in the last few years and the county has not kept up with that.

Table 9.2a   Penlyn High Budgets 1990–95 (LEA Indicative Formula)

	1990/91	1991/92	1992/93	1993/94	1994/95
Teachers	£1 463 612	£1 742 809	£2 038 393	£2 080 000	£2 154 300
Premises	£243 981	£249 936	£277 236	£254 931	£284 118
Teaching materials	£95 255	£117 079	£121 260	£87 016	£91 161
Net expenditure	£1 953 220	£2 249 751	£2 596 378	£2 585 900	£2 722 659

Table 9.2b   Percentage of Total Expenditure

	1990/91	1991/92	1992/93	1993/94	1994/95
Teachers	74.90%	77.46%	78.50%	80.43%	79.12%
Premises	12.49%	11.10%	10.67%	9.85%	10.43%
Teaching materials	4.87%	4.52%	4.67%	3.36%	3.32%

Tables 9.2a and 9.2b show Penlyn's escalating budgets for the years 1990–95 for teachers, premises and teaching materials. In particular, the 1993/94 budget on which the study focuses, reveals that in spite of three full-time members of staff leaving the school, the salary budget for the school still stood at 80.43 per cent of the total expenditure. Alongside the rising percentage of teacher costs over total net expenditure over the five years, the tables reveal that reductions were made on premises costs and on teaching materials in the LEA indicative formula.

Like Allyn High, Penlyn made savings on actual sums spent on teaching materials: in 1993, £65,000 was allocated for spending on teaching materials. In addition to this, £5109 was available for library books and £4690 for physical education and maintenance of gym equipment, making a total of £74,799 which was substantially less than the sum suggested by the LEA indicative formula allocated for the year that is shown in Table 9.2a (£87,016). The headteacher explained the deficit between allocated and actual expenditure on teaching materials in a staff meeting in May 1993:

> Failure to meet these targets will have repercussions on other vital items of expenditure including the ability to afford supply cover, or even a deficit in staffing costs.

An examination of the school budgets establishes some of the parameters for decision-making, but further insights into the degrees of flexibility that could be found within budgets, the range of decision-making opportunities that were available, and the rationale that underpinned choices were provided by interviews with headteachers and administrative staff. It is to an examination of these issues that we now turn.

Budget Management

Providing a Rationale

Effectiveness in terms of maintaining or increasing human resources can be conceptualized in a number of ways. First, there is a generally accepted but unproven assumption regarding the efficacy of smaller classes. Thomas's (1990) research into the effectiveness of different forms of provision at sixth form level suggests that the number of pupils in a group has no significant effect on outcomes. However, it can be argued that it is less stressful for members of staff to prepare work, control, teach and assess when there are fewer numbers to deal with; that pupils in smaller classes receive more attention and meaningful interaction with their teachers. (Private, fee-paying schools are often marketed as offering just these advantages.) Interviews with members of staff confirmed that staff were readier to accept cuts in their expenditure and to make the necessary economies if they were aware that a chief priority of the school was to maintain their jobs. It was no coincidence that announcements made at the schools regarding cuts in budgets for teaching materials were invariably preceded by reminders of the possible consequences for staffing if economies were not achieved. LMS and the restrictions of a budget imposed by external agencies became the enemy from without and provided cohesion within the group. The maintenance of staffing levels and acceptable pupil–teacher ratios was viewed by the head of Penlyn as a whole-school policy issue which would necessitate considerable debate before it could be altered. He describes how budgets were formulated at the school:

> But where we really start is always with our policies – What do we want for staffing, conditions of service, non-contact time? – issues like that . . . decisions we make on staffing maintain these parameters as much as we can. Otherwise we're into a big debate. Say there were cuts in money. What gives? Do we have bigger classes, or do we cut our non-contact time? That's a staff debate; it's not for me to decide. The teachers who do the work 20 lessons a week out of 25 need to make up their minds. Do they want 32 in a class and maintain a relatively good non-contact ratio or do they give up a free period and have smaller classes? Since they do the work, they have to decide.

This is an example of the kind of 'mental production function' (Simkins, 1994) that can underpin the allocation of resources and that can incorporate organizational judgments of effectiveness. Many of these decisions may be explained in terms of cultural values that can be general and related to whole school situations, or particular and related to norms vested within subject areas (Hargreaves, 1994). As the quotation above suggests, the 'mental production functions' involved in decision-making could be traced through an examination of the heads' reactions to the options that were available to them.

The options open to the school will be examined by using and developing Knight's (1977: 13) concepts. His 'tactical options' included 'economies' – doing what we do now at less expense; 'cuts' – cutting out some of the things we do now; 'transfer of expenditure' – persuading someone else, probably pupils or parents to pay for some things; 'seeking value for money' – obtaining better education returns on the same money spent. The 1988 Education Reform Act and LMS in particular has widened the decision-making arena for schools considerably. The discussion will include some consideration of the effects that these increased powers have had on the options open to schools to improve the efficiency and effectiveness of their decision-making.

Economies

Levacic and Marren (1994) found that schools in difficult or 'losing' situations were likely to concentrate on efficiency strategies rather than on attempts at improving effectiveness since these were difficult to evaluate anyway. It would seem, however, that both Allyn and Penlyn's strategies were driven more by the need to economize rather than a desire to be efficient. Economy enabled both schools to attain one of their chief objectives which was to maintain existing staffing and satisfactory pupil–teacher ratios as far as possible.

Economizing was by far the option most utilized by the schools. Both schools transferred monies into their salary budgets from supplies and services, which meant substantially reducing their teaching materials' budget; premises costs were also reduced. In the case of Penlyn, the 'natural' loss of three full time equivalents (FTEs) who left the school in 1992 was compensated for by the appointment of a member of staff in 1993 so when economies paid off, improvements could be made.

Cuts

It was harder for the schools to judge the likely consequences of making cuts. Schools are restricted by the national curriculum in what they are able to do in terms of cutting the number of subjects and therefore classes taught. An elimination of below average size classes, particularly remedial groups, sixth form groups or less popular option groups, which Knight (1977) suggests are all possibilities, could result in opposition from parents as well as staff and may not be in keeping with notions of educational effectiveness that are part of the prevailing culture within the school which, as Hargreaves (1994: 164) observes, are embedded within

> The substantive attitudes, beliefs, habits and assumptions and ways of doing things that are shared within a particular teacher group or among

the wider teacher community . . . the content of teacher cultures can be seen in what teachers think, say and do. It is 'the way we do things around here'.

Although larger class sizes can improve unit costs, there may be other costs of cutting the number of classes that are not so easily quantifiable. From a practical and instrumental point of view, forward planning in terms of numbers of staff required could be overturned by fluctuations in numbers on roll or by subject option decisions made by pupils. However when suitable opportunities arose, the schools did manipulate numbers of staff employed and classes taught. These cuts were made as the result of staff leaving the school voluntarily and were often prompted by the need to deploy staff who remained. For these reasons, they are considered in terms of 'achieving value for money'.

Time

A reduction in administrative time, which members of staff reported had escalated since the 1988 Education Reform Act, may be achieved at the expense of the smooth running of the organization and a disruption of relationships. Allyn allowed heads of departments five non-teaching periods and subject staff had four. Senior staff taught 15 out of 30 periods (half a time-table); the deputy head taught 10 out of 30 and the head four out of 30. The head felt that there was a possibility that these non-teaching periods could be cut although he had observed that there seemed to be a tremendous amount of administration involved in the national curriculum, assessment and examination marking. He had been interested in studying how the staff spent their time but his attempt to make a survey had met with union opposition and had to be abandoned. The head's indecision regarding the amount of non-contact time teachers should be allowed might well have resulted from the fact that he had only very recently been promoted to acting head. Hargreaves (1994: 107) describes 'the separation of interest, responsibility and associated time perspective' that exists between the administrator and the teacher.

Transfer of Expenditure

The schools' parent–teacher associations (PTAs) were relied upon to augment curriculum resourcing. Other sources of funding such as local industry were sought, and these provided occasional boosts to individual subject areas.

Unlike Allyn, Penlyn had formulated a charging policy. Items for which the schools were unable to charge followed local and central government policies. These included admission, education during school hours, education out of school hours drafted to national curriculum or prescribed public examination for which a pupil had been prepared.

Also unlike Allyn, Penlyn charged for individual music tuition if not part of public examination or national curriculum or covered by county council policy. Penlyn also charged for materials for use in school if parents wished to own the product made by their children, board and lodging costs of residential trips outside school time, other activities outside school hours, and wasted examination fees.

Transfer of expenditure had limited application as a strategy to save funds; this strategy could also have repercussions and consequences for pupils. Materials for use in school which were not paid for by parents could place children at a disadvantage. Such pupils would not necessarily have any choice over the items they produced or over the quality of materials used. It meant that the school had control over both aspects. Pupils were not deprived of the education and training in whatever skill was required to produce the items but they were denied ownership of the results of their efforts:

> If parents do not wish to own the finished product, no pupil will be excluded from any course. However, while receiving the same education and skill training, they may be asked to produce different items which will be the property of the school. (Penlyn' School Prospectus: 26)

At Penlyn, financial assistance was offered by the schools from the School Fund or other charitable funds for children of parents who were unable to meet the costs of extracurricular activities and field trips. No such assistance was offered to parents at Allyn.

Interview data revealed the differences that catchment area made, especially to the ability of parents to provide resources for their children. In the case of Allyn High it could mean the ability to provide children with essentials such as pens and coloured pencils. Homework and coursework material prepared by pupils could not only suffer from a lack of essential materials but also from the fact that pupils did not have anywhere to work at home or any place where they could safely keep their work. Such disadvantages were found to be more critical for subjects such as art and technology which entail a heavy use of resources.

Value for Money

Deciding on what is value for money in education can be problematic. Value for money could be viewed as being dependent on the skill and attitude of the teacher as Knight (1977) suggests and have more to do with expenditure on training needs than on the allocation of resources. The value placed on teaching expertise was implicit in the decisions that both schools made during the course of the study, when they transferred money from their teaching materials budgets in order to preserve the jobs of members of staff.

Knight concluded that as far as tactical measures on teachers' salaries were concerned, there was little scope except cuts and thereby worsening the service provided (1977: 15). However, it is not within the power of schools to cut teachers' salaries. Making teachers redundant can involve the school and LEA in negotiating costly redundancy claims as well as demotivating members of staff who remain.

However, LMS has increased the school's power over both the appointment and deployment of staff. Replacing expensive staff who leave the school with less expensive staff has been used as a way of achieving economies under the cloak of value for money (Audit Commission, 1993; Huckman and Hill, 1994) since the same job is being done at less cost. Under the same cloak, cuts in a school's salary bill can be made by not replacing staff who leave. This may not be considered to have the same adverse effects as redundancy on the motivation of members of staff. As the following extract from an interview with the acting head of Allyn shows, these decisions involve a detailed consideration of the impact of the decision in terms of the school's organization of staffing, the curriculum and timetabling, but less consideration of the results of decisions in terms of educational effectiveness. Although Allyn had lost four senior members of staff and saved in the region of £110,000 on staffing salaries during the previous year (1993–94), falling rolls had meant that there still remained a deficit on the budget which had to be dealt with. The head described how the budget was formulated in April 1994.

> We started off this financial year with a deficit budget on staffing salaries even without those four. If those four had remained here we would have been in a desperate plight and I mean a desperate plight. By January 1994 we had a drop of 56 students and our budget came out at a deficit of £53,000. So then I had to go to the drawing board with the governors, to look at areas where we could cut and save money. We are losing our head of science, so we've asked the head of biology to take that responsibility over at no extra cost. We are appointing a .5 chemist to take over. This makes a saving of about £25,000. Because of the lack of numbers in the school, we were able to cut two classes which means that we have saved something like £16,000. Mrs B who is second in the music department is retiring. She would have been earning nearly £20,000. We're not replacing her and we've cut music from a part of the timetable from two to one period a week. Not ideal, but rather than lose existing staff through redundancy, this is a natural sort of wastage, plus the fact that we have some surplus periods in some department areas. One of the departments is technology, so what we've done is we've increased the allocation of technology time in the curriculum to three periods instead of two, accounting for the one period of music that we're losing. We will save in the course of a financial year about £20,000. That together with the science and little bits here and there – a .4 instead of a .5.

We've cut the business studies part-timer down to a .2. It's brought us to a balanced budget – it's unsatisfactory really; it's all kept near the margins.

As Knight (1977) suggests, a consideration of value for money leads to a questioning of the relative values that can be placed on different areas of the curriculum in terms of future benefits to society, and to the individual student. As far as flexibility and choice for the school is concerned, the national curriculum restricts the choices that schools have in terms of the content and organization of the curriculum and consequently the deployment of staff. In the case of Allyn High, the need to deploy surplus members of the technology staff was a driving force in the head's decision-making described above. A second interview with the head revealed the rationale underpinning these choices:

> Although we are cutting science by one period in years 7/8/9, it still gives us an overall number of hours within the range [laid down by national curriculum guidelines]. So we've moved that one period to extra technology because we have more technology staff. I've obviously got to deploy the technology staff. There are four members of staff in technology. If we had stuck to last year's curriculum, it would have meant the technology department would have had surplus something in the region of 20 periods a week which is almost a full time member of staff . . . Heads look at their number of periods in a day; they look at the staffing, they look at the number of periods on the curriculum that is needed to teach the subject in the year in the key stage and they will work it accordingly.

A deeper consideration of educational benefit or educational effectiveness was abrogated by the need to avoid redundancies and balance the budget. Depending on the circumstances, rising pupil–teacher ratios could be viewed as an unsatisfactory but unavoidable consequence of a tight budget:

> If we're in a contracting situation in maths in year 11, instead of us having six sets this year, we've got five sets, so I've saved three periods; the group size becomes correspondingly bigger but it is only a ploy to be able to save a little bit here and a little bit there. There's a lot of flexibility, but it's all geared around to whether it's a plus or a minus on your budget in the first place . . . Without this flexibility, you'd be talking about a redundancy situation because really, if we looked at the timetable, bearing in mind the technology situation where it is not compulsory anymore, we could possibly do without a technology teacher.

Only if a technology teacher had opted to leave, would the head consider appointing another chemistry teacher which the school needed and which would enable the school to reinstate the lost science period for years 7/8/9.

Reorganization – Back to Streaming

The loss of staff at Allyn High meant that pupil–teacher ratios that had been 20/21:1 had by 1994/95 escalated to 26:1. Mixed ability teaching, which had been set in motion in 1989 with the appointment of a new head, was no longer viewed as being acceptable by the new acting head. Staff had reacted both to the difficulty of producing differentiated work for large groups of pupils with a wide range of abilities, as well as to the school's position at the bottom of the much publicized league tables of results by calling for a reorganization of special needs teaching at the school:

> We are at the bottom of the league tables and no matter what anybody can say to defend the fact that we're a difficult school, and it's inevitable we're going to finish up at the bottom tiers of this system, we've still got to make efforts to improve our situation, so we've decided now to make a fast track at the top/middle ability band and then a special needs class at the bottom. That's going to increase the top class to 28 because we felt that a class of 28 brighter kids will not cause us the problems that we've had in mixed ability classes. So the staff wanted that . . . We've got to look at some strategies to improve our exam results somehow. So we thought, if we can keep one group together and push them hard, in a few years' time, it may pay dividends. (acting head, Allyn High)

However, the reorganization was not to be achieved without some expenditure on resourcing. In previous years the special educational needs (SEN) allocation on the formula budget (about £5000 in 1994), had been placed into the general teaching materials budget, but for 1994/95 SEN would receive a larger portion in order to facilitate the setting up of separate SEN units within the school. To achieve this, further reductions needed to be made in the allocations designated to other departments.

Generating Income

As well as the funds from the PTA reported earlier, the schools were able to let out their premises during non-teaching times. Obviously, the more facilities the school could offer the better the chance of obtaining extra revenue. Although Penlyn did not consciously set out to accrue reserve funds, it was fortunate in having a youth centre and a Dutch barn on the campus which had proven very popular. Usage of the school's premises resulted in the school being able to carry forward a balance of about £9000 in 1993/94 from a gross income of £10,023. This sum, of course, was liable to some fluctuation and the schools could not rely upon it. The financial administrator at Allyn described how she viewed and used this income when formulating the school's budget:

> I always work above the line, first taking out fixed and unavoidable costs. I disregard figures which can go way down, e.g. lettings figures. If they do well it's a windfall. That's how I get my carry-overs. They'll come back next year; we're not going to lose them.

The gross income from lettings for Allyn was £9,919 in 1993/94 and £8,637 in 1994/95.

Carry-Overs or Contingency Funds

At Allyn, budget deficits were alleviated by sums of money that the school had managed to carry over from the previous year. The Audit Commission's Report (1993) found that the average balances held by the schools ranged from 5 per cent to 15 per cent. Allyn's carry-over sum at 1.87 per cent was modest in comparison with the average for most secondary schools which the Audit Report recorded as being 3.5 per cent. However, the head of Penlyn viewed the contingency money accrued by many LMS secondary schools, not only to be unnecessary but also morally wrong. He believed it to be the result of inadequate management training received by the majority of heads, many of whom were frightened of overspending, or who viewed large reserve funds as a proof of their management skills:

> It's a macho symbol, isn't it? If you've managed to save a bit of cash then you've done rather well. We've had it drummed into us that it's the money that's important rather than the children. They only get one chance. If we save money on them for the next generation, then people get a poorer chance than they ought to have.

However, his confidence in the LEA to provide, that the money provided 'should be spent now because there will be a new lot next year', was not shared by his financial administrator. While agreeing that the money should be spent for the benefit of children currently at the school, she also wondered whether it was 'sensible to carry forward a balance – it must look as if we don't need the money.'

The Audit Report (1993) agreed with the head of Penlyn on the efficacy of a strategy based on accruing funds against unforeseen needs to spend:

One effect of balances is that a sum approaching 5% of the annual grant for schools is not being used. Another effect is that schools are seeking to achieve 100% of the required output with 95% of the resources.

Keeping Small Reserves – What's in the Office Account?

At both the schools, budgets were monitored monthly. Once the main transfers from premises and services had taken care of large deficits, smaller deficits on budget headings during the year were made up by tapping pockets that had been set up to cover miscellaneous expenditure. At Penlyn this was designated as the office account. The head's fund of about £1000 at Allyn served a similar purpose.

Non-Teaching Appointments

The increased usage of non-teaching personnel was observed by the Audit Commission Report (1993). At Penlyn three non-teaching staff were appointed during 1993/94. Applicants who could offer the school more than one skill were viewed as providing value for money. Thus caretakers who had abilities in electrical, plumbing and building skills were especially welcomed. Penlyn had appointed a clerk/first aider, since, like the other schools in the area, the LEA no longer supplied a nurse who was based permanently at the school and a great deal of valuable teacher-time could be taken up with sorting out minor injuries. Penlyn had also appointed someone to help with photocopying and a technician to help out in technology.

Conclusion

Since the 1988 Education Reform Act and LMS, therefore, schools were able to expand the 'tactical options' outlined by Knight (1977) in order to achieve a degree of flexibility in their budgets. The key to this increased flexibility rested in the power to decide on the numbers of staff employed and how they were deployed within the school, even though making teachers redundant was avoided at all cost. The evidence would suggest that efficiency in terms of balancing budgets rather than effectiveness in terms of educational outcomes for pupils was more easily achieved and evaluated. Many of the choices open to the schools were restricted and were viewed by heads and financial administrators alike as being inevitable in the circumstances. A consideration of opportunity costs (other uses for the money or resources) or other possibilities was not always possible. Costing exercises were more easily done in global terms, i.e. the amount saved on teachers' salaries rather than as a calculation of the cost of altering specific curricular programmes. Although some attempts were made to place allocations to subject departments on a more rational footing, it would seem that the paucity of attempts to analyse situations in terms of costs or benefits resulted from the dynamic nature of resource decision-making in educational organizations. Budget situations and priorities could alter even within a term as staff and students left or joined the school, or as a result of changes made by the LEA. A comparison of the schools' financial situations over the four years in which LMS had been operating revealed a worsening situation alleviated by fortuitous rather than planned events, and contained by strategies which the acting head of Allyn High appropriately described as 'decisions made at the margins'.

References

AUDIT COMMISSION (1993) *Adding Up the Sums: School Management of Their Finances*, London, HMSO.

BROCKMAN, F.J. (1989) 'Program budgeting: Implications for secondary school principals', in LEVACIC, R. (ed.) *Financial Management in Education: Emerging Function*, Milton Keynes. Open University Press.

CALDWELL, B. and SPINKS, J. (1988) *The Self-Managing School*, London, Falmer Press.

CALDWELL, B.J and SPINKS, J.M. (1992) *Leading the Self Managing School*, London, Routledge.

COOMBS, P.H. and HALLAK, J. (1972: 1985) *Cost Analysis in Education*, (rev. edn) published for the World Bank, Baltimore, MD, The John Hopkins University Press.

DAVIES, B. and ANDERSON, L. (1992) *Opting for Self Management*, London, Routledge.

DAVIES, B. and BRAUND, C. (1989) *LMS: An Introduction for Teachers, Governors and Parents*, London, Resources in Education, Northgate House.

DENNISON, W.F. (1984) *Educational Finance and Resources*, London, Croom Helm Ltd.

DENNISON, W.F (1990) 'The management of resources: Limited research effort on major issues', in SARAN, R. and TRAFFORD, V. (eds) *Research in Education Management and Policy*, London, Falmer Press.

FULLAN, M.J. (1985) 'Change processes and strategies at the local level', *Elementary School Journal*, **85**, 3, pp. 391–421.

GRAY, J. (1980) *The Search for More Effective Schools: Problems and Progresson Studies Related to British Schools*, Division and Institute of Education, University of Sheffield.

HARGREAVES, A. (1994) *Changing Teachers, Changing Times*, London, Cassell.

HOUGH, J.R. (1981) *A Study of Educational Costs*, Windsor, NFER-Nelson.

HUCKMAN, L. (1994) 'LMS in the primary school: Winners and losers', *Management in Education* **8**, 2, pp. 32–34, June.

HUCKMAN, L. and HILL, T. (1994) 'Rationality in the employment of teachers', *Oxford Review*, **20**, 2, pp. 185–97.

INTERNATIONAL INSTITUTE FOR EDUCATIONAL PLANNING (IIEP) (1972) *Educational Cost Analysis in Action: Case Studies for Planners*, an IIEP research project, Paris, UNESCO/IIEP.

KNIGHT, B.A.A. (1977) *The Cost of Running a School*, Edinburgh, Scottish Centre for Studies in School Administration.

KNIGHT, B.A.A. (1983) *Managing School Finance*, London, Heinemann.

LEVACIC, R. and MARREN, E. (1994) 'Senior management, classroom teacher and governor responses to local management of schools', *Educational Management and Administration*, **22**, 1, pp. 39–53.

MACLURE, S. (1988) *Education Reformed*, London, Hodder and Stoughton.

NIAS, J. (1980) 'Leadership styles and job satisfaction in primary schools', in BUSH, T., GLATTER R., GOODY, J. and RICHES, C. *Approaches to School Management*, London, Harper and Row.

REYNOLDS, D. (ed) (1985) *Studying School Effectiveness*, Lewes, Falmer Press.

REYNOLDS, D. and CUTTANCE, P. (1992) *Improving the Urban High School*, London, Cassell.

SIMKINS, T. (1987) 'Economics and the management of schools', in THOMAS, S. and SIMKINS, T. (eds) *Economics and the Management of Education: Emerging Themes*, London, Falmer Press.

SIMKINS, T. (1994) 'Efficiency, effectiveness and the local management of schools', *Journal of Educational Policy*, **9**, 1, pp. 15–33.

STRAIN, M. (1990) 'Resource management in schools: Some conceptual and practical considerations', in CAVE, E. and WILKINSON, C. (eds) *Local Management of Schools: Some Practical Issues*, London, Routledge.

THOMAS, H. (1990) *Education Costs and Performance: A Cost Effective Analysis*, London, Cassell.

Chapter 10

Educational Change in the United Kingdom: A North–South Divide

Sally Brown

One State, Two Nations

It is tempting for those of us in Scotland to imagine that an embattled and embittered English education system looks north with envy on better ways of doing things; while bemoaning our own fate, we reassure ourselves about how much worse things are south of the border. Whether others agree with that will depend on their own educational values. They may well regard us as self-satisfied, complacent, old-fashioned whingers who can never get away from the idea that we somehow 'lost' in the Act of Union in 1707 and so must continually assert our superiority in areas such as education and the law, both of which remain unassimilated to the English systems.

The separation of education systems does, of course, have a major impact on the ways in which the common aspects of 'British' policy are implemented in the two nations. That implementation will depend fundamentally on the distinctive cultural and political climates of the two settings. In an attempt to explore this one state/two nations set of circumstances, this chapter looks at six of the many stories that can be told about how education is in Scotland.

Educational Consumerism, Competition and Control

This first story is short, familiar and commonplace in recent educational literature throughout the UK. It elaborates the ways in which Scotland, like the other nations, has been subjected simultaneously to both libertarian and highly centralist policies (often referred to as free-market Stalinism) by a long running Conservative government. The market ideology of consumerism, competition, efficiency and enterprise alongside that of central control is as evident in the ruling party in the Scottish Office as it is in Whitehall. Matters of equity, social justice, public good and public responsibility to provide a common entitlement for all young people take second place. The ideas on which attention has been focused will have a familiar ring to those south of the border:

- self-governing schools (in England grant maintained);
- school boards (in England governing bodies);
- parental choice of schools;
- a national curriculum, in Scotland the 5 to 14 Programme and Standard Grade;
- the technical and vocational education initiative (TVEI);
- performance indicators and publication of schools' performance records (cf. league tables in England);
- national testing;
- technology academies (city technology colleges in England);
- devolved school management (local management of schools in England);
- initial teacher education becoming more school-based.

There are, of course, some differences in the two market places. For example, early efforts to set up Scottish technology academies, despite support from individuals (notably Lord Forte) in the private sector, were abandoned largely because the 20 per cent of finance from that sector was not forthcoming and the government was reluctant to establish new institutions in areas where there was already a surplus of places in maintained schools. Furthermore, there have been rumours of private companies from south of the border enquiring about the possibility of supporting technology academies in Scotland but then withdrawing their interest, apparently for two reasons: that they did not perceive a substantial Scottish market for their own products and the existing homogeneity of provision in Scottish schools weakened the case for the new kind of academy.

Despite these differences there is clearly a common ideological framework; we have to ask, therefore, whether we should conclude that the Scots and the Sassenachs are in the same boat?

Policy Hysteria

A second short story, told by Ian Stronach and his colleagues (Maclure and Stronach, 1994; Stronach and Morris, 1994), is of 'policy hysteria'. This hysteria takes no account of Hadrian's wall and is illustrated by these authors through analyses of current approaches to evaluation and of educational vocationalism. It could be happily accommodated, however, by other discourses of crisis that characterize the current British government's policy moves. It is identified as a 'cluster of related features in educational policy development':

- shortening cycles of recurrent reforms;
- multiple innovation;
- frequent policy switches, involving inconsistent aims and means;

- scapegoating of systems, professionals and client groups;
- shifting meanings within the central vocabulary of the reform;
- rotations of themes of blame and cure;
- innovations suffering from endemic credibility problems;
- displacing of professional expertise by managerial and centralized control. (Maclure and Stronach, 1994: 3)

A postmodern deconstruction of this kind is enticing. This is not the place to provide lengthy exemplification, but the strains and insecurities on professionals brought about by multiple innovations, without educational coherence except at the most superficial of administrative levels, are all too apparent. A manifestation of that in Scotland was voiced by several regional authorities and the main teachers' union – the Educational Institute of Scotland (EIS) – against the 'unworkable' timetable for the implementation of *Higher Still* reforming the Scottish Certificate of Education Higher Grade (SOED, 1994). There was considerable concern that new principles implicit in the proposals (e.g. earlier specialization) had not been considered and debated, but particularly important were: 'the strains of introducing the changes at a time when the system is having to cope with the 5–14 programme, devolved management, staff appraisal and local government reform' (report in *Times Educational Supplement Scotland*, 8 April 1994: 3).

During the summer of 1995 Michael Forsyth, the new Secretary of State for Scotland, announced a delay in the implementation of *Higher Still*. This image of rapprochement, with an educational community still largely hostile to Forsyth as the former Scottish Minister for Education, could be seen as a strategy to calm (temporarily at least) the fears of those conservative Conservatives in Scotland who were concerned about continuing conflict in education. In this interpretation, the responsive gesture fulfils a ritual rather than an educational function. Such arguments appear elsewhere. For example, the idea of scapegoating educators has become commonplace. As we slipped deeper into recession it was assumed that young people did not have the right knowledge, skills and attitudes to ensure economic recovery and prosperity, and that these deficiencies must be laid at the door of those who teach them. In another publication, Ian Stronach (1988: 56) questioned the 'cause/effect assumption that relate the modern education and training of the individual to broad economic goals', argued that messages of this kind were unbelievable – 'after all, attempts to blame a military defeat on indiscipline in the Brownies would be discounted' (1988: 57) – and concluded that the persuasiveness of the case lay in its ritualistic aspect – 'it centres on a need to reassure the powerful as much as it seeks to mystify the powerless' (1988: 67). One of the interesting omissions from these rituals as enacted in the UK is any concern to give education credit for the emergence, real or imagined, of the country from recession.

So does this second story reinforce the idea that English and Scottish education are 'of that ilk'? Are we talking about the same policies and developments on both sides of the border? Or does the process of taming those developments in Scottish circumstances produce a distinctive educational experience?

Differences on the Ground

The third story is very long and only snippets will be offered here. It is an account of how things have turned out in practice to be different in Scotland than England.

The legal systems are separate, but education acts have tended to come in pairs; the 1945 Education Act (Scotland) had clear links with the 1944 Act for England, and there were two 1981 Acts addressing issues for children with special educational needs. That is not to say, however, that these form pairs of identical acts. As Lindsay Paterson (1994: 125) has argued, 'The Scottish Office has had more independence in educational policy than in any other sphere, inheriting the autonomy that had been enshrined in the Union'.

The 1981 Acts, for example, differed in that English local education authorities were made legally responsible for the integration of children with special needs into mainstream schools (albeit with generous let-out clauses); in the Scottish act there was no corresponding requirement although parents were given the choice of mainstream or special schools for their children. Perhaps the most striking contrast is that between the legislation of 1988 for England and 1989 for Scotland. The former enacted the national curriculum and testing in law, the latter did not.

It appeared that the government's decisions not to enact the national curriculum in Scottish legislation were taken in the belief that teachers and schools in Scotland were well used to doing what they were told by HMI or through the arrangements set out by the single Scottish Examinations Board (SEB, subsequently complemented by the Scottish Vocational Education Council – SCOTVEC). While a bit of trouble from the unions over workload was anticipated, it was assumed that schools and teachers would follow the usual pattern. In the event, compliance seems to have been achieved over the curriculum, but not on national testing. Regional education authorities and teachers made it clear that tests were to be fiercely resisted and so regulations on requirements to test at 8 and 12 years were immediately brought in by central government. Subsequently (1992) these legal measures were relaxed, largely because of a powerful alliance of parents, teachers and education authorities in opposition to external testing of children in the primary period of their education.

The '5 to 14 programme', as the Scottish version of the national curriculum is called, is rather different from that in England. It consists of 'guidelines' rather than 'orders' and is less prescriptive in form. However, the non-compulsory aspect is, in practice, illusory: all regional authorities and maintained schools, together with a high proportion of independent schools, are locked into the programme. Its lack of extension to 16 years of age reflects the secure position of Standard Grade, in the Scottish Certificate of Education, which is designed to promote certification for *all* pupils. The structure of '5 to 14' does not have the 'subjects' nature of the English national curriculum. Its curriculum areas of English language, environmental studies, expressive arts, mathematics, personal and social development and religious and moral education reflect the way primary education has been conceptualized in Scotland since the Primary Memorandum put out by the then Scottish Education Department (now the Scottish Office Education Department) in 1965. The guidelines have, moreover, been repeatedly described by Her Majesty's Inspectorate (HMI) as an articulation of existing best practice and not a radical reform. That is, of course, comforting to schools who may assume that since they are already engaged in the best of practice, life will not be seriously disrupted. Evidence of some complacency of this kind and of meagre levels of innovation are already emerging (Goulder *et al.*, 1994; Harlen and Malcolm, 1994).

On the assessment side, things were less readily welcomed. A somewhat fierce battle was fought (and won?) to achieve an approach to national testing in which external test material was to be used by teachers as and when they believed each pupil had reached a particular level. The intention was to use these (barely) external measures to verify the teachers' own assessments of achievement and there were to be no published league tables of test results. There was, however, a considerably greater demand than in the past for teachers to record and report on assessments generally to parents, and the added workload was keenly felt. The move away from an imposed external testing programme, of the kind implemented south of the border, was largely achieved through teachers, with the support of education authorities and parents, simply not being prepared to administer the tests. Testing was achieved in 1991 and 1992 in less than one-third of schools. Interestingly, although official figures are not available, it looks as if the new softer version of the testing programme has been implemented even more sparsely in subsequent years.

Much of the way things have turned out has rested on the still powerful regional authorities in Scotland; they have been particularly energetic in opposing external testing. However, as in England, there has been encouragement from central government for Scottish schools to opt out of local authority control. Indeed, the 1989 act for Scottish education went under the curious title of *Self-Governing Schools etc.* In England, in early 1995 (Fitz *et al.*, 1995) some 633 secondary and 415 primary schools had become grant maintained. In Scotland, one secondary school became self-governing by 1 April 1996.

Edwards and Whitty (1994: 7) have argued that although the government hoped that opting-out schools would provide greater diversity for the market through distinctive specialization, the early evidence from England has suggested these schools were instead seeking 'to resist such changes as becoming non-selective, co-educational, losing their sixth form, being merged with another school or being closed down'.

There has been a hint of this on the Scottish scene where some schools threatened with closure as part of local authority rationalization following falling school rolls, also took steps to opt out. The former Secretary of State (Ian Lang), however, did not allow their applications. Nor did he support a case where it was suspected that opting out was a mechanism for establishing a religious school (Islam). One school which became self-governing was a two-year secondary school (age 12 to 14) with a heavily rural population where older pupils travelled to two other six-year schools for their education post-14. The major reason for the application appeared to be the desire for change to become a full six-year secondary. Undermining the enterprise was the reported small roll of only 80 pupils in a school with a capacity for 120, and the below capacity rolls of the other two schools which catered for the more senior classes. Furthermore, after the opt-out the local authority provided a free bus service for pupils to travel to the other two schools from the *start* of their secondary careers (age 12) and a substantial number took advantage of this (Heron, 1994). The self-governing school's subsequent application to the Scottish Office to change its status to a six-year secondary was turned down. At the time of writing it is expected it will make further application to the new Secretary of State (Michael Forsyth). This general stramash, the embarrassment of the Scottish Office and the acrimony within the local community were all cause for concern, or hilarity, or 'I told you so'. How these events turn out will have considerable significance for a small coastal community in the north of Scotland, but as things stand there are few implications for Scottish education generally.

Lindsay Paterson (1994: 1–2) has used this example of controversial legislation, in the 1989 proposals to allow schools to leave the control of local authorities, as an illustration of how those from the full spectrum of politics seek to defend what is distinctively Scottish about education when articulating diametrically opposed positions. He pointed to the way opponents (especially Scottish Labour and Scottish Nationalists) saw the proposals as alien to, and an anglicization of, the educational heritage of Scotland, and juxtaposed this with Scottish Conservatives' defence of the policy as being in accord with the virtues of traditional Scottish education and its basis in the local community.

There is a variety of other ways in which Scottish practice stands apart from English. School Boards have, unlike governing bodies of schools in England, a majority of parent members; but they have more limited powers and the devolution of financial control has been targeted to headteachers rather than the boards. Devolved school management (DSM) is being introduced with schemes tailored to the needs of individual local authorities, rather than to centrally determined formulas of the kind that have characterized local management of schools (LMS) in England. No technology academies (city technology colleges) have been established; again, the relative homogeneity of the Scottish system has presented some difficulties in finding ways to ensure that such academies' curricula could offer something distinctively different that would be sought after by parents. Parental choice of school was introduced earlier in Scotland than England. Although there are similarities between the two (Adler *et al.*, 1989; Adler, 1993; Edwards and Whitty, 1994) the Scottish scene is influenced by the rural isolation of major tracts of the country, the general commitment of parents and professionals to education at the local comprehensive school and a much lower level of education in the independent sector (with the exception of Edinburgh). At a more specific level, Scotland has yet to see effects of the kind observed in England where some children with special needs have difficulty in being accepted into the market-oriented competition of schools, and those with emotional and behavioural difficulties are subject to increasingly higher rates of exclusion as they are seen to endanger the schools' academic achievement records (prospective concern about possible increases in exclusion rates has, however, prompted the Scottish Office to commission research in this area). The initial training of secondary teachers had the period of students' experience in schools raised from 18 to 22 weeks (out of 36) for a Post Graduate Certificate of Education (PGCE) and a pilot study prior to change on a broad scale was financed by the SOED; recently, however, the period of school experience has been reduced again and there are, as yet, no schemes for basing such training entirely in the hands of schools as there are in England.

This third story reminds us that the Scottish outpost of the Union is not simply geographically, but also historically and attitudinally removed from Westminster. Despite the shared free market framework of the first story, what about the politics? For that, we move on to the fourth story.

The Political Complexions

There are very obvious party political differences between Scotland and England. Despite 81 per cent of the Scottish electorate voting for parties other than the Conservatives at the last general election, and 84 per cent of the Members of Parliament from Scottish constituencies being members of these other parties, it is the Tories who rule Scotland from the Scottish Office in Edinburgh. However, Labour MPs hold 52 of the 72 Scottish seats and control most of the power in the regional councils. *None* of those councils, nor any of the new unitary authorities which take over in 1996, is Conservative controlled.

The pattern of education policy in the regions has traditionally been one of working *with* the Scottish Office, especially HMI, in Scotland's more centralized system. That is not to say that there have not been tensions and dramatic confrontations (especially over national testing), but there seems to have been a general wish to create an appearance of consensus, sustain a sense of collective responsibility and maintain lines of communication. Indeed, it could be imagined that the development of alternative institutions like technology academies might well have proceeded through the collaboration among, and resourcing by, regional authorities, central government and the private sector if the legislation had not precluded the involvement of local government. This relatively cooperative pattern developed over a period when local authorities and civil servants were powerful in Scotland, not least because many former ministers were in London for most of the week and only came back to do their Scottish business on Fridays, and none of the authorities behaved in ways that made it credible to apply the adjective 'loony' as has happened elsewhere.

That kind of consensual comfort can be scuttled by a new cast of characters, however. In the late 1980s the minister with responsibility for education in Scotland, Michael Forsyth, introduced New Right policies with speed and energy. His ideological commitment seemed so strong that he was unworried about damaging the already tenuous foothold of the Conservatives in Scotland. He flourished in combat with regional authorities, teachers' unions, academics, parents and, indeed, members of his own party (his subsequent appointment as Chairman of the Scottish Conservatives was short-lived). No doubt he also intimidated civil servants; they certainly became secretive and defenders (rather than the traditional describers and explainers) of government policies. In particular, he took on the local authorities and the unions over the matter of national testing and displayed considerable ingenuity and mental agility in the battle. Perhaps his major misjudgment was to assume that he could take the majority of parents with him. He underestimated their power (though he was never caught out in public using phrases like 'Neanderthal' or 'ballot-fodder' as others have been).

The change of leadership in the Conservative party and the subsequent general election in 1992 saw Mr Forsyth off to Whitehall and brought new characters into the Scottish Office play. The new Secretary of State, Ian Lang, and his minister with responsibility for education, Lord James Douglas-Hamilton, appeared to have more paternalistic, traditional, Scottish Tory leanings, to welcome rather than deride consensus and to be committed to restoration of Conservative popularity in Scotland. The civil service once again appeared to assert itself and HMI was, unlike its English brotherhood, remarkably successful in retaining its size and role more or less unchanged. The government still had to contend, however, with education authorities in the regional councils which remained outwith Conservative control. Their hope was that under local government reorganization in 1996 the new and much smaller authorities would place a sprinkling of power in Tory hands. Blatant gerrymandering of boundaries was used in order to capture a few diminutive Conservative heartlands. It was unsuccessful; Conservatives won only a very small proportion of seats and took control of none of the new authorities. Their efforts to achieve some power at local level, however, were at the cost of creating tiny authority units with such reduced resources that coping with education might become an unmanageable task. For example, school catchment areas will be maintained even where they cut across the new boundaries. To change these areas the new authorities will have to go through the statutory procedures which will include serious consultation with parents, school boards, churches and the communities more generally. This will be least cost-effective for those authorities with lowest staffing levels. At the same time of writing, the politicians in control at the Scottish Office have changed again. Michael Forsyth, regarded as a stark Thatcherite in his former role there, is now Secretary of State for Scotland. His initial statements imply a greater readiness to listen to, and collaborate with, professionals and education authorities. We shall see.

The political preferences of Scotland's population is, of course, an aspect of its identity. Lindsay Paterson (1993a), editor of *Scottish Affairs*, has challenged the popular monolithic, leftist, democratic, radical picture of the Scottish identity as inaccurate and pointed to the uncomfortable multiplicity of identities that are apparent. The fifth story, therefore, is taking some risks in generalizing about the culture within which educational change takes place, so the dip in this pond will be brief.

The Culture of Scottish Education

Some time ago in *The Scotsman* Bob Campbell (1994: 11), a journalist, reported Siri Neale's reactions to acting before a Scottish audience:

> Scotland is a different country. That is quite clear. It has its own identity, a stoic people. That can often be alienating if you're English . . . [The population is] not so cosmopolitan – it's not really mixed-race, it's very much Scottish – and the education that people have had is very similar, so you get that the audience is picking up on certain things in the play. But they're picking up as one mind, one body. The energy isn't dispersed . . . people are very cultured here.

This is, of course, an actress saying the things she thinks the readers of a major Scottish paper want to hear. Even if one accepts the general thrust, however, thinking and speaking as one mind is a great exaggeration of reality. It is interesting, however, that words like 'consensus' are still regarded with favour in education north of the border. On a visit from the south to a one-day conference in the late 1980s, Duncan Graham and Philip Halsey, the then Directors of the National Curriculum Council and the Schools Assessment and Examination Council respectively (and nowadays regarded by few as extreme right wingers), expressed astonishment at ideas of consensus which they regarded as outrageously outmoded. Such astonishment tends to entrench Scottish solidarity and commitment to those ideas. In passing, one might add that the economical Scots have not found it necessary to create new agencies like NCC, SEAC or their successors.

One aspect of consensus is the priority that is given to the involvement of practising teachers in curriculum and assessment developments. A very considerable number have been engaged in the formulation of 5 to 14 guidelines, Standard Grade arrangements and test item collections. Their contributions, however, are strictly within the hierarchical framework which assigns the important decisions to the professional élite of HMI and (though less so) officers of the Scottish Examination Board and the Scottish Consultative Council for the Curriculum. Whether teachers in general feel more kinship to the developments as a result of their colleagues' involvement is a moot point, but it ensures that the language of innovation is acceptable and demonstrates some measure of official trust of teachers.

This trust of the profession appears to extend to parents (Munn, 1993). Much of the parental support for schools in resisting national testing rested on confidence that teachers' own assessments were satisfactory and less likely to intrude into, or take time from, teaching (whether this confidence is justified is another matter). Clearly parents were sufficiently persuaded by schools to join together and make a successful demand for change; at an anecdotal level, however, some parents have complained of being pressurized by a concerted effort on the part of the profession. Much of that effort was orchestrated by the Educational Institute of Scotland, the teachers' union to which a large majority of teachers belong. So despite a few dissenting voices, collectivism and comprehensive education still get most of the Scottish vote.

Views of this kind tend to attach themselves to the belief that not only have a substantially higher proportion of Scots than English gone on to higher education in recent years, but also historically relatively larger numbers from the most humble of backgrounds were able to read and write as public schools in every parish were established in the seventeenth century. That takes us to the final story about what counts as progress in school.

Progress in School

Scottish society shares within itself what academics like to call the myth of the 'lad o' pairts' tradition whereby it was possible

> by dint of discipline, hard work, frugality and the support of the Dominie and local community, the gifted son of poor parents could 'make it' up through university to a successful career, particularly in teaching or the ministry. (MacLean, 1994: 38)

As Catherine MacLean has pointed out, however, this upward mobility was available only to 'talented and dedicated male individuals' (there was no 'lass o' pairts'), and these young men tended not to come from *very* poor homes. In the 1860s, although nearly one-quarter of the university students were the sons of the skilled working classes very few came from crofting or labouring backgrounds. The value put by the Scots on this individualism (of the self-supporting, self-improving man) *and* on collectivism (as identification with public systems), on both egalitarianism *and* élitism, on competition *and* cooperation, on meritocracy *as much as* democracy has been explored by several writers (e.g. McPherson, 1973; Paterson, 1983; MacLean, 1994). This tradition, rather than bald matters of wealth and class, has certainly promoted the careers of many men with modest small town backgrounds (the 'Kirriemuir' career) and this is not least apparent in the higher echelons of education itself (see McPherson and Raab 1988). This group has had a powerful influence and, as Lindsay Paterson (1994: 126) has argued,

> the distinctive Scottish curricula and examinations – devised by the professional élite – helped to shape the cultural outlook of Scottish society: the dominant view of learning valued curricular breadth, intellectual rigour and meritocratic competitiveness for the academically able, but also dull conformity and limited horizons for the majority.

Not surprisingly, one effect of all this has been the powerful association between notions of student progress and formal qualifications. The pedigree of the Scottish 'Highers' is over 100 years old in comparison with the 40 years of the youthful English A-level. The shift to GCSE from O-levels in England was predated by the development work on Standard Grade to replace O-Grades in Scotland (the 'Munn and Dunning Programme'), and the Scottish Vocational Education Council had introduced its National Certificate modules at a time when National Vocational Qualifications south of the border were just a bright idea for replacing an existing plethora of vocational certificates. This reform of vocational education has been described by Paterson (1994: 127) as an example of the Scottish educational community closing ranks 'against a perceived threat from outside' in the form of the Manpower Services Commission. HMI built upon teachers' union and education authority views to develop an alternative framework (to Mrs Thatcher's vocationalism) 'designed to preserve Scottish autonomy, and to defend comprehensives by maintaining a link between vocational and general education'.

There is, of course, a great emotional resistance to suggestions that Scottish education should fall into line with English. Ideas that children should transfer from primary school to secondary at 11 years as they do in England rather than 12 as in Scotland, or 'our Highers' should be replaced by 'their A-levels', or our young people should go to university at 18 for a three-year programme rather than 17 for a four-year programme, all get the thumbs down. But the reverse is also true; despite rhetoric that has applauded the 'breadth' of Highers, the English have remained wedded to the specialization of A-levels, and issues like changing the age of transfer are rarely mentioned in public. (Whether curricular breadth in Scotland is, indeed, achieved is a moot point. Rather few pupils actually sat the 'nine O-grades and five Highers' that was so frequently asserted for the majority.)

The language of progress in the 5 to 14 programme has similarities with that of England's national curriculum. Unfortunately there are confusing if minor semantic differences with the Scottish 'attainment outcomes' (referring to the main areas of skills, knowledge and understanding) being the equivalent of 'attainment targets' in England, and Scottish 'targets' the equivalent of English 'statements of attainment'. What they share is a heavy emphasis on academic criteria, rather than affective or social growth, and a conceptualization as a hierarchy – that is, a ladder to be climbed or stages of the high jump. The idea that there can be national scales of attainment to which children and schools can be nailed shows a lack in understanding of the complexity and sophistication of school learning both north and south of the border. Further- more, the language of 'delivery' of the curriculum is rife; implicit in this is a behaviourist conception of how children learn (Brown, 1992), which strikes chords with criticisms that people like Margaret Brown (1991) and Wynne Harlen (1991) have made of the English national curriculum orders.

There are, however, differences. The absence of the threat of league tables associated with 5 to 14 testing has enabled schools not to become obsessed with a unidimensional concern to manipulate their pupil populations and so maximize school scores. It is still the case that pupils living within school catchment areas, or, in the case of secondary schools, those who have attended associated primaries, are expected to go to the local school, and that for those with special educational needs or emotional and behavioural difficul- ties it is the parents' wishes for special or mainstream schools that are central (although not final in every case). Devolved school management has not, in contrast with England's LMS, based funding so heavily on student numbers, and the individual local authority schemes which are only just becoming public appear to be retaining central funding for special educational needs, particu- larly those children with a Record (*cf.* England's Statement) of Needs. Under these circumstances there is less opportunity for the transfer of funding sup- port from less privileged area schools to leafy suburb, high achieving schools.

At a somewhat speculative level, it might be claimed that the Scottish system has the potential to encourage broader curricula and concepts of what pupils' progress in school should be. The lower levels of prescription certainly give teachers an opportunity to perceive growth in more comprehensive terms than simply formal academic attainments. Furthermore, it can be argued that the 5 to 14 programme has made a significant step towards an entitlement for *all* children to the same broad and balanced curriculum (Brown, 1994); chil- dren with learning difficulties have to be negotiated (if necessary) *out of* the full offering, rather than having to *gain access to* it (the design of Standard Grade was also envisaged as a means of certification for all, but the implica- tions of that were not thought through). In principle, this provides the flexibility to pursue wider notions of progress, which our own research on teachers' constructs suggests are also concerned with matters such as improvement in pupils' self-confidence, sense of responsibility, self-esteem and social skills as well as academic achievement.

How things turn out is, of course, another matter. The academic tradition of the lad o' pairts dies hard. Indeed, HMI in 1980 (SOD, 1980) expressed concern that teachers in Scottish primary schools were concentrating too heav- ily on the basics of language and number and, they suggested, this was result- ing in distortion of the curriculum and of the primary school experience. Everyone was encouraged to pursue much more broadly based programmes, and this at a time when the rest of the world was weighed down with 'back to basics' exhortations. So whatever the potential breadth that is offered, Scotland may be trapped in its meritocratic and academic model. We can be very irritated by evidence of academic decline. For example, the proportion of Fellows of the Royal Society (FRSs) in Scotland has greatly reduced over this twentieth century, and this infuriates us even if at the same time we assert that the Royal Society is an 'English' institution. But of course, as Lindsay Paterson (1993b) suggested in addressing the idea of Scottishness, the acceptance 'that Scotland is full of contradictions . . . might be a sign of cultural maturity'.

Conclusion

The stories that have made up this chapter have, implicitly at least, been spoken to an English audience. The difficulties that may be encountered in trying to fit them together reflect some of the complexities of the north–south divide. Scotland's autonomy is only partial and while many place emphasis on the priorities of Scottishness being mobilized and defended, equal opportunities within the UK and Europe are just as important for Scotland's negotiations for the resources of the social and educational worlds. Despite a great sense of national allegiance in Scotland, its institutions (schools, colleges, universities) and bureaucracies (especially the Scottish Office) are in many ways not so different from those south of the border.

It is by no means easy to judge, therefore, whether the differences between the Scottish and English scenes are more or less real and significant than are their commonalities. From north of the border, it appears that features like a desire for solidarity (and even consensus), greater homogeneity of provision, belief in comprehensive education, educational authority power and political colour, clearer trust of teachers and semi-autonomous definitions of the educational agenda do make Scottish education distinctive. This distinctiveness is reinforced because the domestication of general UK government policies has to proceed through a double process of translation: at a national level the Scottish Office imposes its interpretation before the professionals have their go. It is not surprising, therefore, that educational practice in Scotland looks (and probably is) significantly different, given the increased variety of pressures and opinions to which policies are subjected.

Explaining the differences and considering where we go from here is even more problematic. Ian Stronach (1992) has argued that the differences may, to a considerable extent, be a logical inevitability of a Scottish identity that is itself a largely negative dialectic based on an insistent non-Englishness; 'being Scottish' requires a 'difference from English'. In those circumstances

> The Scottish myths . . . are set *implicitly* against English norms –
> egalitarian/élitist; breadth/narrowness; Scottish identity/anglicization
> . . . Arguably these defining polarities are sharpened by recent Tory
> government policies . . . The nature of the dialectic points to the need

to compare in order to *be* – implying a lack of cultural confidence and political power in the face of more powerful neighbours . . . Thus the identity is dependent, incomplete, and pathological, although certainly lively. (Stronach, 1992: 101–3)

As he goes on to point out, an identity of this kind based on distinctiveness *from* rather than distinctiveness *in*, 'needs the denial or self-denial involved in dependent relations in order to remain dynamic'. What would our education look like if we were *not* looking over our shoulder at the rest of the UK or Europe?

This kind of argument may or may not be seen as convincing. What it does little for, however, is the debate about where we go from here. There continues to be great ambivalence among many in Scottish education on the extent to which we should be looking for complete separation and dissolution of the various aspects of the UK common framework for education. As yet, alternative images of the possible impact of wider, overarching European agencies are still in a primitive state, but when they are clarified we will be, no doubt, still 'in two minds'.

References

ADLER, M. (1993) *An Alternative Approach to Parental Choice*, London, National Commission on Education, Briefing Paper 13.

ADLER, M., PETCH A. and TWEEDIE, A. (1989) *Parental Choice and Educational Policy*, Edinburgh, Edinburgh University Press.

BROWN, M. (1991) 'Attainment targets and children's mathematical learning', *Open University Course E271 Curriculum and Learning*, Block B Learning Part 3 Learning in Action, Milton Keynes, Open University, pp. 27–32.

BROWN, S. (1992) 'Raising standards: Factors influencing the effectiveness of innovations', SCRE Fellowship Lecture, in *Critical Reflections on Curriculum Policy*, Edinburgh, SCRE Fellowship Lecture.

BROWN, S. (1994) 'The Scottish national curriculum and special educational needs', *The Curriculum Journal*, **5**, 1, pp. 83–94.

CAMPBELL, B. (1994) 'Two by two, side by side: Siri Neale and Brian Cox', *The Scotsman*, 31 March: 11.

EDWARDS, T. and WHITTY, G. (1994) 'Choice in English Secondary Education: Lessons for America?' paper presented to the annual meeting of the American Educational Research Association, New Orleans, LA, April.

FITZ, J., HALPIN, P. and POWER, S. (1995) 'Opting into the Past? Grant Maintained Schools and the Reinvention of Tradition,' paper presented to the annual meeting of the American Educational Research Association, San Francisco, CA, April.

GOULDER, J., SIMPSON, M. and TUSON, J. (1994) 'The 5–14 development programme in Scottish secondary schools: The first phase', *Curriculum Journal*, **5**, 1, pp. 69–81.

HARLEN, W. (1991) *Research Directions at a Time of Change in Curriculum and Assessment*, NICER Occasional Paper No.6, Belfast, NICER.

HARLEN, W. and MALCOLM, H.C. (1994) 'Putting the curriculum and assessment guidelines in place in Scottish primary schools', *Curriculum Journal*, **5**, 1, pp. 55–67.

HERON, L. (1994) 'Highland skirmish: The controversy surrounding Scotland's first opted out school', *The Independent*, 31 March: 33.

MACLEAN, C. (1994) 'The theory and practice of equal opportunities in Scotland', *Scottish Affairs*, **6**, pp. 36–51.

MACLURE, M. and STRONACH, I. (1994) 'Deconstructing the notion of "Policy Hysteria"; Five readings, some unprincipled coupling, and no happy endings', paper presented to the annual meeting of the American Educational Research Association, New Orleans, LA, April.

MCPHERSON, A. (1973) 'Selections and survivals: A sociology of the ancient Scottish universities', in BROWN, R. (ed), *Knowledge, Education and Cultural Change*, London, Tavistock.

MCPHERSON, A. and RAAB C.D. (1988) *Governing Education*, Edinburgh, Edinburgh University Press.

MUNN, P. (ed) (1993) *Parents and Schools: Customers, Managers or Partners?* London, Routledge.

PATERSON, H. (1983) 'Incubus and ideology: The development of secondary schooling in Scotland, 1900–1939', in HUMES, W.M. and PATERSON, H. (eds) *Scottish Culture and Scottish Education 1800–1980*, Edinburgh, John Donald.

PATERSON, L. (1993a), 'Editorial: New thinking and new politics', *Scottish Affairs*, 2, pp. 1–4.

PATERSON, L. (1993b) 'Editorial: Scottishness', *Scottish Affairs*, 4, pp. 1–4.

PATERSON, L. (1994) *The Autonomy of Modern Scotland*, Edinburgh, Edinburgh University Press.

SCOTTISH EDUCATION DEPARTMENT (SED) (1965) *Primary Education in Scotland*, Edinburgh, HMSO.

SCOTTISH EDUCATION DEPARTMENT (SED) (1980) *Learning and Teaching in Primary 4 and Primary 7*, Edinburgh, HMSO.

SCOTTISH OFFICE EDUCATION DEPARTMENT (SOED) (1994) *Higher Still*, Edinburgh, SOED.

STRONACH, I. (1988) 'Vocationalism and economic recovery: A case against witchcraft', in BROWN, S. and WAKE, R. (eds) *Education in Transition: What Role for Research?* Edinburgh, SCRE, 55–70.

STRONACH, I. (1992) 'The "Howie Report": A glossary and a commentary', *Scottish Educational Review*, **24**, 2, pp. 93–104.

STRONACH, I. and MORRIS, B. (1994) 'Polemical notes on educational evaluation in the age of "policy hysteria"', *Evaluation and Research in Education*, **8**, 182, pp. 5–19.

Chapter 11

When 'Breadth and Balance' Means 'Balancing the Books': Curriculum Planning in Schools Post-ERA[1]

Dawn Penney and John Evans

Introduction

Since 1990 we have been exploring the impact of the Education Reform Act (ERA) 1988 on the provision of physical education (PE) and sport in schools, and specifically, the implementation of the national curriculum for physical education (NCPE) in England and Wales. In the course of our research both survey and case study data (see Evans and Penney,1992; Penney,1994) have drawn attention to the fact that local management of schools (LMS) has not only changed the relationships between schools, and between schools and other policy sites (specifically relationships between schools and local education authorities (LEAs) and central government), but has also led to parallel changes in the structures and relations *within* schools. Essentially, what we have seen in schools is the development of an internal market[2]. In response to changes in the education structure, rules and relations beyond them, schools have changed their own structures, rules and internal relations. Economic efficiency and the need to survive in the education market are not only critical concerns for schools post-ERA, but also for departments within them. In this chapter we pursue the implications of the internal market, the structures, rules and relationships within schools post-ERA, in terms of its impact on curriculum planning, and specifically, schools' delivery of the NCPE. In doing so we highlight the inherent inequalities of the policy process within schools post-ERA and the imperfections of the internal market conditions. We focus on the position of PE and its relative ability to compete with other curriculum subjects to illustrate the implications of the inequalities for curriculum design and delivery post-ERA. As we will see, PE is a subject in which its status relative to others and its position in the phased implementation of the national curriculum (NC) mean that certainly in some schools it has not been well placed to compete with other subjects in the internal market, and these disadvantages are in turn being reflected in what children are experiencing as a national curriculum for physical education (NCPE).

The Market and Internal Market Post-ERA

The market has been the focus of much recent literature in education, but as Ball (1993) and his colleagues (Bowe *et al.*, 1992) have pointed out, the literature has largely focused on 'the demand side, on choice'. The mechanisms of the market, the operation and effects of competition have been overlooked (Ball, 1993). Furthermore, the focus of attention has essentially been confined to the exploration of the relationships *between* schools post-ERA. The effects of the introduction of the education market on the relationships *within* schools has received little attention. It is these latter relationships – the structures, rules and mechanisms created within schools in response to the ERA, that are our focus in addressing the internal market.

In addressing these issues, we certainly acknowledge that competition between subjects within schools for resources is an established feature of state education, and is not something that has arisen as a consequence of the ERA. However, like Bowe *et al.* (1992) we see the ERA as having changed the values that are now the primary focus of attention within schools, and as having accentuated and made explicit the competition. While financial concerns may have always played some part in decision-making within schools, we see them as now framing decision-making within schools (Lungren, 1977; Penney, 1994; Penney and Evans, 1995), such that educational concerns are subordinated. Similarly, in addressing the implications of resource decisions, we do not deny that curriculum content and delivery has always to some degree reflected the constraints of resourcing within schools. What we draw attention to, however, is the extent of these constraints post-ERA and the pressures for teachers to increasingly focus on resource issues in designing their curricula. Essentially what we see in the process of framing is resource pressures creating increasingly narrow boundaries within which decisions within schools are set (see Penney, 1994).

The Fight for Funding

The introduction of local management of schools (LMS) was portrayed by the government as providing schools with financial freedom from LEAs, as offering them a new degree of control in the allocation and use of their resources (see DES, 1988). In our research we have seen that this freedom and control is illusory or very seriously constrained, with schools being offered the opportunity to make decisions about the allocation of severely limited funds. Post-ERA, as has always been the case, subjects are competing for scarce resources within schools. However, what we have also seen is the formalization of this competition, with clear rules being established in the internal market.

Essentially, our exploration of the funding of PE post-ERA has shown that the allocation of funds within schools (like that between schools, see DES

1988) is being driven by a formula relating primarily to pupil numbers. The number of pupils taking a subject now has a direct bearing on the financial fortunes of the department. Subject contact time is another factor that has been incorporated in some schools' formulas and in some instances arrangements within schools are mirroring those of formula funding more vividly, by also incorporating an age weighting factor (see Penney and Evans, 1995). Often accompanying the allocation of funds by such formulas is the opportunity for departments to bid for funds, for example for curriculum development or support for in-service training.

However, under these conditions, the competition for funding is certainly not a competition amongst equals. What the rules fail to challenge and in some instances actually explicitly reinforce themselves, are the inequalities inherent in the competition, the fact that all players are not equally placed to play this game. With the application of formulas within schools, the ability of subjects to attract pupils will, at least to some extent, influence their financial fortunes and security, as will subject contact time if this is also a factor in calculations. But subjects are very differently placed in terms of their ability either to attract pupils or win bids and are accorded different amounts of timetable time. Subject status, both historically and in the eyes of those influencing choices and determining allocations, unavoidably and inevitably plays an important role in the operation of the market. Furthermore, we have seen that differences between subjects in terms of their perceived status or value may not remain a hidden influence in the allocations of funding within schools. In some formulas subject weightings are incorporated in calculations (see Penney and Evans, 1995). What this clearly illustrates is the way in which the discourse of the market has entered and is interacting with, and arguably legitimating and reinforcing, existing inequalities within schools. Although the status assigned to different subjects varies between institutions and over time, and our research has highlighted considerable variations between schools in the status and priority accorded to PE, we would nevertheless support Ball's (1990: 222) view that 'None the less, there are typical patterns, and clearly the expectations of influential outside audiences do enhance the claims made by certain subjects and detract from those of others'. These differences between subjects will be reflected in their ability to attract pupils, who wins and loses bids and the weightings assigned to subjects.

However, as well as historical status, we point to the national curriculum as itself influencing funding allocations and specifically reinforcing and legitimating the traditional hierarchy of subjects within schools and the pattern of rewards then mirroring this hierarchy. This hierarchy was inherent in the distinction between core and foundation subjects and then in the order for NC subjects being introduced (see DES, 1989), and our research has shown that certainly in some schools, priorities in resource allocations then mirrored the order in which NC subjects were introduced, with this introduction being a critical factor in decisions. In these circumstances, those subjects coming later in the implementation process, with PE amongst them, were disadvantaged relative to curriculum subjects ahead of them (see Penney, 1994; Penney and Evans, 1995).

What we see then, is that with the introduction of LMS, not only are there clear winners and losers amongst schools, which will in turn impact upon all departments, but that the impact will be differential; there will also be clear winners and losers amongst departments within schools. We again stress that curriculum provision has always occurred within financial constraints. However, the tightening of those constraints post-ERA has meant that increasingly, financial considerations, over and above educational issues, are directing and shaping curriculum design and delivery. Such constraints and their effects on curriculum planning have to be viewed in the light of the stated aims of one of the key policies within the ERA: the national curriculum.

A 'National' Curriculum?

The national curriculum would, it was stated, establish as an entitlement, the provision of a broad and balanced curriculum for all pupils in all state schools in England and Wales, and, it was said, 'be an effective way of ensuring that good curriculum practice is much more widely employed' (DES 1989: 3.1). Sadly, as some of the following text will illustrate, much of our research has led us to question the extent to which these aims are being realized in the context of PE. In addressing the extent of such realization, there is a need to look not only at schools' delivery of the NCPE, but also at the text of the NCPE itself.

Arguably, in the process of making the NCPE (and specifically in the progression from the NCPE working group's interim report, to their final report, to the National Curriculum Council consultation document and finally the statutory order; see Evans *et al.*, 1993a; Talbot, 1993; Penney, 1994), much of the ability of the NCPE to ensure breadth and balance expressed in the PE curricula of all schools, was lost.[3] Increasingly, and with the possible resource implications of requirements being a primary concern, flexibility became a critical feature of the text of the NCPE, such that under the requirements in the statutory order schools have considerable choice with respect to the activities they include in their curricula and the time that they devote to various activities. As a text, the NCPE legitimated the pattern of variation between schools with respect to what pupils experience and the opportunities they enjoy in PE. What the flexibility also effectively ensured was that those experiences and opportunities, what children experienced as an NCPE, would be shaped by the very different resources available within schools. It is in this light that we draw attention to and reflect upon the impact and implications of the operation and inequalities of the internal market in schools.

Counting Costs

Certainly our research has highlighted differences between PE departments in terms of the resources they have been able to draw on in implementing the NCPE, and has illustrated how, in turn, these differences are reflected in what pupils are experiencing as an NCPE (see Evans *et al.*, 1993b; Penney, 1994). Equipment for PE, hire of facilities and travel to off-site facilities are all areas of expenditure that have been repeatedly highlighted by heads of PE departments as matters of concern and issues that impact directly upon their curriculum design. One head of PE vividly illustrated the link between the mechanisms of the internal market and the curriculum provision that could be made, explaining that with 'number of students on GCSE course increasing rapidly' there was 'extra money available to purchase equipment for outdoor education'. Others showed that inadequacies in funding could clearly constrain opportunities, with reports of, for example, year 7 (pupils aged 11) swimming having been 'abandoned' due to a 'lack of funds for pool hire and transport'.

The use of and resourcing to enable access to off-site facilities is a critical issue to consider in addressing the breadth and balance inherent in the NCPE. Here we should highlight that schools vary considerably in the range of the on-site facilities they have available and some lack what can be regarded as the most basic of facilities, being without a gymnasium or on-site playing fields (see Penney, 1994). For many schools, use of off-site facilities enables them to extend the breadth and balance of their PE curriculum, with pupils experiencing activities that could not otherwise be provided by the school. In some instances it is the means of overcoming major shortcomings in their on-site facilities and making what could be seen as a minimal response to the demands of the NCPE. Support for PE in funding allocations is thus critical in enabling the expression of breadth and balance and facilitating curriculum development in PE.

However, levels of subject funding are by no means the sole or necessarily the most influential factor in curriculum planning. In the case of PE, the moves towards greater flexibility in the text of the NCPE reflected in part, the role of *staff expertise* in shaping the curriculum. Without support for the implementation of the NCPE in terms of extensive in-service training of PE teachers (in for example, the teaching of dance) if schools were to be able to meet the requirements of the NCPE, there was a critical need for the requirements to provide schools with a degree of choice with respect to the activities they included within their curricula. Essentially the text of the NCPE accommodated rather than challenged differences between schools with respect to the resources they have available for PE and particularly, different levels of staffing and expertise amongst staff. It legitimated the design of PE curricula being shaped by or towards the expertise of staff available to teach PE. What we draw attention to below is not only the link between such shaping and the expression of breadth and balance in the NCPE, but also the way in which post-ERA staffing within schools (and the expertise therefore available for delivery of the NCPE) is being assessed primarily on the basis of *financial* rather than educational concerns.

A Model of Efficiency?

Essentially what we have seen in our research is that funding is by no means the only aspect of resourcing to be the subject of accentuated pressures and changing rules post-ERA. Neither are the competition between and prioritizing of subjects for allocations matters applicable only relevant to subject funding. The appointment and allocation of staff and allocation and arrangement of timetable time (see below) are equally important issues to pursue in addressing the conditions and arrangements within schools post-ERA, and their implications for curriculum planning.

As the largest budgetary item in school expenditure, staffing within schools has been subject to critical scrutiny post-ERA. With the introduction of LMS, avoiding either replacing staff leaving, or making any additional appointments, represents an important and sometimes critical saving for schools (see Penney, 1994). Faced with a falling roll and thus a reduced income some headteachers have little alternative but to 'lose' a member of staff. Increasingly, the pressures are for schools to operate with economic efficiency, which in terms of staffing equates to a pattern of all teachers teaching at all times. Unfortunately, subject timetabling and specialisms are unlikely to match such a model. Instead, what we have observed in our research is a demand for increased flexibility in staffing, with gaps in staffing being filled with non-specialist input. Non-specialist input is certainly not a new phenomenon in secondary schooling, but again we highlight it as an apparently increasing and worrying trend, certainly in the context of PE. Furthermore, we again suggest that not all subjects may be equally effected by this trend and the pressures on staffing in schools. Again market mechanisms interact with and further reinforce the different status of subjects. Certainly we would question whether non-specialist input is regarded as acceptable in some other subjects as it appears to be in PE and suggest that in staffing decisions, the differential status and priority given to subjects again comes into play. The issue here is not only from which areas staff can be 'lost' or appointments or replacements avoided, but also the timetabling of staff and priority given to different subjects (and specialisms) in this process. In investigating staff timetabling within schools post-ERA we again observed both the historical status of subjects and the NC (and specifically the phased introduction of subjects) playing a part in resourcing decisions. One head of PE explained that a PE specialist was 'being taken' to teach more humanities, and that this was 'taking precedence to PE because of NC implications'. In other instances, the low status and priority accorded to PE was evident in future staffing being a matter of uncertainty, dependent on the 'demands of the rest of the curriculum' and with PE therefore being taught by 'different staff each year' (see Penney, 1994).

The implications of these patterns of staffing and particularly the low status accorded to PE in staffing decisions were matters of concern to both LEA PE inspectors and heads of PE departments in our research. In both instances, non-specialist input was regarded as threatening the ability of schools to deliver a broad and balanced PE curriculum and maintain quality in their provision. Seventeen (38 per cent) of 44 (56 per cent) heads of PE commenting on staffing inadequacies specifically drew attention to the specialist/non-specialist balance in PE teaching. The potentially damaging impact on PE of the increased mobility of staff within schools was very apparent. One head of PE explained that 'The amount of curricular time taught by non-specialists has increased. Consequently *the standard of teaching is lower, as is the quality of learning*' (our emphasis). Another stated 'We have non-specialists in the dept. *This "leads" the timetable*' (our emphasis), while a third respondent indicated that this 'lead' may be towards a games bias in the PE curriculum, saying 'We have lost a full-time member of PE in the last two years. *We are staffed by non-specialists with an interest in games*' (our emphasis) (see Evans *et al.*, 1993b; Penney, 1994).

For many years games has been recognized as dominating the PE curriculum within many schools, receiving a far greater percentage of PE curriculum time than other areas of activity, such as dance or outdoor and adventure activities. In its early texts, the NCPE seemed destined to challenge such practice and force schools to look critically at the breadth and balance of their PE curricula. However, the introduction and increased emphasis of flexibility in requirements largely removed this challenge. Furthermore, accompanying the increased emphasis of flexibility, was a privileging of games within PE. For example, the statutory order identified games as the *only* area of activity that it was compulsory for schools to provide in *each year* of key stage 3 (DES/ WO, 1992). This reinforcement and legitimation of the games bias reflected a dual concern within government. On the one hand, the dominant view of PE within government equated PE with 'sport' and in turn saw competitive games as the defining and dominant feature of PE. On the other, this political and ideological stance can be seen as compatible with the economic concerns surrounding the development of the NCPE with respect to the resource implications of recommendations. Typically, games is regarded as a cheap area of activity to provide, being an area that can invariably be provided on-site and for which non-specialist input is frequently used and seen as acceptable (see Evans, *et al.*, 1993a, 1993b, 1994; Talbot, 1993; Penney, 1994).

Tight for Time

A further issue influential in both the making of the NCPE texts and in subsequent implementation was timetable time. Here again it is worth acknowledging that there has always been an element of competition between subjects for resourcing. However, post-ERA this was certainly accentuated. With the introduction of the NC, many schools found themselves struggling to accommodate what appeared to be excessive and growing demands for time (see Graham with Tytler, 1993). What our research showed was timetables being progressively squeezed as more NC subjects were introduced. Once again pressures were not equally felt by all subjects and the phased introduction of subjects seemed to again reinforce historical differences between subjects in resource allocations. Some heads of PE were feeling pressures from the claims being made from other subjects and in one head of PE's view the 'justification of subject' being 'more and more crucial' if PE was 'to have a chance of retaining PE time allocation compared to other subjects, i.e. science, maths, English' (see Penney, 1994). Here, as in the process of bidding for funding and making a case for staff appointments, replacements and arrangements, we see pressures for heads of departments to adopt the discourse of the market. As Ball (1990: 237) explains, 'In the contemporary jargon, heads of departments are "middle managers" with all the implications of "line" responsibility that that suggests' (see also Penney, 1991).

Critically the ERA precluded the time to be devoted to individual subjects being prescribed in statutory orders, and in turn, these orders contained no prescription with respect to the allocation of time within a subject. In these circumstances, breadth and balance, as expressed in terms of curriculum time, are matters determined in individual schools. Obviously the breadth of a subject's curriculum will depend to some degree on the total time allocated to the subject. In considering time allocations to PE, as indicated above, in some schools those subjects accorded lower status and coming later in the introduction of the NC appeared disadvantaged in this respect. However, this disadvantage was reflected not only in implementation of the NCPE, but also in the NCPE statutory order itself. The NCPE was designed at a time when the timetable overload in schools was increasingly apparent (see Graham with Tytler, 1993) and certainly, the NCPE working group were aware that the requirements for the NCPE had to be such that they would be able to be accommodated within invariably very little timetable time in schools (see Penney, 1994). The text thus again legitimated the inadequacies in resourcing of the subject, but also differences between schools in terms of the level of resourcing.

Our data lent clear support to the view that there is a direct link between the time available for PE and the breadth of the curriculum offered to pupils. Typically less time was devoted to PE in year 11 than in year 9 and this was reflected in the different scope of the year 9 and 11 PE programmes. Fewer departments offered dance, gymnastics and athletics in year 11 than year 9, and fewer weeks allocated to these areas of activity in year 11 than in year 9 (see Penney, 1994). However, our data also highlighted that opportunities for curriculum development were effected by other aspects of timetabling and in particular the length of school periods and how they are then positioned in the timetable. The former concern again drew attention to the pressures created by the ERA. Changing the length and therefore number of periods in school days and weeks has been one means by which schools have attempted to overcome the overload created by the NC. Our research has highlighted the potential impact of such decisions on the PE curriculum, particularly in relation to either facilitating or curtailing the use of off-site facilities. The length of lessons and whether they are timetabled as 'singles' or 'doubles' were clearly critical issues in heads of PE departments' decisions about whether or not to utilize off-site facilities. The concern was not only the cost incurred in facility hire and/or transport (see above), but also the fact that 'travelling time lessens teaching time', such that staying on-site, even if this means reducing the range of activities offered, may be regarded as the preferable option (see Penney, 1994). Obviously where comparable facilities do not exist on site, such curtailment will also be reflected in the curriculum provided. Our concern with respect to the likely expression of breadth and balance in the NCPE is that the combined and greatly increased pressures with respect to both finance and time will increasingly be reflected in the facilities used for PE and in turn the range of activities incorporated in the PE curriculum. This was already the reality for some heads of PE, with one head of PE reporting, for example that 'as a school we are not using [sports centre name] so much', this being due to the 'lack of time available and cost of hiring', and another that 'lack of time' had 'curtailed use of off-site facilities, hence more on-site use' (see Penney, 1994).

A further issue impacting upon the feasibility of off-site use is the position of PE periods within the school day and the structure of the school day. Timetabling PE immediately prior to or following a break, or at the end of the day, may effectively 'create' additional time that means the journey off-site is considered feasible and worthwhile or that allowing time for pupils to change at the end of a lesson is not such a concern for the PE teacher. Equally, a failure to adopt such sympathetic timetabling can effectively preclude use of off-site facilities and lessen the time in which pupils are engaged in activities. The priority accorded to different subjects and specifically whether or not the headteacher and/or deputy head responsible for timetabling arrangements make efforts to accommodate the specific needs of PE, is therefore critical in shaping curriculum opportunities. Unfortunately for PE, breaks between periods are another area in which the pressures of the introduction of the NC have been felt, with some restructuring of school days significantly reducing such breaks in an attempt to create more teaching time. With only minimal time between lessons, teaching time for PE can actually be seen to have been lost in these circumstances, with lessons having to be drawn to a close sooner to enable pupils to change and get to their next lesson on time (see Penney, 1994).

Conclusion

What we have outlined is how in their allocation of resources to subjects, schools have responded to the combined demands of LMS and the NC. We have seen the ways in which the discourse of the market, its pressures and demands (particularly for efficiency in economic terms) have been adopted by schools and become embedded in their internal rules and relationships. In this respect we see the responses of schools (and particularly headteachers) as being framed by the context in which they are operating, the conditions imposed upon them by the ERA (see also Penney, 1994). Certainly we would agree with Bowe *et al.*, (1992: 28–9) in seeing 'self-delusion' in 'the notion that budgetary control is somehow liberating and inevitably more efficient without attention to the simple but crucial question of the size of the budget'.

In addition, we see some delusion in the likelihood of the stated aims of the NC being fulfilled in this context. In the case of PE, we have drawn attention to not only potentially worrying and damaging implications of market decisions for curriculum design and delivery, but also critically, the way in which as a policy text the statutory order for the NCPE has itself legitimated the effects we have highlighted as arising from market pressures. In the delivery of the NCPE we see the subtle interaction of text and context and between policies, with the NCPE, NC and LMS all playing a part in determining what children ultimately experience as an NCPE. Despite the rhetoric of ensuring quality and of providing opportunities for *all* pupils, in the context of PE post-ERA, we sadly see continued diversity in provision and opportunities and a picture of many teachers facing an apparently increasingly difficult task with respect to the possibilities and support they have for curriculum review and development. Certainly, such review and development has not been a notable feature of the implementation of the NCPE to date (see Evans *et al.*, 1993b; Penney, 1994). How PE survives in the market and what children experience as an NCPE are issues we continue to pursue in our research.

Acknowledgment

This chapter draws on data from research funded by the Sports Council and Economic and Social Research Council (Project No. ROO 23 3269). We are grateful to these organizations for their support and for the time and cooperation of the many individuals who have participated in the research.

Notes

1   This chapter is a development from the paper 'Changing Structures; Changing Rules: Implications for Curriculum Planning in Schools' presented at the CEDAR International Conference 'Changing Educational Structures: Policy and Practice'; University of Warwick, 15–17 April 1994. Following that presentation, the aspect of the paper focusing on the nature of the 'internal market' within schools was developed for publication in *School Organisation*. Readers are therefore also directed to that article (in press) 'Changing Structures; Changing Rules: The Development of the "Internal Market"' (Penney and Evans, 1995).

2 In addressing the situation within individual institutions our use of the term internal market is notably distinct from its use in other literature addressing recent changes in either the health service or education. Previously internal market has been a term used to refer to the development of competition within a service, and thus *between* institutions (see Pollitt, 1990).

3 In our theoretical analyses of policy we have highlighted the danger of a contradiction between a conceptualization of policy as a process and use of the terms policy, practice, making and implementation. We have stressed that in a view of policy as a process, all of these can be seen as featuring throughout the process and should not be regarded as distinct phenomena associated only with particular policy sites (see Evans *et al.*, 1993c; Penney, 1994).

References

BALL, S.J. (1990) *The Micro-Politics of the School. Towards a Theory of School Organization*, London, Routledge

BALL, S.J. (1993) 'Education markets, choice and social class: The market as a class strategy in the UK and the USA', *British Journal of Sociology of Education*, **14**, 1, pp. 3–19.

BOWE, R. and BALL, S.J. with GOLD, A. (1992) *Reforming Education and Changing Schools. Case Studies in Policy Sociology*, London, Routledge.

DEPARTMENT OF EDUCATION AND SCIENCE (DES) (1988) *Education Reform Act: Local Management of Schools*, Circular No. 7/88, London, DES.

DEPARTMENT OF EDUCATION AND SCIENCE (DES) (1989) *National Curriculum – From Policy to Practice*, London, DES.

EVANS, J., DAVIES, B. and PENNEY, D. (1994) 'Whatever happened to the subject and the State? *Discourse, Australian Journal of Educational Studies*, **14**, 2, pp. 57–64.

EVANS, J. and PENNEY, D. (1992) 'Investigating ERA qualitative methods and policy oriented research', *British Journal of Physical Education, Research Supplement*, **11**, pp. 2–7.

EVANS, J. and PENNEY, D. (1995) 'The politics of pedagogy', *Journal of Education Policy*, **10**, 1, pp. 27–44.

EVANS, J., PENNEY, D. and BRYANT, A. (1993a) 'Playing by market rules: Physical education in England and Wales after ERA', in McFEE, G. and TOMLINSON, A. (eds) *Education, Sport, Leisure: Connections and Controversies*, Eastbourne, Chelsea School Research Centre, University of Brighton.

EVANS, J., PENNEY, D. and BRYANT, A. (1993b) 'Improving the quality of physical education? The education reform act, 1988 and physical education', *Quest*, **45**, pp. 321–38.

EVANS, J., PENNEY, D. and BRYANT, A. (1993c) 'Theorising implementation: A preliminary comment on power and process in policy research', *Physical Education Review*, **16**, 1, pp. 5–22.

GRAHAM, D. with TYTLER, D. (1993) *A Lesson for Us All: The Making of the National Curriculum*, London, Routledge.

HILL, M. (1980) *Understanding Social Policy*, Oxford, Basil Blackwell.

LUNDGREN, U.P. (1977) *Model Analysis of Pedagogical Processes*, Stockholm Institute of Education, CWK Gleerup.

PENNEY, D. (1991) 'Making a case for physical education: Preparing for the National Curriculum', *British Journal of Physical Education*, **22**, 4, pp. 36–9.

PENNEY, D. (1994) 'No Change in a new ERA?: The impact of the Education Reform Act (1988) on the provision of PE and sport in State schools', PHD thesis University of Southampton.

PENNEY, D. and EVANS, J. (1995) 'Changing structures: Changing rules: The development of the "Internal Market"', *School Organisation*, (in press).

POLLIT, C. (1990) 'Doing business in the temple? Managers and quality assurance in the public services', *Public Administration*, **68**, pp. 435–52, Winter.

TALBOT, M. (1993) 'Physical Education and the National Curriculum: Some political issues', in McFEE, G. and TOMLINSON, A. (eds.) *Education, Sport, Leisure: Connections and Controversies*, Eastbourne, Chelsea School Research Centre, University of Brighton.

Notes on Contributors

Margaret Arnott is lecturer in British government and politics at Glasgow Caledonian University. Previously she was a research fellow at the Universities of Birmingham and Edinburgh. Her research interests include devolved management of schools and the governance of education.

Carl Bagley is senior lecturer in sociology at Staffordshire University. His present research interests include the quasi-market in education and social welfare provision for minority groups.

Eric Blyth is principal lecturer in social work and director of the Centre for Education Welfare Studies at the University of Huddersfield. Prior to taking up his current post, he was a practising social worker in a child guidance clinic.

Sally Brown is professor of education at the University of Stirling. Previously she was director of the Scottish Council for Research in Education. Her current interests are in the areas of curriculum policy and practice, school effectiveness, teachers' constructs of teaching, gender issues and special educational needs.

Rita Chawla-Duggan is a former research fellow in CEDAR at the University of Warwick, where her teaching and research interests were in the study of primary school curriculum and social research methodology. She now teaches English as a foreign language.

Rosemary Deem is professor of educational research and dean of social sciences at Lancaster University. She has published extensively on gender and education, women and leisure, and school governance, and is currently chairperson of the British Sociological Association. At present she is working on feminist methodology and epistemology, and on a project about women, time and holidays.

Caitlin Donnelly is a doctoral student in the School of Public Policy, Economics and Law at the University of Ulster, studying the impact of changing governance on schools in Northern Ireland.

John Evans is professor of physical education in the Department of Physical Education, Sports Science and Recreation Management at Loughborough University, and co-director with Dr Dawn Penney of a Leverhulme Trust-funded project investigating the impact of the Education Reform Act (1988) on the provision of physical education and sport in schools in England and Wales. He has published widely in the sociology of education on teaching and teacher education.

Julia Evetts is senior lecturer in the School of Social Studies at the University of Nottingham. For a number of years she has been doing research into teachers' and headteachers' careers and has published two books, *Women in Primary Teaching* and *Becoming a Secondary Headteacher*. Currently she is writing about careers in science and engineering, and is beginning a new research project on the internationalization of professional regulation.

John Fitz is senior lecturer in education policy and management in the School of Education, University of Wales, Cardiff. Within the broad field of educational policy analysis he has been involved in research on the assisted places scheme, grant maintained schools, parental choice and institutional autonomy. He is currently researching modes of school inspection.

John Fletcher teaches education management up to doctoral level at the University of Wales, Cardiff, having practised in head of department and vice-principal roles in further education. His research interests currently focus on aspects of change in educational organizations.

Ron Glatter is professor of education and director of the Centre for Educational Policy and Management (CEPAM), School of Education, the Open University. He also directs the University's ESRC-funded Parental and School Choice Interaction (PASCI) study. He is a former national chair of the British Educational Management and Administration Society (BEMAS), and took part in the OECD's International School Improvement Project (ISIP). His publications are mainly in the fields of institutional change, educational management development and school-environment interactions.

David Halpin is professor of education at Goldsmiths College. He has undertaken extensive research into the grant maintained schools policy, at both primary and secondary level, as well as comparative work in the United States. In addition to education policy analysis, other research interests include comprehensive schooling and special educational needs.

Lynda Huckman is a research fellow and lecturer in education management at the University of Wales, Cardiff. Her research interests include local management of schools, financial and resource management and school governance.

Ian Jamieson is professor of education and pro-vice-chancellor at the University of Bath where he currently directs the Centre for School Improvement. He is the founder and editor of the *British Journal of Education and Work.* His major books include *Capitalism and Culture* (Gower, 1980); *Schools and Industry* (Methuen, 1982) with Martin Lightfoot; *Industry in Education* (Longman, 1985); *Mirrors of Work* (Falmer, 1988) with Andy Miller and Tony Watts, and *Rethinking Work Experience* (Falmer, 1991) with Andy Miller and Tony Watts.

Penny McKeown is lecturer in public policy and management in the School of Public Policy, Economics and Law at the University of Ulster. Her main research interests lie in the areas of education management and policy and she is currently engaged in an ESRC-funded project with colleagues from the University of Birmingham and from Canterbury Christchurch College, Kent: 'New Forms of Education Management: A Comparative Study Across the UK.'

Judith Milner is senior lecturer in social work and co-founder of the Centre for Education Welfare studies at the University of Huddersfield. Prior to taking up her current post, she was a practising teacher and social worker.

Pamela Munn is professor of curriculum research at Moray House Institute of Education, Heriot-Watt University, Edinburgh. She is currently researching exclusions from school, a project funded by the Scottish Office Education Department. This work is a continuation of a long-standing research interest in school discipline, truancy and bullying. SOED has also extended the work of the team researching devolved school management, to chart its continuing impact in schools in Scotland.

Bob Osborne is professor of applied policy studies in the School of Public Policy, Economics and Law at the University of Ulster. His major research interests lie in the areas of education policy, higher education and equal opportunities policies. He is currently working with colleagues from Queen's University, Belfast on behalf of the Standing Advisory Commission for Human Rights on an evaluation of the implementation of government guidelines for policy appraisal/fair treatment in departments in Northern Ireland.

Dawn Penney is lecturer in the Department of Human Movement Studies at the University of Queensland, Australia. She is co-director with Professor John Evans of an ongoing research project funded by the Leverhulme Trust, investigating the impact of the Education Reform Act (1988) on the provision of physical education and sport in schools in England and Wales. She has authored and co-authored many publications addressing policy in physical education and education and methodological issues in policy research.

Christopher Pole is lecturer in sociology/CEDAR at the University of Warwick. His research is concerned primarily with higher education, in particular, the socialization and training of research students. He has recently completed a feasibility study on the Internationalization of Research Training for the European Union, and is currently conducting an ESRC-funded follow-up study of social and natural science PhD students which focuses on the later stages of doctoral research processes.

Sally Power is research officer in the Department of Policy Studies, Institute of Education, University of London, where she is currently working on a project which explores differences in the opportunities and experiences of state and private schooling. As well as the grant maintained schools policy, her research interests include education policy analysis in general, the secondary school curriculum and homelessness and education.

Charles Raab is reader in the Department of Politics, University of Edinburgh. He has published many articles and contributions to books on education policy, and on methodological and theoretical issues. Under grants from the Economic and Social Research Council and the Scottish Office Education Department, he has co-directed comparative research projects on the devolved management of schools in England and Wales and Scotland. His book (with Andrew McPherson), *Governing Education: A Sociology of Policy Since 1945* (Edinburgh University Press, 1988), won the 1989 Annual Book Prize of the Standing Conference on Studies in Education. He is a member of the editorial board of the *Journal of Education Policy*.

Philip Woods is a research fellow in the Centre for Educational Policy and Management (CEPAM), School of Education, the Open University, and principal investigator for the ESRC-funded PASCI (Parental and School Choice Interaction) study being conducted at the centre. He has written extensively on the new education quasi-market and on parental involvement in schooling, and has developed the notion of the consumer-citizen. He is also engaged in research on values and spirituality in education.

Index